Rational Decision-making for Managers

Rational Decision-making for Managers

An Introduction

Sarah Keast and Michael Towler

A John Wiley and Sons, Ltd., Publication

Other Wiley Editorial Offices

John Wiley & Sons Inc., 111 River Street, Hoboken, NJ 07030, USA

Jossey-Bass, 989 Market Street, San Francisco, CA 94103-1741, USA

Wiley-VCH Verlag GmbH, Boschstr. 12, D-69469 Weinheim, Germany

John Wiley & Sons Australia Ltd, 42 McDougall Street, Milton, Queensland 4064, Australia

John Wiley & Sons (Asia) Pte Ltd, 2 Clementi Loop #02-01, Jin Xing Distripark, Singapore 129809

John Wiley & Sons Canada Ltd, 6045 Freemont Blvd. Mississauga, ONT, L5R 4J3, Canada

Wiley also publishes its books in a variety of electronic formats. Some content that appears in print may not be available in electronic books.

Library of Congress Cataloging-in-Publication Data

Towler, Michael.
    Rational decision making for managers : an introduction / Sarah Keast and Michael Towler.
       p.   cm.
    Includes bibliographical references and index.
    ISBN 978-0-470-51965-3 (pbk.)
    1. Decision making.   I. Keast, Sarah.   II. Title.
    HD30.23.T69 2009
    658.4′03—dc22

                                                                                        2008042467

British Library Cataloguing in Publication Data

A catalogue record for this book is available from the British Library

All screenshots from Microsoft are © Microsoft Corporation

ISBN 978-0-470-51965-3

Typeset in 9/13pt Kuenstler by Integra Software Services Pvt. Ltd, Pondicherry, India
Printed and bound in Great Britain by TJ International, Padstow, Cornwall

Contents

About the Authors

Sarah Keast is a lecturer in information management at the University of Plymouth Business School. Sarah has formed an interest in the use of mathematical modelling and quantitative analysis techniques in both the economic and the general business environments. She has developed and delivered courses in quantitative analysis techniques at postgraduate and undergraduate levels.

Mike Towler began his career in research and development. An initial period in the UK public sector was followed by several years in the private sector, moving from R&D to R&D management. He joined the University of Plymouth Business School in 2002, where he lectured in operations management and in business decision-making. In 2008 this was followed by a move to BPP Business School. Mike has a PhD in physics from the University of Exeter and an MBA from the University of Aston.

Acknowledgements

The authors would like to acknowledge the University of Plymouth Business School for support during the writing of this text, and in particular the kind assistance of some students who read early drafts of parts of the manuscript. We are also appreciative of the helpful comments made by the anonymous referees of a draft text.

Preface

In recent years there has been a lessening of the focus on simply rational decision-making in business and management education (e.g. a growing appreciation of naturalistic decision-making). Nevertheless, there remains a requirement for a basic understanding of rational decision-making techniques, not least to recognise when they are appropriate. Once managers have this ability, they then need to be able to identify the characteristics of the decision to be made to guide them in their choice of techniques.

The primary aim of this text is to provide managers and students with an introduction to some of the most common decision-making techniques. Following a discussion of the decision context, the approach followed is to divide the techniques into sections according to the types of decision for which they are most appropriate.

This text begins, in Chapters 1 to 3, by introducing the nature and context of decisions. In particular, the consideration of futures is developed, while both quantitative and qualitative techniques for describing continuous or discrete models of the future are expounded. These first three chapters aim to familiarise readers with the potential nature of the future, whether it is certain, uncertain, or strictly uncertain.

The second section of the text, Chapters 4 to 7, and the third section, Chapters 8 to 10, are divided to stress that, while some decisions are singular in nature in that they will be taken once or will be repeated after a finite period of time, some decisions are sequential in nature, opening up future decision-making opportunities in which managers may add value. This is a simple yet important conceptual step.

The role of the nature of the future introduced in the first section is seen throughout the later chapters. The future may be certain, as highlighted in Chapter 6 with examples from linear programming, it may be uncertain owing to uncontrollable events and considered discrete (e.g. Chapter 5 considers payoff matrices and Chapter 9 considers decision trees), it may be uncertain and considered continuous (exemplified in Chapter 4 with inventory management decisions), or it may be uncertain owing to the actions of a competitor (e.g. Chapters 7 and 10 consider game theory). The discrete or continuous characteristics of the decision are also drawn out.

A single option from several discrete choices (e.g. payoff matrices or decision trees), a single option from a continuum of choices (e.g. inventory management), or a combination of discrete choices (e.g. linear programming and mixed strategy games) may be appropriate.

The appendix summarises some basic mathematics, although it is not necessary to read and understand the entirety of the mathematical theories and methods presented in order to understand and benefit from the rest of the text. Rather, the reader is encouraged to refer to the Appendix as and when required.

The Decision Context

CHAPTER 1

Introduction to Decision-making

Objectives

- *To understand the overall process of taking decisions.*
- *To appreciate the differences between certainty, risk, and strict uncertainty.*
- *To be able to differentiate between the descriptive, normative, and prescriptive approaches to decision-taking.*
- *To appreciate those issues that affect the decision-taking process, including biases, models, and decision roles.*

Introduction

Even though they are likely to be taking between 10 and 20 breaths per minute, most reading this sentence are unconscious of their breathing rate. Yet, should a reader decide to hold her breath, a conscious decision to act will have been taken. Often, decisions to act are taken with an intent or purpose to achieve a goal. The ways in which such decisions are taken interest philosophers, psychologists, scientists, and business leaders alike, whether purely to understand the decision-taking process or to improve the process, leading to better decisions. This text aims to present some of the techniques developed to assist in the decision-making process. These are particularly useful for many types of problem commonly faced within both large and small organizations. Before these techniques are discussed, it is vital to appreciate some of the broad context in which decisions are taken and factors that need to be borne in mind when making decisions.

What is a Decision?

Taking a decision precedes a period of implementation. It seems reasonable to ask what precedes taking a decision, and to reply a process of inference from the available evidence. Several processes of assessment and inference come to mind:

- a recognition process;
- an argumentation process;
- a selection from alternatives process.

It is the third of these that is of predominant interest in this text; however, a familiarity with the others can be beneficial.

Recognition

In researching dynamic environments requiring rapid decision-taking, Klein (1989, 1998) found that the decision process of experts was one of recognition. The process is now called *recognition primed decision-making*, or RPD for short. RPD commonly occurs in situations in which experts are taking decisions with ill-defined goals under time pressure within a changing context; for example, decisions taken by members of the emergency services such as firefighters. Such a process occurs much less frequently in situations requiring justification, optimisation, or conflict resolution. In dynamic situations, the expert experiences the situation in a changing context and perceives it as typical by recognising relevant cues. This recognition includes the identification of plausible goals and a typical action. The action being typical within the context has associated expectancies. At its simplest – if P, then do Q and expect R to occur – there are no initially specified goals, and alternative actions are not generated and assessed. While the action is being implemented in the recognised situation, the expert has expectancies, such that, if atypical cues begin to occur, the expert can change the action or even the goals. In the case of firefighters, an initial goal in some recognised situation might be to contain the fire and an action is followed; however, if the expectancies do not occur, then the goal might shift to, for example, evacuating a building.

Argumentation

As noted above, RPD generally does not occur in situations requiring justification. Justification is often associated with argumentation: a decision taken is a conclusion justified by an underlying argument. Imagine a government wanting to protect its people from the potential epidemic outbreak of a virus for which a vaccine is available. The reasoning might be as follows:

> For the vaccine to be effective, at least 80 % of people need to be vaccinated. There is a small risk of side effects from the vaccination, so some individuals are not being vaccinated but instead rely on everyone else to do the right thing. Consequently, only 60 % are voluntarily being vaccinated. A law should be passed to make vaccination mandatory.

There are two well-known approaches to mapping arguments that have a more complex form than the one above. Firstly, the approach of Toulmin (2003) introduced the basic structure of an argument as a *claim* that is supported by *data* (i.e. evidence) and a *warrant* that clarifies why the claim follows from the data. The claim is the conclusion to the argument. In the case above, the claim is to pass a law to make the vaccination mandatory, the data is that only 60 % of people are being vaccinated voluntarily, and the warrant is that, for a vaccine to be effective, at least 80 % need to be vaccinated. To this basic argument structure are added modal *qualifiers*, *rebuttals*, and *backing*. Qualifiers indicate the strength of the claim, i.e. the claim is stated with qualification. Rebuttals refute the link between data and claim, restricting the generality of when the data support the claim. Backing offers supporting reasons to the warrant.

The second approach to argument mapping is to be less specific about the role of the elements of an argument and simply to recognise that a conclusion or claim is hierarchically supported or contested by a series of reasons and objections (see, for example, Kelley, 1998). Each reason or objection may be built up from more than one component premise. A simple case of hierarchical reasoning would be to state a reason that *the bus is late*, draw a preliminary conclusion that *the bus has broken down*, treat this as a reason, and finally conclude to *take the car*.

A complex, multilevel argument may contain elements of deductive, inductive, and abductive reasoning. Deductive reasoning is from population to sample; for example, if everyone in a bar is drunk and a person is ejected from the bar, then it is concluded that the person is drunk. Given the truth of the two premises, the conclusion is valid. Inductive reasoning is from sample to population. Suppose one or several people are ejected from a bar and the alcohol level in their blood is tested and found to be high. Then inductive reasoning would conclude that the people in the bar are drunk. Abduction reasons between population and sample. Suppose it is known that everyone in a bar is drunk and then a drunk person is found in the locality of the bar. Abductive reasoning would conclude that the person comes from the bar.

Although argumentation can be used to offer justification for taking a decision, this can also be achieved by making a selection from alternative choices. It is such an approach that is followed in this text. This type of selection process is also suitable for optimisation and conflict resolution.

Selection from Alternatives

Many types of decision can be defined by:

- situation;
- alternatives;
- outcomes.

The *situation* describes the context in which the problem is set. It identifies the features that affect and are affected by the eventual outcome of the decision-making process. *Alternatives* refer to the identified choices available to the decision-taker, and *outcomes* are the predicted results of choosing each of the alternatives. Essentially, the decision-making process is the act of differentiating between the alternatives, given the situation, in order to arrive at an optimal outcome. The decision tools presented in this text assist the decision-taker to differentiate between the alternatives and to move towards an optimal choice.

Essentially, the decision-taking process involves:

1. Identifying the situation, alternatives, and outcomes.
2. Differentiating between outcomes.
3. Choosing the alternative that results in an outcome that is optimal by some chosen definition.

The techniques presented in this text assist with steps 2 and 3. One must, however, spend some time considering step 1 prior to implementing an appropriate decision-taking technique. It is imperative that the decision-taker(s) have a detailed knowledge of the environment in which the decision is being taken, all the possible or likely alternatives that can be taken, and the outcomes of each of these alternatives. Nevertheless, anticipating the characteristics of the decision-taking situation is difficult. Any representation of the situation will necessarily be an approximation of reality at some level, and the key is to identify the features that are instrumental in determining the situation. Regardless, the real problems arise when defining the alternatives and outcomes, and this is where both risk and uncertainty arise.

Uncertainty and Risk in Decision-taking

Difficulties are frequently encountered when identifying all alternatives and outcomes owing to a lack of complete knowledge of the situation and a lack of perfect foresight. Since access to perfect knowledge of both the past and present is impossible, uncertainty is inherent in the decision-taking process. This uncertainty arises from several sources, among which are:

- the subjectivity of the decision-takers where individuals may interpret outcomes in different ways;
- incomplete information about the situation, alternatives, and/or outcomes;
- undifferentiated or poorly differentiated alternatives.

Further complications arise from the uncertainty in the definition of uncertainty itself, where both interdisciplinary and intradisciplinary variations in the definition can be observed. One of the most common classifications of uncertainty and risk is due to Knight (1921) who makes a clear distinction between risk and strict uncertainty:

- Decisions involving risk are those where the decision-takers can assign probabilities or probability distributions to describe the randomness they face.
- Decisions that are strictly uncertain are those for which probability distributions cannot be assigned to the possible outcomes of the decision.

This distinction implies that risky decisions are those for which the situation, alternatives, and/or outcomes can be anticipated, whereas strictly uncertain decisions are those for which the situation, alternatives, and/or outcomes cannot be anticipated.

At first glance this appears to be a reasonable distinction between circumstances where the possibilities have a known degree of certainty and those where at least some of the possibilities are unknown. Given a little more thought, however, problems begin to surface.

One might begin to wonder about situations for which not all the possibilities can be anticipated, but those that are known with some degree of certainty can be expressed using probabilities. This describes many practical decision-taking situations, since information about some elements of the situation, alternatives, and outcomes is unlikely to be available. Although it seems that Knight's description is therefore not an applicable construct, this is not the case. The distinction is often an important assumption in a decision-taking process. It is first worth considering the notion of probability in more detail.

Probability

Probability refers to the measurement and estimation of relative frequencies or likelihoods of events. Although the mathematical formulation of probability, first developed in the sixteenth century, is widely accepted, there has been a prolonged historical discussion on the concept of probability itself. Although there are several interpretations of probability, they largely fall into two dominant camps, that of epistemic probability and that of aleatory probability (Hacking, 2006; Gillies, 2000).

The first of these includes ideas related to belief or credence in a implying b, among other things, including the concept of subjective probability assigned by personal judgement based on the available evidence. Or, rather, epistemic probabilities are subjective because of the lack of complete knowledge of the processes that influence events.

The aleatory camp is associated with the idea that the probability is connected with the object and it is the object's behaviour that leads to stable long-run frequencies and hence objective probabilities. Thus, aleatory probabilities arise from random processes, the natures of which are known with some degree of certainty. It is often the aleatory interpretation that is used to introduce probability for the first time, through repeated rolls of a die or tosses of a coin.

On the face of it, this distinction seems quite reasonable, and yet the argument is long lived, with various authors, and disciplines, falling into both, one, or other of the camps.

If the reader is not yet uncomfortable with the distinction between epistemic and aleatory uncertainty, consider two coins, one that has been tossed and landed on the ground, the other still spinning in the air. If the coin that has landed is covered, then its state, heads-up or tails-up, has already been defined, but until the coin is uncovered the caller is in a state of epistemic uncertainty, not knowing whether the coin is heads or tails. When the caller looks at the spinning coin, she might consider that the coin could land heads-up or tails-up, and this uncertainty is aleatory, it is in the object of the spinning coin. Nonetheless, if the caller knew the exact conditions of position, linear and angular momentum, wind speed, etc., and had an appropriately fast-running piece of code, she could calculate how the coin would land. Under this interpretation, the probability returns to subjective, and the caller has epistemic uncertainty, simply not knowing the initial conditions. Perhaps the reader might now consider that all probabilities are epistemic, but would this remain the case if radioactive decay were considered?

Of course, taking the epistemic view might lead the reader to consider that all follows causally (Woodward, 2003; Psillos, 2002), it is simply that the decision-taker does not possess some knowledge. Following this route, though, the problem of the free will of the decision-taker arises. If the universe is simply unfolding, what is this concept of an agent taking rational decisions? A mechanism is then sought for the decision-taker to be non-random but undetermined.

The preceding paragraph may *cause* the reader to dwell a moment, but, as a future decision-taker, the reader *must* make progress, and so this text proceeds by requesting the reader to make some bold assumptions.

From the evidence at hand (or that which might come to hand) a decision-taker aims to infer a course of action. Under an assumption of certainty, a specific outcome is assumed to follow from a specific course of action. Under an assumption of risk, one of several outcomes with knowable/estimable probabilities is assumed to follow from a specific course of action, and the laws of probability are assumed to hold. Under an assumption of strict uncertainty, one of several outcomes with unknowable probabilities is assumed to follow from a specific course of action. In developing a model to aid the decision-taker, one of these assumptions is usually taken as a starting point of investigation. For example, in Chapter 6 the technique of linear programming begins with an assumption of certainty; this is an example of a programmed decision. In the discussion of expected values in Chapter 5, and in Chapter 9 on decision trees, the starting point is that of an assumption of risk. Within Chapter 8, and in the first half of Chapter 5, decision approaches start with an assumption of strict uncertainty.

The concepts of causation and probability are important to decision-taking; however, a detailed appreciation is beyond the scope of this text and beyond the capacity of the authors, requiring a detailed understanding of at least physics and philosophy. The interested reader is directed to Hacking (2006), Gillies (2000), Woodward (2003), and Psillos (2002).

Rational Decision-taker

Many of the decision-taking techniques rely on the notion that decision-takers are rational. Rationality has a variety of interpretations dependent upon the field in which the description arises. In the context of decision-taking, rationality implies that the decision-taker is able to distinguish between outcomes, rank outcomes according to some measure, and then choose the optimal outcome. For example, if, according to some measure, A > B and B > C, then the rational decision-taker would choose A. Although one might consider the rationality assumption to be perfectly acceptable and even obvious, reality often deviates dramatically from this model. Humans have developed cognitive schema, known as heuristics, that aid the rapid solution of problems. There is, however, substantial evidence that heuristics can generate detrimental biases in some decision-taking.

Biases

Cognitive Biases

When the choices of decision-takers deviate from what would be expected under the assumption of rationality, cognitive biases are very often the root cause. Cognitive bias is an umbrella term for a wide variety of distortions in judgement that result from partiality to particular ideologies or frames of reference.

Decision-taking is affected by biases which are manifested by the way in which groups or individuals view probabilities, differentiate between alternatives, formulate beliefs and ideas, and express these beliefs and ideas. Some of the more common are outlined here;[1] the least that a decision-taker should do is to consider these as a checklist and ask whether they could have affected the decision-taking process.

Four heuristics that give rise to common cognitive biases are *availability*, *representativeness*, *anchoring and adjustment*, and *framing*.

Availability

Frequently occurring events are easy to recall, and hence it is natural to associate a high probability with them. However, peripheral events can modify information that is available from memory, causing inappropriate probabilities to be assumed. For instance, peculiar events often receive high publicity, giving the impression that they are more common than they are in actuality. When statistically considering association between events, many would use Pearson's chi-squared test, in which expected and observed occurrences of all possible outcomes would be considered. Such thoroughness may not occur, though, without statistical guidance. If the reader classes days as *sunny* or *grey*, and classes her mood as *happy* or *sad*, then, in recalling an association, she may try to recall sunny–happy days and grey–sad days; the other pairings that would be considered by the chi-squared analysis are not available to recall.

Representativeness

The representativeness heuristic supports rapid assessment based on stereotypical classification. If a newly proposed product has similar characteristics to an earlier success or failure, then it will be similarly classified. Such thinking may not be an unreasonable starting point but may lead to unnecessarily rapid conclusions when resource is available to gather further information, and it can lead to fallacies from not

---

[1] For a more detailed survey of heuristics and biases, see Bazerman (2006), Kahneman, Slovic, and Tversky (1982), and Kahneman and Tversky (2002).

appreciating Bayes' theorem, the nature of chance, or sample size effects. Television commercials used to be run with statements such as 'eight out of 10 owners who expressed a preference said their pet preferred the advertised pet food'. Would such a claim be more readily found by asking 10 pet owners or a million pet owners?

Anchoring and Adjustment

To reach a zero-order budget quickly, many managers have approximated by adding or subtracting a percentage from a previous year's budget. This is an example of adjusting away from an initial start point. Once more the heuristic can be useful, but, if an initial value or viewpoint is unreasonable, then the adjustment is often insufficient to overcome the anchor.

Framing

Kahneman and Tversky's (2002) prospect theory shows that the framing of inform-ation modifies the attitude to risk of an individual. There is a tendency to be risk seeking to negatively framed choices, those perceived as losses, and risk averse to positively framed choices, those perceived as gains. Without any substantive change, the way of describing a situation can affect the decision taken. Many framing effects beyond those of loss and gain have been observed; the interested reader is directed to Chapter 3 of Bazerman (2006).

Motivational Biases

Heuristics very often lead to cognitive bias, but these are not the only sources of bias. It is generally assumed that *motivational bias* arises from human desire rather than from information processing. Four common biases identified with motivation are *momentary desire, positive self-view, predispositional tendency*, and *regret avoidance* (Bazerman, 2006).

Often, a short-term want self will give rise to a momentary desire that can dom-inate a long-term should self, particularly if choices are only considered one at a time rather than presented together. Nevertheless, which of these selves optimises is not always clear; Bazerman (2006) advises a negotiation between the selves. For the persistent salesperson, positive illusions may have some value. Ordinarily, though, a positive self-view can have a deleterious effect on decision-taking; for example, turn-ing down an offer while expecting a better one to materialise. Objective data may be required to temper this bias. Faced with the identical data and range of choices, it might seem that all rational agents should tend towards taking the same decision; however, a predispositional tendency can exist first to make a choice and then to adapt the relative importance of the decision characteristics to convince that the preference has been reasonably concluded. Finally, a bias can exist to distort behaviour to avoid feelings of regret. If it is easy to imagine an alternative outcome arising from following an alternative action, then a bias arising from regret avoidance is more likely. If the 'what if' scenario is difficult to imagine, then the occurrence of the bias is lower.

Group Biases

The biases discussed so far are those that arise from the behaviour of the individual. Nonetheless, the behaviour of the group can also lead to bias. Interacting group biases (Jones & Roelofsma, 2000) include false consensus, groupthink (Janis, 1972), group polarisation, and group escalation of commitment. The first of these, false consensus, occurs when one individual assumes that her view is typical, which is potentially problematic if a decision taken is based upon expectancies of another's action. The remaining three biases follow from social influence. Groupthink occurs when an interacting group tries to find unanimity at the expense of appropriately considering alternatives; that is, maintaining group cohesiveness becomes the objective that is optimised. Group polarisation occurs when members of a group have initially similar views; group interaction strengthens each individual's view, hence shifting the group to a more extreme position. Although individuals are known to escalate commitment, there is at least an equal tendency for groups to do the same. An escalation of commitment occurs when a group continues to support a chosen path even when contrary evidence is growing, a problem of which to be aware in sequential decision-making.

The existence of bias suggests that conditions will exist in which a rational choice is unlikely, whether the decision is taken as an individual or as a group. Consequently, the development of mathematical, statistical, and structured approaches to aid decision-taking may be useful to limit the effects of bias.

Descriptive, Normative, and Prescriptive Decision-making

Approaches to decision-making can generally be classified as one of three categories: descriptive, normative, or prescriptive (Bell, Raiffa, & Tversky, 1988). Although the definitions of these three are relatively dynamic within the research literature, they can be loosely described as follows:

- Descriptive methods analyse how decisions are taken and determine optimal choices based on what is or what has been done.
- Normative methods determine what choice(s), in theory, should be taken.

- Prescriptive methods are closely related to normative methods in that they determine optimal choices in theory, but these choices are constrained by limitations of what can be done in reality.

Descriptive techniques analyse how real people take decisions, including how they perceive the situation, how they determine alternatives and the resulting outcomes, and how this is influenced by their biases. These techniques draw on methodologies from several different fields including psychology and statistics.

Normative techniques are based on the assumption that the decision-taker is rational and abstract from cognitive bias. The choice of optimal outcomes identified via normative decision-taking techniques represents rational selection from the alternatives. The process is transparent and is, by and large, without bias.

Prescriptive techniques relax the assumption of rationality of the decision-taker, but, rather than account for bias, these techniques account for real-world constraints and indicate the optimal choice according to these constraints. Hence, prescriptive techniques generate understanding of the choices that should be made given that rationality might not be a possible or optimal mode of operation of the decision-taker and given that some alternatives might not be possible.

The primarily mathematical techniques presented in this text fall into the normative category. Nevertheless, when implementing these approaches to support decision-taking, the prescriptive approach should be taken where the optimal choices resulting from the decision analysis will be tempered by real-world restrictions.

Models

An important aspect of many decision-taking techniques, regardless of whether they are descriptive, normative, or prescriptive, is the construction of suitable models. Models can be considered as ideas or abstractions whose primary function is to question or represent phenomena.

Mental models are those that are formulated by the decision-taker, or other stakeholders, representing personal understanding of a situation. Mental models are how the individual construes the world. Such mental constructs can be used to identify possible objectives and outcomes resulting from strategies that the decision-taker could choose. Kelly (1955) put forward *personal construct theory* (PCT) to capture how individuals make sense of the world. Within this theory, sense is made from both similarity and difference. If one describes a person as, say, a rogue, an appreciation of this is only possible if the opposite *pole* of the personalised *construct* is recognised, for example, *rogue rather than reliable* or *rogue rather than straight-laced*. Within PCT, such constructs are considered to be organised hierarchically, so that above and below each pole of a construct there is another construct. Although each person's construct hierarchy is different, to the extent to which two individuals have the same construct hierarchy, they construe the world in the same way. Two techniques have been used to elicit constructs from individuals and from groups, the repertory grid technique (Fransella, Bell, & Bannister, 2003) and the cognitive mapping technique (Eden & Ackermann, 2001a, 2001b). The latter of these has been widely used in business research and management consultancy as a way into complex or messy problems, those situations in which alternatives and outcomes are not initially obvious.

An abstract model can be useful in interrogating a problem situation so as to draw out key characteristics of concern. If it is to be used in this way, from where does the initial model originate? Two possible approaches are the use of *organizational metaphors* (Morgan, 2006) and the *soft systems methodology* (SSM) (Checkland, 1999). Morgan's organizational metaphors consist of eight different perspective lenses: the organization as machine, organism, brain, culture, political system, flux and transformation, instrument of domination, and psychic prison. An initial diagnostic reading asks how a situation is like each metaphor, each bringing a different view and different theories to bear on the problem situation. The diagnostic reading can then be used to generate one or more storyline readings of a situation. A storyline reading has one metaphor as a dominant frame and others supporting. In the SSM approach, a problem situation is first entered and explored with tools such as rich pictures (using drawings and graphics). Having explored the situation, root definitions are developed of identified purposeful activity systems; at their core are transformations from inputs to outputs. These systems do P by Q to achieve R. Abstract models are then developed from these root definitions; that is, models of the purposeful activity systems are made, not of what is actually done. The models can then be used to interrogate current practice. What is in practice but not in the model? What is in the model but not in practice? From this questioning a greater understanding of situation, alternatives, and outcomes can surface.

Mathematical models are frequently used in order to identify the essence and develop an understanding of the decision-taking situation. The process involves recognising the key aspects of the decision environment and the alternatives, and disregarding those aspects that have little or no influence over the situation at hand. This is often an iterative process. Mathematical models couch the terms of the situation in mathematical equations. These equations are then applied to current data in order to predict future values, are solved simultaneously in order to give an optimal solution, or are altered in some way that mimics changes in the system, providing a path to a possible outcome. The mathematical representation is then used to investigate the decision-taking situation and to inform the decision-taker's consideration. Statistical models are similar but primarily identify patterns and relationships within previous data from the system. The resulting information is then used to predict potential outcomes.

This text presents primarily mathematical representations of systems, the use of which depends upon the decision-taking environment and the nature of the decision itself. For example, the decision-taker may be required to set levels of production in such a way as to minimise costs, and in this case uses linear programming as the preferred approach. Or the decision-taker may be choosing among alternatives, with outcomes from these depending upon the future state of the economy. In this case the decision-taker may choose to consider the situation with a decision tree or a payoff matrix. Very often, however, the techniques require future or predicted values for some variables. The estimation of these requires the use of forecasting methods.

Forecasting

Forecasting methods can be classified very broadly into two categories: time series and explanatory. Time series methods are mathematical techniques that assume previous patterns of behaviour within the data can be used to predict future values. As the name would suggest, these techniques are used when future values are required.

Explanatory forecasting uses both quantitative and qualitative techniques to generate new values rather than exclusively future values. Quantitative explanatory techniques attempt to identify relationships between the variable of interest (dependent variable) and those (independent) variables that are believed to influence the dependent variable. Once these relationships have been quantified, new values for the dependent variable can be generated on the basis of observed changes in the independent variables. Qualitative forecasting techniques seek subjective views to generate either predicted values or potential scenarios. These methods often rely on accessing expert opinion.

Who Should Participate in a Decision Process?

Leaders and Followers

It would be a mistake to consider the decision-taker as one person and decision-taking as one step. A leader has the flexibility to decide how to decide. How to take this decision has itself been discussed for half a century:

> Sometimes new knowledge pushes him in one direction ('I should really get the group to help make this decision'), but at the same time his experience pushes him in another direction ('I really understand the problem better than the group and therefore I should

make the decision'). He is not sure when a group decision is really appropriate or when holding a staff meeting serves merely as a device to avoiding his own decision-making responsibility.

Tannenbaum & Schmidt (1958)

Our research has shown that one of the most critical — and most frequently overlooked — aspects of decision-making is identifying, as early as possible in the decision process, who needs to be involved.

Schwarber (2005)

Vroom and colleagues (Vroom & Yetton, 1973; Vroom & Jago, 1988) have researched the problem of involvement in decision-taking in depth, identifying essentially five styles of participation. In the autocratic styles, a leader either makes a decision with available information or seeks specific information from followers before taking the decision. In the consultative styles, a leader consults on either an individual basis or on a group basis, seeking ideas and suggestions with respect to the problem. Following the consultation, the leader takes the decision. Finally, in the group style the leader facilitates a group decision, and the group makes suggestions and takes the decision. Which approach is most appropriate depends upon features of the situation. Among other features, Vroom and Yetton (1973) identified decision quality, availability of information to the leader, clarity of problem structure, and importance of decision acceptance to the choice of style. Similarly, Schwarber (2005) identified obtaining information, creating alternatives, gaining commitment, and training future generations. Normative situational guidance to leaders is available as graphical trees (Vroom & Jago, 1988) and as matrices or as support software (Vroom, 2003). Since there is evidence that following the appropriate style provides for better decision-taking (Vroom & Jago, 1988; Field & Andrews, 1998) and the above tools exist, it could be hoped that practice closer to the normative model would follow. Unfortunately, the guiding tools require leaders to appraise the input data fairly, but, as introduced earlier, such a step can be susceptible to bias, in particular the predispositional tendency. A leader can first decide how a decision will be taken and then backpropagate to characterise the situation accordingly. Recent work (Vroom & Jago, 2007) has focused on the training of leaders to apply decision styles closer to that of the normative guidance.

Organizational Roles

Looking more broadly, Rogers and Blenko (2006) have considered decision-taking bottlenecks within large international corporations. Decisions are slowed when there is lack of clarity with respect to which part of a decision is to be taken in which part of an organization. Distinctive bottlenecks are global versus local, centre versus business unit, function versus function, and inside versus outside partners. Rogers and Blenko

(2006) suggest that assigning specific decision-taking roles removes the bottlenecks. Five significant roles exist: *recommend*, *agree*, *perform*, *input*, and *decide* (RAPID). Within any decision, some of these roles may be located in different parts of the organization, but this should be clearly specified. For instance, recommending proposals, formally deciding, and agreeing to a recommendation might be globally taken, whereas inputting to a decision and performing may be locally taken. Specifically, Rogers and Blenko (2006) highlight three common sources of difficulty:

1. A lack of clarity about who owns the formal decision (*D*) can lead to unending argument, or, if no one owns it, then no decision will be taken.
2. If there are too many people with veto power (*A*), then few recommendations reach the stage of being performed.
3. If many are giving input (*I*), it is unlikely that all are contributing significantly.

Overview of Text

The remainder of this text aims to present some common decision analysis tools that can be used in a variety of situations.

The ability to predict future and new values is important in the use of many tools. Chapter 2 introduces time series as an approach to forecasting future values and to estimating potential errors in these values.

Chapter 3 examines the prediction of other values required for decision analysis tools. It first considers explanatory forecasting methods, which assume that the variable of interest is statistically related to one or more other variables. Chapter 3 then considers qualitative approaches to understanding the decision-taking situation of interest.

Chapters 4 to 7 consider one-off and repeat decisions. In these cases, the alternatives are not directly influenced by previous decisions and therefore can be considered as individual decision-taking situations. Chapter 4 develops some basic models of inventory management, illustrating how models can develop insight even with quite limiting assumptions. These are then relaxed, e.g. showing how an assumption of certainty may at first be used and then developed to an assumption of risk. Chapter 4 also illustrates the ideas of optimisation, sensitivity analysis, feasible solutions, and discrete or continuous models of risk. Chapter 5 introduces payoff matrices as means to summarise alternatives and outcomes, including decision approaches under strict uncertainty and risk. Chapter 6 begins with an assumption of a certain future and considers the solution of constrained optimisation problems using linear programming, e.g. given limited input materials, labour hours, and market size, what mix of products should be manufactured to maximise profit. Chapter 7 presents approaches to considering interacting agents, e.g. competing organizations, that take simultaneous decisions.

Chapters 8 to 10 introduce methods used for sequential decision-taking. Sequential decision situations are those where previous decisions taken, either by the decision-taker or by others (such as competitors), directly influence the alternatives available and possible outcomes. Chapter 8 presents a framework for sequential decision-making based upon maintaining flexibility, i.e. keeping options open. Chapter 9 discusses the main features of decision tree analysis, particularly focusing on sequential decisions within an assumption of risk. Chapter 10 employs game theory to analyse situations in which one player has the opportunity to choose a strategy before another player makes a choice. In Chapters 8 to 10 the process is one of making several decisions in sequence, with each decision directly affecting subsequent decisions.

Further Reading

- Together with the references cited in this chapter, the following texts provide a more in-depth discussion of the topics covered in this introduction:

  Pidd, M. (2003) *Tools for Thinking: Modelling in Management Science*. John Wiley & Sons, Ltd, Chichester, UK.

  Rivett, P. (1994) *The Craft of Decision Modelling*. John Wiley & Sons, Ltd, Chichester, UK.

  Teale, M., Dispenza, V., Flynn, J., & Currie, D. (2003) *Management Decision-making: Towards an Integrative Approach*. Pearson Education, London, UK.

- Two approachable papers are:

  Hammond, JS., Keeney, RC., & Raiffa, H. (2006) The hidden traps in decision making. *Harvard Business Review* **84**(1), 118–126.

  Smith, JE. & von Winterfeldt, D. (2004) Decision analysis in management science. *Management Science* **50**(5), 561–574.

- The following books are not academic texts but do offer more detailed discussions of some of the issues presented in this chapter:

  Heuristics and Bounded Rationality

  Gigerenzer, G. & Selten, R. (2002) *Bounded Rationality: The Adaptive Toolbox*. MIT Press, Cambridge, MA.

  Gigerenzer, G., Todd, PM., & The ABC Research Group (2000) *Simple Heuristics that Make us Smart*. Oxford University Press, Oxford, UK.

  Gladwell, M. (2007) *Blink: The Power of Thinking Without Thinking*. Penguin Books Ltd, London, UK.

  Decision-taking and Bias

  Thaler, RH. & Sunstein, CR. (2008) *Nudge: Improving Decisions about Health, Wealth and Happiness*. Yale University Press, New Haven and London.

Uncertainty
Ariely, D. (2008) *Predictably Irrational: The Hidden Forces That Shape Our Decisions*. Harpercollins, London, UK.
Taleb, NNT. (2007) *The Black Swan: The Impact of the Highly Improbable*. Penguin Books, Ltd, London, UK.

Activities

A1.1 Read *On Chesil Beach* by Ian McEwan, noting the decisions taken, how they were taken, and the consequences that followed.

A1.2 Investigate the following software packages. Write a brief report on their potential use to decision-takers and managers in general:

- 'Rationale' – www.austhink.com
- 'Decision Explore' – www.banxia.com/dexplore/index.html
- 'EnquireWithin' – www.enquirewithin.co.nz

A1.3 Ask each of 100 people whether the population of Germany is more or less than 70 million, and then ask each for an estimate of the population of Germany. Ask each of another 100 people whether the population of Germany is more or less than 100 million, and then ask the same 100 people for an estimate of the population of Germany. What result would you hypothesise on the basis of the anchoring and adjustment heuristic? Test your hypothesis.

A1.4 View some presentations from the BBC series 'Dragons' Den' (www.bbc.co.uk/dragonsden). Reflect on the positive self-view bias.

A1.5 Reconsider the momentary desire bias and then design a product or a service that targets both the want and should selves.

Milkman, KL. (2008) Tap consumers' desires for 'shoulds'. *Harvard Business Review* **86**(7/8), 22–23.

A1.6 Prepare a brief presentation explaining the criterion of regret (Chapter 5) and criticisms of it, the motivational bias of regret avoidance, and how the latter could be used in a marketing campaign.

A1.7 Read *The Ladies' Paradise (Au Bonheur des Dames)* by Emile Zola. Make notes under the headings of each of Morgan's organizational metaphors as you progress.

CHAPTER 2

Time Series Forecasting

Objectives

- *To understand the different types of data that may be encountered and be able to choose the most appropriate forecasting techniques for each type.*
- *To use moving averages and centred moving averages to identify overall trends within the data.*
- *To use decomposition to identify seasonality within the data.*
- *To use exponential smoothing to create forecasts for time series data.*

Introduction

Time series forecasting is based on the assumption that a particular variable will behave in the future in much the same way as it has behaved in the past. Forecasts are produced by collecting data for the variable of interest, which are then analysed for the existence of historical patterns, and these patterns are then used to predict possible future values.

The use of formal statistical methods for forecasting is often subject to criticism owing to the simplifying assumptions that necessarily have to be made, and also the complexity of many of the techniques. They do, however, offer an advantage over more ad hoc approaches owing to the fact that statistical techniques incorporate a measure of confidence in the reliability of the forecast. The accuracy with which forecasts can be made is improving with advances in both knowledge and computing.

This chapter discusses time series decomposition, which is not an actual forecasting technique but is useful for preliminary analysis of data, and continues by introducing exponential smoothing, which is a method used to eliminate randomness by averaging previous values. Various exponential smoothing methods are introduced enabling the forecaster to predict values for data exhibiting a variety of different behaviours.

Creating a Time Series Forecast – Overview

There are three steps to developing a quantitative forecast:

1. The first step is to decide the type of decision that needs to be made, and thereby the variables that need to be forecast can be identified and appropriate data can be gathered.
2. The next step entails choosing and fitting a suitable model. Preliminary analysis of the data very often suggests the most appropriate model to use or, at the very least, reduces the possible candidates. There is also an element of judgement involved, and hence familiarity with possible techniques is important.
3. The final step involves the use of the forecasting model to generate future values and assess the reliability of these values. At this stage, some measure of success of the forecast can be evaluated to decide whether an alternative method should be chosen.

Data Types

There is a wide variety of quantitative data. Fortunately, for those who are required to analyse it and forecast with it, the majority of quantitative data can be classified according to certain shared characteristics.

A common type of data, often known as *white noise*, is purely random in nature (see Figure 2.1). With this type of data there are no discernable patterns.

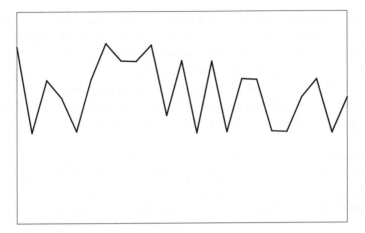

Figure 2.1 White noise.

Although the behaviour of many variables exhibiting white noise characteristics results from measurable changes or actions (e.g. the purchasing choices of consumers), the relationships between the variable of interest and the explanatory factors are extremely complex and as such are essentially random. For example, the behaviour of the stock market depends upon many individual decisions taken during each day, each of these decisions being based on any number of other factors, and so on. Consequently, the fluctuations in the stock market appear to be random.

Another type of data often encountered is called *non-stationary* data (see Figure 2.2). Although these data include random fluctuations, overall the data are

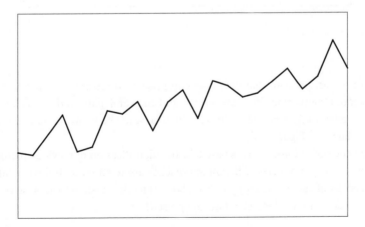

Figure 2.2 Non-stationary data.

increasing or decreasing. In the case of the data illustrated in Figure 2.2, the series is increasing. *Non-stationary* refers to the fact that the data have an overall *trend* indicating the overall direction of movement of data. Hence, the trend is essentially the average change in the value of the data for each unit change in time. Any data without an overall trend (such as white noise), where the fluctuations occur about a horizontal line, are known as *stationary*. The example in Figure 2.2 illustrates data that have a positive trend, meaning that the data are increasing overall.

The final type of data that will be discussed here is *seasonal* data (see Figure 2.3). These data have a general pattern that will repeat over a regular number of time periods. This is often related to data that are influenced by the time of year (hence the term seasonal), time of month, or time of day, such as sales data.

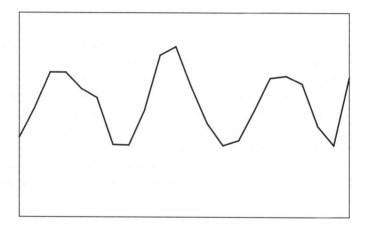

Figure 2.3   Seasonal data.

It is important to note that data may comprise all three types in that they have some random fluctuations but have a trend and an overall pattern that repeats over a regular number of time periods. This type of data would be known as non-stationary seasonal data (see Figure 2.4).

Since time series forecasting is based on the identification of previous patterns of behaviour in the data series, different approaches are required to deal with different combinations of the elements described above. The first task is to analyse the data in order to determine which elements are present.

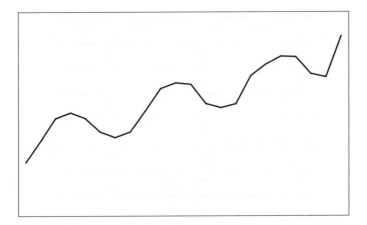

Figure 2.4 Non-stationary seasonal data.

Identifying Trends

The easiest way to identify a trend is to calculate a simple *moving average* (MA), a technique that smooths the random fluctuations in the data, revealing the overall trend of the data. To apply this technique, averages of several consecutive data values in the time series are calculated. The key assumption is that values that are close in time are also likely to be close in value, and therefore the value of a time series at a particular point in time can be represented by an average of the values of the series near that point. The number of data points included in the average defines the order of the MA. For example, consider the quarterly sales volume data shown in Figure 2.5.

A third-order MA is calculated from three data points: the data point upon which the average is centred, the data point immediately prior to the original data point, and the data point immediately following the original data point. So, when calculating the third-order MA for the entire series, the first step is to take the average of the first three data points:

$$T_2 = \frac{1}{3}(Y_1 + Y_2 + Y_3)$$

$$= \frac{1}{3}(6 + 9 + 12)$$

$$= 9$$

This average is centred on the point where $t = 2$.

Y	Year	Quarter	Sales (000 units)
Y_1	1	Q1	6.0
Y_2		Q2	9.0
Y_3		Q3	12.0
Y_4		Q4	8.0
Y_5	2	Q1	8.0
Y_6		Q2	13.5
Y_7		Q3	17.0
Y_8		Q4	13.0
Y_9	3	Q1	12.0
Y_{10}		Q2	20.3
Y_{11}		Q3	30.0
Y_{12}		Q4	19.5
Y_{13}	4	Q1	14.0
Y_{14}		Q2	22.0
Y_{15}		Q3	25.0

Figure 2.5 Quarterly sales data.

The next step involves using the same process but starting with the value of Y_2 rather than Y_1, and so

$$T_3 = \frac{1}{3} (Y_2 + Y_3 + Y_4)$$

$$= \frac{1}{3} (9 + 12 + 8)$$

$$= 9.7$$

This average is centred on the point where $t = 3$ and the process continues until all data points are used (see Figure 2.6).

In general, a third-order MA is given by the following:

$$T_t = \frac{1}{3} (Y_{t-1} + Y_t + Y_{t+1})$$

Y	Year	Quarter	Sales (000 units)	Trend T (third-order)	Trend T (fifth-order)
Y_1	1	Q1	6.0	—	—
Y_2		Q2	9.0	9.0	—
Y_3		Q3	12.0	9.7	8.6
Y_4		Q4	8.0	9.3	10.1
Y_5	2	Q1	8.0	9.8	11.7
Y_6		Q2	13.5	12.8	11.9
Y_7		Q3	17.0	14.5	12.7
Y_8		Q4	13.0	14.0	15.2
Y_9	3	Q1	12.0	15.1	18.5
Y_{10}		Q2	20.3	20.8	19.0
Y_{11}		Q3	30.0	23.3	19.2
Y_{12}		Q4	19.5	21.2	21.2
Y_{13}	4	Q1	14.0	18.5	22.1
Y_{14}		Q2	22.0	20.3	—
Y_{15}		Q3	25.0	—	—

Figure 2.6 Quarterly sales data with trends.

The order of the previous example was chosen arbitrarily, and so it is useful to compare the results of a third-order MA with those of a fifth-order MA.

A fifth-order MA is calculated as follows:

$$T_3 = \frac{1}{3} (Y_1 + Y_2 + Y_3 + Y_4 + Y_5)$$

$$= \frac{1}{3} (6 + 9 + 12 + 8 + 8)$$

$$= 8.6$$

This is centred on the point where $t = 3$. The full results are shown in Figure 2.6. For the effect of increasing the order of the moving average, see Figure 2.7.

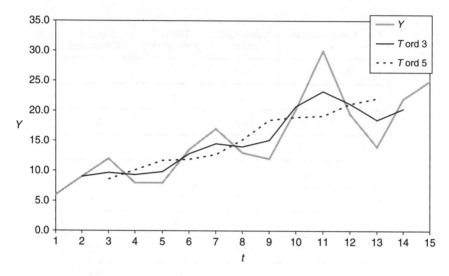

Figure 2.7 Sales data and trends.

From the plot in Figure 2.7 it is clear that increasing the order of the MA creates a smoother trend. Nevertheless, this reduces the amount of information available, since moving averages cannot be calculated for all data values. Specifically, if an mth-order MA is given by

$$T_t = \frac{1}{m} \sum_{j=-n}^{n} Y_{t+j}$$

where $n = (m - 1)/2$, then $m - 1$ data points will be sacrificed.

Centred Moving Averages

Each of the moving averages calculated has been of odd order and has included a data point upon which the average has been centred and an equal number of data points either side of this central data point. This poses a problem if an even order is chosen for the moving average, since an even number of data points will not have a central value.

The calculation of a moving average with an even order number requires a two-step process that involves averaging two consecutive moving averages. This is known as a *centred moving average* (CMA). Written formally, a CMA is given by

$$T_t = \frac{1}{2m} \left(\sum_{j=-n}^{n-1} Y_{t+j} + \sum_{j=-n+1}^{n} Y_{t+j} \right)$$

where $n = m/2$. This will be centred on the data point at time t.

Assuming that a fourth-order CMA is required, this is given by

$$T_t = \frac{1}{8} \left(\sum_{j=-2}^{1} Y_{t+j} + \sum_{j=-1}^{2} Y_{t+j} \right)$$

Before using this equation, it is necessary to determine the data point upon which the first average will be centred. Since the first data value that can be used in the CMA calculation is Y_1, it follows that $t + j = 1$ or $t - n = 1$, and hence $t = 1 + n$. In this example, $n = 2$, and therefore the first average will be centred on the point where $t = 3$. The first CMA is then given by

$$T_3 = \frac{1}{8} \left(\sum_{j=-2}^{1} Y_{3+j} + \sum_{j=-1}^{2} Y_{3+j} \right)$$

Expanding this results in

$$T_3 = \frac{1}{8} (Y_1 + Y_2 + Y_3 + Y_4 + Y_2 + Y_3 + Y_4 + Y_5)$$

Therefore

$$T_3 = \frac{1}{8} (Y_1 + 2Y_2 + 2Y_3 + 2Y_4 + Y_5)$$

and hence

$$T_3 = \frac{1}{8} \left(6 + \{2 \times 9\} + \{2 \times 12\} + \{2 \times 8\} + 8 \right) = 9.0$$

For the full results, see Figure 2.8.

A centred fourth-order moving average is equivalent to a fifth-order moving average, but the weighting of the endpoints of the average are only given half the weighting of the other time periods in the average. This is easier to appreciate by looking again at the fourth-order CMA:

$$T_3 = \frac{1}{2 \times 4} \left((Y_1 + Y_2 + Y_3 + Y_4) + (Y_2 + Y_3 + Y_4 + Y_5) \right)$$

$$T_3 = \frac{1}{8} (Y_1 + 2Y_2 + 2Y_3 + 2Y_4 + Y_5)$$

$$T_3 = \frac{Y_1}{8} + \frac{Y_2}{4} + \frac{Y_3}{4} + \frac{Y_4}{4} + \frac{Y_5}{8}$$

Y	Year	Quarter	Sales (000 units)	CMA
Y_1	1	Q1	6.0	—
Y_2		Q2	9.0	—
Y_3		Q3	12.0	9.0
Y_4		Q4	8.0	9.8
Y_5	2	Q1	8.0	11.0
Y_6		Q2	13.5	12.3
Y_7		Q3	17.0	13.4
Y_8		Q4	13.0	14.7
Y_9	3	Q1	12.0	17.2
Y_{10}		Q2	20.3	19.6
Y_{11}		Q3	30.0	20.7
Y_{12}		Q4	19.5	21.2
Y_{13}	4	Q1	14.0	20.8
Y_{14}		Q2	22.0	—
Y_{15}		Q3	25.0	—

Figure 2.8 Quarterly sales data with trend.

Hence, the middle three time periods are given twice the weighting of the two end periods. This makes a centred moving average an ideal choice when smoothing quarterly or monthly data where the seasonal pattern repeats over a year. The reason for this is that, in a standard fifth-order moving average, each of the time periods is given equal weighting. Considering quarterly data with a seasonal pattern repeating over a year, averaging over five quarters would give a double weighting to one of the quarters. The centred moving average gives a half weighting to the two end periods, making the average equivalent to taking four time periods.

With an annual seasonal pattern and quarterly or monthly data, centred moving averages of order 12, 24, and 36 are very often used, depending upon the quantity of data available, since, the higher the order of the CMA, the greater the degree of smoothing that will be achieved.

Weighted Moving Averages

As the centred moving average has shown, it is possible to calculate a moving average by weighting the contribution of the time periods. The general form for this type of average is

$$T_t = \sum_{j=-n}^{n} a_j Y_{t+j}$$

where $n = (m - 1)/2$, if m is odd or $n = m/2$ if m is even.

The weights are denoted by a_j and must be symmetric $(a_j = a_{-j})$ and sum to 1. A centred fourth-order moving average can then be written as

$$T_t = \sum_{j=-2}^{2} a_j Y_{t+j}$$

such that

$$a_j = \begin{cases} \dfrac{1}{8} & \text{when } j = \pm 2 \\ \dfrac{1}{4} & \text{when } j = 0, \pm 1 \end{cases}$$

There have been many different combinations of weights used in practice; for a brief discussion, see Makridakis, Wheelwright, & Hyndman (1998). Nonetheless, the general rule of thumb is that, the greater the degree of randomness in the data, the larger will be the number of terms required in the moving average.

Decomposition

The methods shown so far are useful for identifying stationary or non-stationary data, but they do not identify patterns of seasonality. Since seasonality is a common characteristic of business and economic data, it is necessary to be able to identify seasonality in addition to identifying stationarity.

The decomposition method assumes that data comprise four elements: a trend, a seasonal component, a cyclic component, and a random component. The cyclic component represents the influence of the business cycle. Since forecast horizons are usually much shorter than the business cycle, it is assumed that the trend and business cycle are combined into one element and known as 'trend cycle' or just as 'trend'. Hence, the data (Y) at any given time (t) are assumed to be a function of the seasonal component (S), the trend (T), and the random element or error (ε), and hence

$$Y_t = f(S_t, T_t, \varepsilon_t)$$

The overall aim of the decomposition method is to isolate each of these components by firstly removing the trend and then isolating the seasonal element. Any residual is then assumed to constitute the error component of the model.

When using the decomposition method, there are two standard forms: the additive and the multiplicative. The additive form is illustrated by the equation

$$Y_t = S_t + T_t + \varepsilon_t \tag{2.1}$$

and the multiplicative form is given by

$$Y_t = S_t \times T_t \times \varepsilon_t \tag{2.2}$$

An additive form would be chosen if the magnitude of the seasonal fluctuations in the data did not change with the level of the trend (see Figure 2.9).

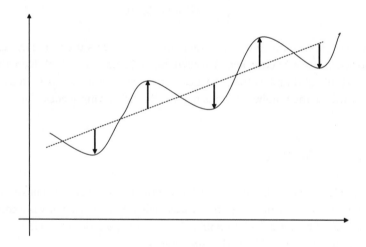

Figure 2.9 Additive decomposition model.

The overall trend of the data is indicated by the broken line, and, the amplitude of the seasonal pattern remains constant as the trend continues to increase.

With the multiplicative form, the magnitude of the seasonal fluctuations changes with the value of the trend (see Figure 2.10).

Again, the trend is indicated by the broken line. In this example, the amplitudes of the seasonal fluctuations increase as the value of the trend increases.

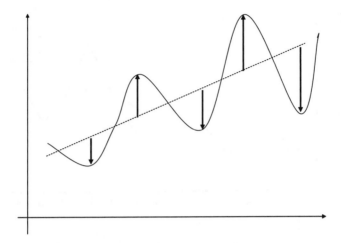

Figure 2.10   Multiplicative decomposition model.

Finding the Seasonal Component

Recalling the equations for the additive and multiplicative decomposition methods and removing the trend from both sides results in the following equation for the additive model:

$$Y_t - T_t = S_t + \varepsilon_t \qquad (2.3)$$

and in the following equation for the multiplicative model:

$$\frac{Y_t}{T_t} = S_t \times \varepsilon_t \qquad (2.4)$$

Hence, by removing the trend from the original data, only the seasonal component and the error remain.

Before using these equations, however, the data need to be examined in order to decide the more appropriate of these two forms. This can be achieved in two ways: the data can be plotted together with the trend and the decision can be made by eye, or both approaches can be used and then the best form can be assessed by analysing the errors between the actual decomposition model and the data.

Plotting the data for the previous example together with the trend given by the centred fourth-order moving average results in the chart shown in Figure 2.11.

An initial inspection would suggest that this follows a multiplicative form, as the amplitude of the seasonal fluctuation is increasing with the trend. Assuming that these data follow a multiplicative form, the next step is to remove the trend from the

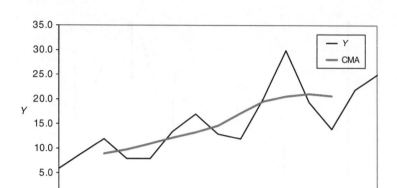

Figure 2.11 Quarterly sales data with a fourth-order CMA.

data as specified in equation (2.4). Therefore, it is necessary to divide the data point by the value of the trend.

When calculating the trend for this particular set of data, a fourth-order CMA was used. This is because the data have been collected quarterly and exhibit seasonality. The results are shown in Figure 2.12. Note that these values are only rounded at the last stage of calculation.

Note that the value of Y/T is greater than 1 where the data point is above the trend line, and less than 1 where the data point is below the trend.

Y	Year	Quarter	Sales (000 units)	CMA (T)	Y/T
Y_1	1	Q1	6.0	—	—
Y_2		Q2	9.0	—	—
Y_3		Q3	12.0	9.0	1.3
Y_4		Q4	8.0	9.8	0.8
Y_5	2	Q1	8.0	11.0	0.7
Y_6		Q2	13.5	12.3	1.1
Y_7		Q3	17.0	13.4	1.3
Y_8		Q4	13.0	14.7	0.9
Y_9	3	Q1	12.0	17.2	0.7

Figure 2.12 Quarterly sales data.

Y_{10}		Q2	20.3	19.6	1.0
Y_{11}		Q3	30.0	20.7	1.5
Y_{12}		Q4	19.5	21.2	0.9
Y_{13}	4	Q1	14.0	20.8	0.7
Y_{14}		Q2	22.0	—	—
Y_{15}		Q3	25.0	—	—

Figure 2.12   (Continued).

Once the trend has been removed from the data, the seasonal and random components remain. The next step requires the removal of the random component. This can be achieved by averaging all values for each quarter. For example, the average for the third quarter of the year is given by

$$\frac{1.3 + 1.3 + 1.5}{3} = 1.4$$

noting that the calculation is rounded at the final stage. The same process is followed for the remaining quarters, resulting in the values shown in Figure 2.13.

Quarter	S_t
1	0.7
2	1.1
3	1.4
4	0.9

Figure 2.13   Seasonal differences.

Plotting these figures results in a clearer representation of the seasonal pattern of the data (Figure 2.14).

At the points above the broken line, the seasonal component brings the data above the trend line. Hence, during quarters 2 and 3, the sales are above the trend on average. During quarters 1 and 4, the sales are below the trend line.

Figure 2.15 illustrates the final values for the trend and the seasonal elements.

In order to determine if the initial assumption that the data exhibit multiplicative seasonality is most suitable, the same process can be carried out using the additive

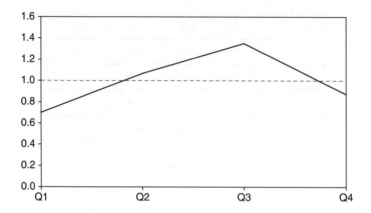

Figure 2.14 Plot of the seasonal changes.

Y	Year	Quarter	Sales (000 units)	CMA (*T*)	*S*
Y_1	1	Q1	6.0	—	—
Y_2		Q2	9.0	—	—
Y_3		Q3	12.0	9.0	1.4
Y_4		Q4	8.0	9.8	0.9
Y_5	2	Q1	8.0	11.0	0.7
Y_6		Q2	13.5	12.3	1.1
Y_7		Q3	17.0	13.4	1.4
Y_8		Q4	13.0	14.7	0.9
Y_9	3	Q1	12.0	17.2	0.7
Y_{10}		Q2	20.3	19.6	1.1
Y_{11}		Q3	30.0	20.7	1.4
Y_{12}		Q4	19.5	21.2	0.9
Y_{13}	4	Q1	14.0	20.8	0.7
Y_{14}		Q2	22.0	—	—
Y_{15}		Q3	25.0	—	—

Figure 2.15 Multiplicative seasonality.

method. A measurement of error can then be used to determine which of the forms matches the data most closely.

Recall for the additive model that $Y_t - T_t = S_t + \varepsilon_t$. The component $S_t + \varepsilon_t$ is calculated, and then the average for each quarter is found, leaving simply the S_t component. The results are contained in Figure 2.16.

Y	Year	Quarter	Sales (000 units)	CMA (T)	Y–T	S
Y_1	1	Q1	6.0	—	—	—
Y_2		Q2	9.0	—	—	—
Y_3		Q3	12.0	9.0	3.0	5.3
Y_4		Q4	8.0	9.8	−1.8	−1.7
Y_5	2	Q1	8.0	11.0	−3.0	−5.0
Y_6		Q2	13.5	12.3	1.3	1.0
Y_7		Q3	17.0	13.4	3.6	5.3
Y_8		Q4	13.0	14.7	−1.7	−1.7
Y_9	3	Q1	12.0	17.2	−5.2	−5.0
Y_{10}		Q2	20.3	19.6	0.7	1.0
Y_{11}		Q3	30.0	20.7	9.3	5.3
Y_{12}		Q4	19.5	21.2	−1.7	−1.7
Y_{13}	4	Q1	14.0	20.8	−6.8	−5.0
Y_{14}		Q2	22.0	—	—	—
Y_{15}		Q3	25.0	—	—	—

Figure 2.16 Quarterly sales data – additive model.

In order to determine which of the two forms matches the data more closely, an error, e, is calculated that is defined as the difference between actual data and the values generated by the decomposition model, $\hat{Y}$. Thus

$$e_t = Y_t - \hat{Y}_t$$

Since the process of constructing the decomposition models has included finding averages at each step, the models essentially represent an average of the data.

Consequently, assuming that the errors are random with a mean of zero implies that the mean of the components, ε_t, is also zero and can therefore be disregarded for the moment.[1] Hence, the decomposition model equations are as follows:

$$\text{Multiplicative}: \hat{Y}_t = T_t \times S_t$$

$$\text{Additive}: \hat{Y}_t = T_t + S_t$$

The error values are shown in Figure 2.17.

Y	Year	Quarter	Sales (000 units)	Errors	
				Multiplicative	Additive
Y_1	1	Q1	6.0	—	—
Y_2		Q2	9.0	—	—
Y_3		Q3	12.0	−0.2	−2.3
Y_4		Q4	8.0	−0.6	−0.1
Y_5	2	Q1	8.0	0.3	2.0
Y_6		Q2	13.5	0.4	0.3
Y_7		Q3	17.0	−1.1	−1.7
Y_8		Q4	13.0	0.1	0.0
Y_9	3	Q1	12.0	0.0	−0.2
Y_{10}		Q2	20.3	−0.7	−0.3
Y_{11}		Q3	30.0	2.0	4.0
Y_{12}		Q4	19.5	1.0	0.1
Y_{13}	4	Q1	14.0	−0.5	−1.8
Y_{14}		Q2	22.0	—	—
Y_{15}		Q3	25.0	—	—

Figure 2.17 Errors.

---

[1] These are not unreasonable assumptions, since, if the errors were non-random and/or non-zero, this would likely imply that there is some relationship between the current data and previous data. Although there are methods of dealing with this, decomposition is not one of them.

Comparing the two columns, it would appear that the additive model has the greatest errors. This can be checked quite easily by calculating a simple average known as the *mean square error* (MSE). The MSE is calculated by squaring the errors to remove negatives and then averaging these squared values, or by the equation

$$\text{MSE} = \frac{1}{p} \sum_{j=1}^{p} \left(Y_j - \hat{Y}_j \right)^2$$

where p is the total number of errors.

This results in a value of 0.7 for the multiplicative model and a value of 2.9 for the additive model, confirming that the multiplicative form is the best choice, as it results in the lowest MSE.

Note that data of the multiplicative form can in fact be transformed into data of the additive form by taking the logarithm. The equivalence of the two forms can be confirmed by taking the logarithm of the multiplicative equation.

Although the decomposition method is not used as a formal forecasting technique, it is useful in assessing the form of seasonality in the data and also the nature of the trend. This allows the forecaster to choose an appropriate approach when actually calculating a forecast, and to deseasonalise (account for fluctuations due to seasonality) data when reporting past performance.

Average and Moving Average Forecasts

The simplest form of forecast that can be calculated is to use the average of the data. If the data have no discernable trend with minimal fluctuations, the assumption that the average of the previous data is a good approximation to the next value in the time series is an acceptable one.

The forecast is given by the following equation:

$$F_{t+1} = \frac{1}{t} \sum_{j=1}^{t} Y_j$$

If a forecast has already been made for the previous time period (i.e. F_t has already been calculated), then the average can be rewritten in terms of the previous forecast. Rearrange the equation above to give

$$F_{t+1} = \frac{1}{t} \left(Y_t + \sum_{j=1}^{t-1} Y_j \right)$$

and so in terms of the previous forecast[2]

$$F_{t+1} = \frac{1}{t}\left(Y_t + (t-1)F_t\right)$$

If the data have a discernable trend but little or no seasonality, then the moving average can be used as a forecast. The moving average used in these circumstances is slightly different from that encountered previously. For decomposition, the moving average is an average of values close to the data point. When used for forecasting, the moving average is calculated for the most recent observations, and hence

$$F_{t+1} = \frac{1}{m}\left(\sum_{j=t-m+1}^{t} Y_j\right)$$

for a moving average of order m. For example, a forecast based on a third-order moving average is given by

$$F_{t+1} = \frac{1}{3}\left(Y_{t-2} + Y_{t-1} + Y_t\right)$$

This type of forecast can also be written in terms of previous forecasts, although it is not quite as straightforward as the simple average. The easiest way to determine how this can be rewritten is to expand the summation

$$F_{t+1} = \frac{1}{m}\left(Y_{t-m+1} + Y_{t-m+2} + Y_{t-m+3} + \cdots + Y_{t-1} + Y_t\right) \tag{2.5}$$

Now consider F_t

$$F_t = \frac{1}{m}\left(Y_{t-m} + Y_{t-m+1} + Y_{t-m+2} + \cdots + Y_{t-2} + Y_{t-1}\right) \tag{2.6}$$

Comparing equations (2.5) and (2.6), it follows that equation (2.5) can be rewritten as

$$F_{t+1} = F_t - \frac{1}{m}Y_{t-m} + \frac{1}{m}Y_t$$

so

$$F_{t+1} = F_t + \frac{1}{m}\left(Y_t - Y_{t-m}\right)$$

---

[2] Note that $F_t = \dfrac{1}{t-1}\sum_{j=1}^{t-1} Y_j$, and so $F_t(t-1) = \sum_{j=1}^{t-1} Y_j$.

This forecast copes better with seasonality than a simple average[3] and can be useful when a quick and simple forecast is required. Nevertheless, these types of forecast are rarely used because exponential smoothing techniques are relatively simple to implement and produce superior results.

Simple Exponential Smoothing

The *simple exponential smoothing* (SES) technique is related to the weighted moving averages previously encountered, and, in order to derive exponential smoothing equations, the assumption is made that a previous forecast, F_t, exists. The forecast error can then be written as

$$Y_t - F_t$$

A simple forecast can be constructed that expresses the new forecast as the previous forecast plus some proportion of the error, or

$$F_{t+1} = F_t + \alpha \, (Y_t - F_t) \tag{2.7}$$

where $\alpha \in [0, 1]$.

Consequently, α is the weighting placed on the forecast error. This forecast will always be lagged by one time period because the error on the previous forecast is used.

Equation (2.7) is not the simplest form, and so the terms are grouped to produce the final form of the forecasting equation:

$$F_{t+1} = \alpha Y_t + (1 - \alpha) F_t$$

where $\alpha \in [0, 1]$.

To examine in detail how this technique works, consider the case where $t = 3$:

$$F_4 = \alpha Y_3 + (1 - \alpha) F_3 \tag{2.8}$$

Now

$$F_3 = \alpha Y_2 + (1 - \alpha) F_2 \tag{2.9}$$

---

[3] Note that $Y_t - Y_{t-m}$ is the difference between the current data point and the last data point at the same point in the seasonal cycle if the length of the seasonal cycle is assumed to be equal to m.

Substituting equation (2.9) into equation (2.8) gives

$$F_4 = \alpha Y_3 + (1 - \alpha)(\alpha Y_2 + (1 - \alpha) F_2)$$
$$= \alpha Y_3 + \alpha (1 - \alpha) Y_2 + (1 - \alpha)^2 F_2$$

Continuing this process results in the following:

$$F_4 = \alpha Y_3 + \alpha (1 - \alpha) Y_2 + \alpha (1 - \alpha)^2 Y_1 + (1 - \alpha)^3 F_1 \qquad (2.10)$$

The effect of choosing different values for α can be assessed using equation (2.10). Note that the values sum to 1 across each row (Figure 2.18), indicating the proportion of the forecast that comes from each of the previous values and the previous forecast.

α	$\alpha (1 - \alpha)$	$\alpha (1 - \alpha)^2$	$(1 - \alpha)^3$
0.0	0	0	1
0.1	0.090	0.081	0.729
0.2	0.160	0.128	0.512
0.3	0.210	0.147	0.343
0.4	0.240	0.144	0.216
0.5	0.250	0.125	0.125
0.6	0.240	0.096	0.064
0.7	0.210	0.063	0.027
0.8	0.160	0.032	0.008
0.9	0.090	0.009	0.001
1	0	0	0

Figure 2.18 Changing α.

It is clear that increasing the value for α reduces the contribution of the older data points and older forecasts. Choosing the most effective value for α requires the use of both judgement and numerical optimisation techniques. Since the forecast equations are non-linear in α, non-linear numerical optimisation techniques need to be used in order to minimise some measure of error such as the mean square error.

These techniques are beyond the scope of this text; however, Chapter 13 of Hillier and Lieberman (2006) is a useful starting point.

Trial and error can also be used to determine an appropriate value for α. For instance, using the data from the previous example, a forecast has been calculated using different values of α, and the MSE has been calculated for each choice. The results are shown in Figure 2.19. Note that the initial forecast (i.e. F_1) is assumed to be equal to Y_1.

| | | Forecasts | | | | | |
| | | α | | | | | |
	Y_t	0	0.1	0.4	0.5	0.6	1
Q1	6.0	6.0	6.0	6.0	6.0	6.0	6.0
Q2	9.0	6.0	6.0	6.0	6.0	6.0	6.0
Q3	12.0	6.0	6.3	7.2	7.5	7.8	9.0
Q4	8.0	6.0	6.9	9.1	9.8	10.3	12.0
Q1	8.0	6.0	7.0	8.7	8.9	8.9	8.0
Q2	13.5	6.0	7.1	8.4	8.4	8.4	8.0
Q3	17.0	6.0	7.7	10.4	11.0	11.4	13.5
Q4	13.0	6.0	8.7	13.1	14.0	14.8	17.0
Q1	12.0	6.0	9.1	13.0	13.5	13.7	13.0
Q2	20.3	6.0	9.4	12.6	12.7	12.7	12.0
Q3	30.0	6.0	10.5	15.7	16.5	17.3	20.3
Q4	19.5	6.0	12.4	21.4	23.3	24.9	30.0
Q1	14.0	6.0	13.1	20.6	21.4	21.7	19.5
Q2	22.0	6.0	13.2	18.0	17.7	17.1	14.0
Q3	25.0	6.0	14.1	19.6	19.8	20.0	22.0
MSE	—	130.6	63.1	30.7	30.0	30.2	31.3

Figure 2.19 Choosing α.

Comparing the MSEs, the optimal value of α is between 0.4 and 0.6. Hence, the best forecast is produced by weighting the calculation more or less evenly between the older forecasts and most recent forecasts. Using 0.5 for the value of α produces a forecast for the next period of 22.4.

The plot of a selection of the forecasts illustrates how poorly the SES technique performs for this type of data (see Figure 2.20).

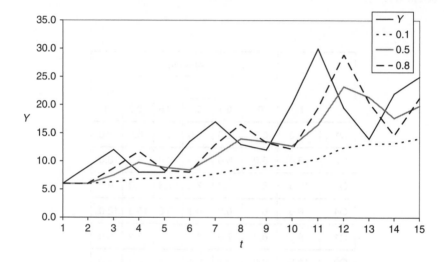

Figure 2.20   SES forecasts.

It is clear that the exponential forecasts are lagged by one time period. Consequently, this approach performs poorly with data that are markedly changing owing to trend or seasonality.

The SES technique works best with stationary data with little or no seasonality. For an example of such data and forecasts, see Figure 2.21.

		Forecasts						
					α			
t	Y_t	0	0.1	0.5	0.7	0.8	0.9	1
1	6.0	6.0	6.0	6.0	6.0	6.0	6.0	6.0
2	6.2	6.0	6.0	6.0	6.0	6.0	6.0	6.0
3	6.2	6.0	6.0	6.0	6.1	6.1	6.2	6.2	6.2

Figure 2.21   Forecasts for stationary data with no seasonality.

4	6.6	6.0	6.0	6.2	6.2	6.2	6.2	6.2
5	6.8	6.0	6.1	6.4	6.5	6.5	6.6	6.6
6	6.4	6.0	6.2	6.6	6.7	6.7	6.8	6.8
7	6.8	6.0	6.2	6.5	6.5	6.5	6.4	6.4
8	7.2	6.0	6.2	6.6	6.7	6.7	6.8	6.8
9	7.2	6.0	6.3	6.9	7.1	7.1	7.2	7.2
10	7.2	6.0	6.4	7.1	7.2	7.2	7.2	7.2
11	6.8	6.0	6.5	7.1	7.2	7.2	7.2	7.2
12	7.2	6.0	6.5	7.0	6.9	6.9	6.8	6.8
13	7.2	6.0	6.6	7.1	7.1	7.1	7.2	7.2
14	7.2	6.0	6.7	7.1	7.2	7.2	7.2	7.2
15	7.0	6.0	6.7	7.2	7.2	7.2	7.2	7.2
Errors	—	0.8	0.3	0.1	0.1	0.1	0.1	0.1

Figure 2.21 (Continued).

Comparing the errors for these data, the optimal choice of α is between 0.5 and 1, so this forecast is weighted in favour of the more recent forecasts. A plot of the data against the best forecast (for $\alpha = 0.8$) is shown in Figure 2.22.

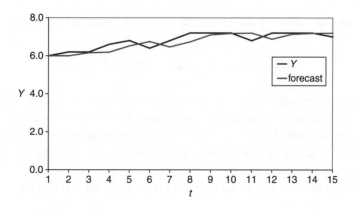

Figure 2.22 Plot of forecasts.

Since the technique is related to moving averages, the result is to smooth the data, and so the SES technique smooths the data to produce the forecast.

It should be noted that the MSE is not the only measure of error that can be used to assess the effectiveness of the forecast, and the choice of error measurement can influence the optimal value of α. A more detailed discussion of measuring forecast error can be found in Makridakis, Wheelwright, and Hyndman (1998).

Exponential Smoothing for Data with a Trend

The SES technique is easy to use and can produce a good forecast for data exhibiting relatively little fluctuation from the average. Nevertheless, business and economic data often reveal both trend and seasonality together with random elements. Fortunately, the exponential smoothing technique can be modified to deal with both a trend and seasonality, either separately or combined.

Holt's method (Holt, 2004), originally developed in 1957, is an exponential smoothing technique suited to dealing with non-stationary data and can be understood by first considering the standard SES forecast equation:

$$F_{t+1} = \alpha Y_t + (1 - \alpha) F_t$$

Since the data has a trend, the previous forecast, F_t, may not necessarily be a good approximation to the new data. If, however, the slope of the trend line can be approximated, the previous forecast plus the value of the trend would be a better approximation to the value of the data. Holt's method approximates the slope of the trend line and uses this together with a smoothed value of the data to produce a forecast.

The first equation of Holt's method gives a smoothed approximation of the data:

$$V_t = V_{t-1} + T_{t-1} + \alpha \left(Y_t - (V_{t-1} + T_{t-1}) \right) \tag{2.11}$$

Hence, the current value is approximated by the sum of the previous smoothed value (V_{t-1}) and the value of the trend (T_{t-1}) in the previous time period plus a proportion of the error between the current value (Y_t) and the estimate of the current value $(V_{t-1} + T_{t-1})$. This means that the forecast will not be lagged, since the current value is incorporated into the forecast.

Grouping terms in equation (2.11) leads to the final form of the equation:

$$V_t = \alpha Y_t + (1 - \alpha) (V_{t-1} + T_{t-1}) \tag{2.12}$$

Note that the time indices are slightly different to the original exponential smoothing equation: the smoothed value at time t is expressed in terms of the actual value at time t.

The next equation gives the value of the trend T at time t:

$$T_t = T_{t-1} + \beta \, (V_t - (V_{t-1} + T_{t-1})) \tag{2.13}$$

In this case, the current value of the trend is given by the previous value plus an adjustment which is a proportion of the difference between the current smoothed value of the data and the previous smoothed value plus the trend. Note that $V_t - (V_{t-1} + T_{t-1})$ is equivalent to the error term in equation (2.11). To confirm this, subtract $V_{t-1} + T_{t-1}$ from both sides of equation (2.11).

Equation (2.13) is also rearranged to give the final form

$$T_t = \beta \, (V_t - V_{t-1}) + (1 - \beta) \, T_{t-1} \tag{2.14}$$

The forecast is then given by

$$F_{t+m} = V_t + mT_t \quad \text{for } m = 1, 2, 3, \ldots$$

Hence, the forecast values are equal to the smoothed value plus a multiple of the trend where the multiple is the number of periods into the future for which the forecast is required.

To summarise, Holt's method is defined by the following set of equations:

$$V_t = \alpha Y_t + (1 - \alpha) \, (V_{t-1} + T_{t-1})$$

$$T_t = \beta \, (V_t - V_{t-1}) + (1 - \beta) \, T_{t-1}$$

$$F_{t+m} = V_t + mT_t \quad \text{for } m = 1, 2, 3, \ldots$$

Note that, since the equations require data for time period $t - 1$, an initial estimate needs to be used for time $t = 1$. The easiest approach is to set V_1 equal to Y_1 and T_1 equal to $Y_2 - Y_1$. Holt's forecast equations when $m = 1$ are shown in detail in Figure 2.23.

A numerical example of Holt's forecast using non-stationary data is shown in Figure 2.24.

The values for α and β should be chosen by optimising some choice of error function using non-linear optimisation techniques. These particular values were chosen by trial and error using the MSE as a measure of the error.

Plotting the actual data values together with forecast values using Holt's method (Holt) and using simple exponential smoothing (SES) with $\alpha = 1$ (the most effective

t	Y_t	V_t	T_t	F_t
1	Y_1	$V_1 = Y_1$	$T_1 = Y_2 - Y_1$	—
2	Y_2	$V_2 = \alpha Y_2 + (1 - \alpha)(V_1 + T_1)$	$T_2 = \beta(V_2 - V_1) + (1 - \beta)T_1$	$V_1 + T_1$
3	Y_3	$V_3 = \alpha Y_3 + (1 - \alpha)(V_2 + T_2)$	$T_3 = \beta(V_3 - V_2) + (1 - \beta)T_2$	$V_2 + T_2$
$\vdots$	$\vdots$	$\vdots$	$\vdots$	$\vdots$
n	Y_n	$V_n = \alpha Y_n + (1 - \alpha)(V_{n-1} + T_{n-1})$	$T_n = \beta(V_n - V_{n-1}) + (1 - \beta)T_{n-1}$	$V_{n-1} + T_{n-1}$

Figure 2.23 Holt's forecast equations.

t	Y_t	V_t	T_t	F_t
1	6.0	6.0	0.0	—
2	6.0	6.0	0.0	6.0
3	7.0	6.9	0.3	6.0
4	9.0	8.8	0.8	7.2
5	8.0	8.2	0.3	9.6
6	9.0	8.9	0.5	8.5
7	11.0	10.8	0.9	9.4
8	12.0	12.0	1.0	11.7
9	13.0	13.0	1.0	12.9
10	14.0	14.0	1.0	14.0
11	16.0	15.9	1.3	15.0
12	18.0	17.9	1.5	17.2
13	20.0	19.9	1.7	19.4
14	20.0	20.2	1.2	21.6
15	19.0	19.2	0.6	21.4
16	—	—	—	19.8
17	—	—	—	20.4[a]

[a] $m = 2$.

Figure 2.24 Holt's forecast – $\alpha = 0.9$, $\beta = 0.3$, $m = 1$.

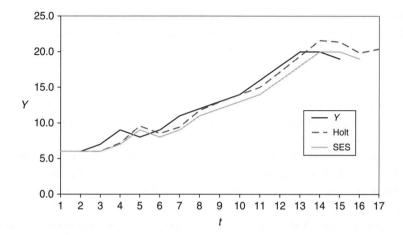

Figure 2.25 Plot of Holt's forecast versus SES forecast.

value of α for this particular dataset) shows that Holt's method appears to perform better than SES for non-stationary data (see Figure 2.25).

Note that Holt's method is also referred to as double exponential smoothing or Brown's double exponential smoothing if $\alpha = \beta$.

Exponential Smoothing for Non-Stationary Data with Seasonality

Since neither of the techniques considered so far has been able adequately to forecast non-stationary data with seasonality, the final version of exponential smoothing considered here does just that. This approach is very often known as the Holt-Winter's method and can incorporate seasonality of both multiplicative and additive form.

Exponential Smoothing for Multiplicative Seasonality

Recalling that for the multiplicative model

$$Y_t = T_t \times S_t \times \varepsilon_t$$

the actual data, Y_t, includes trend, seasonality and error (or random) elements. It is therefore necessary to modify the equations of Holt's method to account for the seasonality in the data.

For multiplicative seasonality, the modification is achieved firstly by replacing Y_t with Y_t/S_{t-s} in the equation estimating the smoothed value of the data:

$$V_t = V_{t-1} + T_{t-1} + \alpha \left(\frac{Y_t}{S_{t-s}} - (V_{t-1} + T_{t-1}) \right) \qquad (2.15)$$

where S_{t-s} is the estimate of the 'value' of the seasonality multiplier at the most recent equivalent time period in the seasonal pattern, s being the number of time periods in the full seasonal pattern.

Dividing the actual current value by the estimate amounts to 'removing' the seasonality from the data, leaving just the trend and error elements. Consequently, the bracketed element of equation (2.15) is now equivalent to the bracketed element of equation (2.11).

As with Holt's method, equation (2.15) is rearranged to give the following form:

$$V_t = \alpha \frac{Y_t}{S_{t-s}} + (1 - \alpha)(V_{t-1} + T_{t-1})$$

For the Holt-Winter's method, the equation for the trend remains the same:

$$T_t = \beta(V_t - V_{t-1}) + (1 - \beta)T_{t-1} \qquad (2.16)$$

The next equation estimates the seasonality of the data. This is given as the estimate of seasonality at the most recent equivalent time period in the seasonal pattern plus a proportion of the error. This error is the difference between the data with the smoothed trend removed and the seasonality estimate from the equivalent seasonal period:

$$S_t = S_{t-s} + \gamma \left(\frac{Y_t}{V_t} - S_{t-s} \right)$$

The terms are grouped to give

$$S_t = \gamma \frac{Y_t}{V_t} + (1 - \gamma)S_{t-s}$$

Finally, the forecast is determined by

$$F_{t+m} = (V_t + mT_t)S_{t-s+m}$$

where m is the number of time periods required for the forecast.

In summary, the full forecast is given by the following set of equations:

$$V_t = \alpha \frac{Y_t}{S_{t-s}} + (1 - \alpha)(V_{t-1} + T_{t-1})$$

$$T_t = \beta(V_t - V_{t-1}) + (1 - \beta)T_{t-1}$$

$$S_t = \gamma \frac{Y_t}{V_t} + (1 - \gamma) S_{t-s}$$

$$F_{t+m} = (V_t + mT_t) S_{t-s+m}$$

Providing initial estimates for this forecast is a little more involved than for Holt's method, since the data exhibit seasonality. The initial estimate for V is calculated as an average of the data over the first complete seasonal pattern:

$$V_s = \frac{1}{s} (Y_1 + Y_2 + \cdots + Y_s)$$

where s is the number of time periods in a complete season. Note that the initial period is not $t = 1$ but $t = s$. This is because data for a complete season are required in order to estimate the seasonality.

To provide an initial estimate for the trend, the actual trend over each season is calculated and an average is taken of these estimates. Two complete seasons of data are used in order to supply an estimate. The first trend is given by $(Y_{s+1} - Y_1)/s$ and is the trend between the first data point and the consecutive equivalent season. Similarly, the second trend is given by $(Y_{s+2} - Y_2)/s$, and so on, until the final season when the two complete seasons have been used, yielding the final trend $Y_{s+s} - Y_s/s$.

The average of these trends is taken to give an initial estimate for T, and therefore

$$T_s = \frac{1}{s} \left(\frac{Y_{s+1} - Y_1}{s} + \frac{Y_{s+2} - Y_2}{s} + \cdots + \frac{Y_{s+s} - Y_s}{s} \right)$$

The estimates for the seasonality multipliers are given by the ratio of the actual data to the smoothed value, and hence

$$S_1 = \frac{Y_1}{V_s}, S_2 = \frac{Y_2}{V_s}, \ldots, S_s = \frac{Y_s}{V_s}$$

Note that V_s is used as the denominator because this is the first estimate for the smoothed data.

An example of the use of the Holt-Winter's forecast for non-stationary data with multiplicative seasonality (period 4) is given in Figure 2.26. The parameter values used for this example are $\alpha = 1$, $\beta = 0$, $\gamma = 0$ and $m = 1$ (except for the final forecast where $m = 2$). Consequently, the best approximation to the trend is a constant (linear trend), and there is a constant repeating seasonal pattern.

The success of this method for non-stationary data with multiplicative seasonality can be seen more clearly in the plot of the data in Figure 2.27. For non-stationary data with seasonality, it is clear that the Holt-Winter's method provides the most accurate forecasts when compared with both SES and Holt's method.

t	Y_t	V_t	T_t	S_t	F_t
1	6.0	—	—	0.7	—
2	9.0	—	—	1.0	—
3	12.0	—	—	1.4	—
4	8.0	8.8	1.0	0.9	—
5	8.0	11.7	1.0	0.7	6.7
6	13.5	13.1	1.0	1.0	13.1
7	17.0	12.4	1.0	1.4	19.4
8	13.0	14.2	1.0	0.9	12.3
9	12.0	17.5	1.0	0.7	10.5
10	20.3	19.7	1.0	1.0	19.1
11	30.0	21.9	1.0	1.4	28.4
12	19.5	21.3	1.0	0.9	20.9
13	14.0	20.4	1.0	0.7	15.3
14	22.0	21.4	1.0	1.0	22.1
15	25.0	18.2[a]	1.0	1.4	30.7
16	—	—	—	—	17.6
17	—	—	—	—	18.6

[a] $m = 2$.

Figure 2.26 Holt-Winter's forecast.

Exponential Smoothing for Additive Seasonality

The set of equations in order to forecast data with additive seasonality are similar to those for multiplicative seasonality:

$$V_t = \alpha \, (Y_t - S_{t-s}) + (1 - \alpha) \, (V_{t-1} + T_{t-1})$$

$$T_t = \beta \, (V_t - V_{t-1}) + (1 - \beta) \, T_{t-1}$$

$$S_t = \gamma \, (Y_t - V_t) + (1 - \gamma) \, S_{t-s}$$

$$F_{t+m} = V_t + mT_t + S_{t-s+m}$$

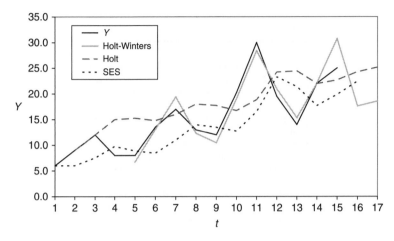

Figure 2.27 Plot of forecast comparisons.

In order to initialise the forecast, the same estimates for the initial values and trends of the series are identical to those used for multiplicative seasonality. The seasonal estimates, however, are slightly different and are given by

$$S_1 = Y_1 - V_s, S_2 = Y_2 - V_s, \ldots, S_s = Y_s - V_s$$

An example of the additive forecast is shown in Figure 2.28.

t	Y_t	V_t	T_t	S_t	F_t
1	26.0	—	—	3.5	—
2	21.0	—	—	−1.5	—
3	18.0	—	—	−4.5	—
4	25.0	22.5	−1.3	2.5	—
5	23.0	20.4	−2.1	3.1	24.7
6	16.5	18.2	−2.2	−1.6	16.8
7	13.0	16.7	−1.5	−4.1	11.5
8	17.0	14.9	−1.8	2.3	17.7
9	17.0	13.5	−1.4	3.3	16.1

Figure 2.28 Holt-Winter's forecast for additive seasonality ($\alpha = 1, \beta = 0, \gamma = 0$).

10	9.8	11.7	−1.7	−1.7	10.5
11	7.0	10.5	−1.2	−3.8	5.9
12	10.5	8.8	−1.7	2.0	11.6
13	10.0	6.9	−1.9	3.2	10.3
14	5.0	5.9	−1.1	−1.3	3.2
15	5.0	6.8	0.7	−2.8	0.9
16	—	—	—	—	9.6
17	—	—	—	—	10.3[a]

[a] $m = 2$.

Figure 2.28 (Continued).

A plot of the Holt-Winter's forecasts against the other forecasting methods[4] demonstrates its superiority for non-stationary data with seasonality (see Figure 2.29).

Standard Deviation of the Forecast

For many decision-making techniques that rely on forecasts of variables, it is simply not enough to provide a point forecast of the data. It is also necessary to provide an estimate of the variability in the forecast, the most common measure being the standard deviation. A specific case being the newsvendor problem, an example of inventory management that will be encountered in Chapter 4.

There are various approaches to developing a measure of the standard deviation, one of these being based on the error measure known as the *mean absolute deviation* (MAD), which is the mean absolute (non-zero) difference between the forecast and actual data, and hence

$$\text{MAD} = \frac{1}{n} \sum_{t=1}^{n} |Y_t - F_t|$$

The standard deviation, σ, of a dataset is defined as the square root of the average squared difference from the mean, or

$$\sigma = \sqrt{\frac{1}{n} \sum_{i=1}^{n} (x_i - \bar{x})^2}$$

---

[4] For Holt's forecast, $\alpha = 0.3$ and $\beta = 0.3$, and for the SES forecast, $\alpha = 0.5$.

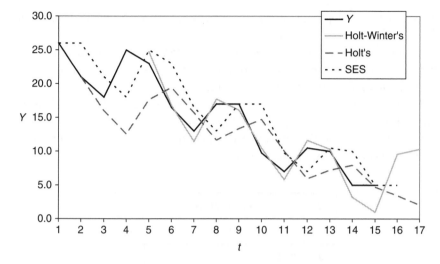

Figure 2.29   Plot of the Holt-Winter's forecast for additive seasonality.

where x_i is the data point and $\overline{x}$ is the mean. For the forecast, it is necessary to have a measure of the deviation of the data from the forecast, so it is useful to define the standard deviation in terms of MAD. It can be shown that

$$\sigma = \sqrt{\frac{\pi}{2}}\text{MAD} \qquad (2.17)$$

This derivation is via the use of integrals and is left as an investigation for the interested reader.

The question as to why the MAD should be used here rather than just calculating the standard deviation of the forecast directly is largely answered by the fact that the MAD is less sensitive to outliers. This implies that a forecast of a standard deviation based on the MAD will be more robust, as it is less likely to be influenced by occasions when the value happens to be unusually high or low.

The measure for the standard deviation given by equation (2.17) is for the current series of data. As more data become available, the MAD is usually updated using the exponential smoothing method. Consequently, not all the data need be stored, just the most recent calculation of the MAD.

The equation for the MAD updated at time t is given by

$$\text{MAD}_t = (1 - \delta)\,\text{MAD}_{t-1} + \delta|Y_t - F_t|$$

This can be developed in much the same way as the exponential smoothing techniques discussed previously.

It is usual to use a figure for δ close to zero, since the absolute deviations tend to vary considerably, and this ensures that the MAD is not sensitive to unusually large or rapid variations in the absolute difference.

The initial value for the MAD is usually taken from historical data of forecast errors. For a numerical example using the non-stationary data with additive season-ality used in the Holt-Winter's forecast calculation, see Figure 2.30. Note that the initial value for the MAD is the first forecast error.

t	Y_t	F_t	MAD ($\delta = 0.1$)	σ
1	26.0	—	—	—
2	21.0	—	—	—
3	18.0	—	—	—
4	25.0	—	—	—
5	23.0	24.7	1.7	2.2
6	16.5	16.8	1.6	2.0
7	13.0	11.5	1.6	2.0
8	17.0	17.7	1.5	1.9
9	17.0	16.1	1.4	1.8
10	9.8	10.5	1.4	1.7
11	7.0	5.8	1.3	1.7
12	10.5	11.6	1.3	1.7
13	10.0	10.3	1.2	1.5
14	5.0	3.2	1.3	1.6
15	5.0	1.0	1.5	1.9

Figure 2.30 Standard deviation of forecast.

Plotting the standard deviation against the forecast (Figure 2.31) shows that the error in the forecast decreases over time until $t = 14$, when the forecast and data

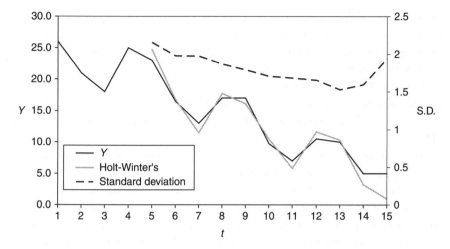

Figure 2.31 Standard deviation of forecast.

begin to diverge. So it would appear that the forecast is slightly less reliable in the most recent time periods than in the earlier time periods.

Choosing Appropriate Forecasting Models

When forecasting with the data used in the examples given here, it has been relatively easy to see which of the methods is the most appropriate. However, in practice this is usually a more difficult task. Decomposition can be used to identify the trend and the existence or otherwise of seasonality, and, if it does exist, what form the seasonality takes.

There are also statistical techniques available to help in the data investigation process. The primary technique used to identify seasonality is known as autocorrelation. This is a measure of the correlation (strength of the linear relationship) between different time periods in the same time series. Several different autocorrelations are usually calculated for each time series. The first is calculated for data that are one period apart (i.e. successive time periods), the second is calculated for data two periods apart, and so on, up until the point where the correlation is being calculated between seasonally equivalent time periods.

If the data are random, the average correlation between different time periods should be zero. There are statistical tests that can be used to ascertain whether the set of autocorrelations for the dataset of interest is significantly different from zero. These tests are known as Portmanteau tests, and a common example of these is the Ljung–Box test.

Autocorrelations can also be used to assess the accuracy of forecasts. In order to do this, autocorrelations of the forecast errors are calculated. Forecast errors should be random; non-random errors indicate a systemic problem with the forecast. Hence, if the autocorrelations of the forecast errors are significantly different from zero, this indicates that the forecast could be improved either by altering parameters or possibly by altering the form of the forecast.

Microsoft Excel does not include an autocorrelation function, which makes it a non-trivial process to carry out in that software package. There are, however, dedicated data analysis packages that do incorporate such functions, such as SPSS or E-views.

In order to analyse the trend, the data are very often differenced, meaning that the difference between successive time periods is calculated, i.e. $Y'_t = Y_t - Y_{t-1}$. Using a set of differenced data, unit root tests (a common example being the Dickey–Fuller test) can be used to test for the existence of a trend. These tests have a less intuitive explanation than the Ljung–Box test, and the reader is directed to Makridakis, Wheelwright, and Hyndman (1998) for a more detailed discussion of the use of both autocorrelations and differencing.

Transforming Data

Holt's method and Holt-Winter's method are both useful for developing forecasts with data exhibiting linear trends. If the trend happens to be non-linear, however, these forecasting techniques become less accurate. This does not always mean that more sophisticated forecasting techniques need be sought. Recalling that multiplicative seasonality is equivalent to additive seasonality under a logarithmic transformation, data with a non-linear trend can also be transformed in a similar fashion, and the forecasting techniques presented here can be applied to the transformed data.

Owing to its versatility, the logarithm is one of the most common functions used to transform data. The logarithm changes the data so that, instead of being measured on a linear scale, it is measured on a percentage scale. Hence, if the data are increasing at a constant percentage rate, the logarithm of the data will produce a linear series.

If transformed data are being used for the forecast, the forecast values will be transformations of the actual values that are required. Consequently, when choosing a function, it is necessary to be aware of the inverse of the function in order to change the forecast values back to the form that is required. If more than one type of function is used to transform the data, it is vital to keep track of the order in which the transformations are applied so that the inverse functions can be applied to the forecast values in the correct order.

There are a variety of transformations that can be used other than the logarithm function, and Pecar (1994) introduces the most common functions, together with the types of data that can be changed to linear form using these functions.

Alternative Time Series Forecasting Techniques

This chapter has discussed forecasting methods for data with seasonality and linear trends. There are, however, a wide range of other types of forecasting method available for use with data that are more complex in nature, such as those exhibiting non-linear trends.

Autoregressive models, such as the *autoregressive moving average* (ARMA) models, calculate the forecast by relating current values of the variable to values at previous time periods by means of regression. Several of the exponential smoothing methods are specific cases of autoregressive models, but there are many more than have been covered in this chapter. The advantage with using these techniques is that there is a clear approach for assessing the most appropriate forecasting model.

The techniques presented so far have been linear in nature, in that the models are expressed as a linear combination of previous data and some measure of error. Different techniques have been developed that use a non-linear approach to modelling, allowing for a greater variety of data to be modelled, such as the class of models known as *autoregressive heteroskedasticity* (ARCH) models. These allow for the standard deviation of the error in the model to vary according to the value of the forecast and are often used when forecasting financial markets.

Other time series forecasting techniques have been adapted from many different fields. A relatively recent development in forecasting has come from the field of artificial intelligence. The same technique that is used to model neuron networks in the central nervous system can also be applied to forecasting non-linear time series. Nevertheless, this still remains the subject of research.

Summary

This chapter has introduced some common time series forecasting methods and demonstrated how to implement these techniques. It is, however, important to choose the most appropriate method according to the type of data that is to be forecast.

The chapter introduced a method for identifying the main characteristics of the time series data, including ways in which to isolate the trend (underlying linear behaviour) and the seasonal component (regular fluctuations about the linear trend). This method, known as decomposition, indicates whether the data exhibit seasonality and also the form of the seasonality, whether multiplicative or additive.

For data exhibiting no trend (stationary), no seasonality and few random fluctuations, simple moving average forecasts can be employed, which use the most recent data as an indicator of the likely behaviour of future data.

A slightly more sophisticated technique is simple exponential smoothing, which is best used for stationary data (no trend) that exhibit no seasonality. This method smooths the data in order to forecast future values and so can be used for data that exhibit some random fluctuations.

The exponential smoothing technique can be augmented in such a way that it can forecast non-stationary data (data that exhibit a trend). This is often known as Holt's method. This technique incorporates an estimate of the slope of the trend line into the forecast while still including the smoothing component of the simple exponential smoothing method. Although this method can forecast data that have both random fluctuations and trend, it cannot forecast data with a seasonal component.

In order to forecast non-stationary seasonal data, the Holt-Winter's technique is often used. This is a further extension of the exponential smoothing method, incorporating both an estimate of the trend and an estimate of the seasonal component into the forecast. This method can forecast both forms of seasonality by using slightly different equations derived from the decomposition models demonstrated earlier in the chapter.

For some decision-making techniques that use forecast data, it is necessary to provide an estimate of the variability in the forecast. The method presented here uses the *mean absolute deviation* (MAD), which is the average absolute difference between the forecast and the actual data. This can then be used to estimate the standard deviation of the forecast.

The chapter concluded with a discussion of other issues that may arise when forecasting data, such as using data that include a non-linear trend. There are alternative methods that can be used to check the seasonality of the data (autocorrelation) and also ways in which data can be transformed so that the standard techniques demonstrated in this chapter can be used. If, however, the data cannot be manipulated into a suitable form, there are many alternative forecasting techniques that can be employed, although they are beyond the scope of this text.

Further Reading

- Alternative presentations of the material presented in this chapter can be found in the following texts:

  Render, B., Stair, RM., & Hanna, ME. (2005) *Quantitative Analysis for Management*. Prentice Hall, Upper Saddle River, NJ, Chapter 5.

  Waters, CDJ. (1989) *A Practical Introduction to Management Science*. Prentice Hall, Englewood Cliffs, NJ, Chapter 14.

Questions

Q2.1 Consider the following data:

		Quarter			
		Qtr 1	**Qtr 2**	**Qtr 3**	**Qtr 4**
Year	**1**	1048	1032	1034	1040
	2	1039	1001	1042	1012
	3	982	1024	1018	1048
	4	1017	1030	1007	944
	5	880	899	867	1002
	6	873	843	863	954

(a) Plot the data.
(b) Use decomposition to determine the trend and add this to the plot of the data. From the plot, estimate whether the data are of multiplicative or additive form.
(c) Complete the decomposition method to determine whether your answer to part (b) was correct.
(d) Use the most appropriate forecasting method to generate forecasts for the next 2 years.

Q2.2 A manager of an online travel agent has collected data regarding the number of holidays that have been sold by the sales department each day over a 4 week period. The data are shown in the table below.

		Monday	**Tuesday**	**Wednesday**	**Thursday**	**Friday**	**Saturday**	**Sunday**
Week	**1**	108	109	110	106	103	108	114
	2	122	118	121	120	116	126	127
	3	137	133	139	136	135	135	143
	4	142	149	151	149	143	148	158

The sales manager wishes to forecast the number of holidays that will be sold over the next 14 days.

(a) Plot the data.

(b) Use decomposition to determine the characteristics of the data and add the trend to the plot of the data.

(c) Use the information you generated in part (a) to help you choose the most appropriate form of the forecast, and use this method to generate a sales forecast.

(d) Calculate the MAD for your forecast and plot this on the chart of the data. Write a brief report discussing the accuracy of your forecast.

(e) Write a short report discussing the factors that might influence this particular dataset and how these factors might influence the way in which you choose to forecast the data.

Further questions for this chapter are available online.

Activities

A2.1 Download a times series of the claimant count (unemployment rate) for the UK from the Office for National Statistics website (www.statistics.gov.uk). Use the techniques developed in this chapter to forecast the unemployment rate for the next month. Compare your forecast with those created by the professional forecasting companies, which are summarised every month by HM Treasury in the document *Forecast for the UK Economy* which is available on the Treasury website (www.hm-treasury.gov.uk). Keep a note of your forecast and compare it with the actual unemployment rate when it is released.

A2.2 Investigate the types of software package available that are either dedicated forecasting packages or that can be used for forecasting. Prepare a presentation to identify the merits and drawbacks of each package. The presentation should also indicate the types of forecasting technique that can be implemented using each package.

A2.3 Download the historical house price data from the HBOS plc website. Create a forecast for house prices in your own region over the next year using the most appropriate forecasting method. Survey the local and national press to find out any estimates for changes to house prices and compare these with your forecasts. Who do you think will be most accurate and why?

A2.4 Activity A2.3 asked you to forecast house prices and to consider whether you thought your forecast was accurate. In reality, house price forecasters make use of more complex methods than those presented in this chapter. Why do you think that this is the case? Think about the key assumption regarding the behaviour of time series data that these methods rely upon, and then consider the external influences on the behaviour of the housing market. Do you think time series forecasting is a valid approach to forecasting house prices? Investigate the methods used by commercial and academic forecasters to forecast house prices.

CHAPTER 3

Explanatory and Qualitative Forecasting

Objectives

- *To appreciate the need for explanatory forecasting.*
- *To be able to carry out linear regression with Excel.*
- *To appreciate the need for qualitative forecasting.*
- *To recognise approaches to eliciting an expert's probability estimates.*
- *To understand the nominal group technique.*
- *To understand the Delphi technique and its associated issues.*
- *To understand the scenario analysis technique.*

Introduction

In many decision-taking situations, a combination of techniques is required to populate a mathematical decision aid with suitable values. For example, if decisions are being taken whose outcomes will depend on a contextual environment several years into the future, then a reasonable prediction of that context may be impossible. Time series techniques used for generating some model parameters, as discussed in Chapter 2, become less reliable when suitable historical data are unavailable, when the forecast horizon is long, or when the dynamics of a forecast variable are complex. Equally, if a decision situation is uncommon, not being similar to any previous decisions, then frequency-based data will be unavailable to estimate required probabilities.

Under long-time-scales, complex, or dynamic circumstances, quantitative explanatory forecasting techniques and/or the beliefs of experts may be used. This chapter first presents linear regression modelling as an introduction to explanatory forecasting, and then outlines several means to elicit and structure expert knowledge.

Quantitative Explanatory Forecasting

Explanatory forecasting is a quantitative forecasting technique that seeks to explain the behaviour of a variable of interest (dependent variable) in terms of at least one but usually many explanatory variables (independent variables). In other words, these methods seek to quantify functional relationships between the variable of interest (dependent variable) and the variables that are believed to influence it (independent variables).

Explanatory forecasting techniques are mathematical models that predict the behaviour of the dependent variable and in addition provide a measure of confidence in the applicability of the model. Consequently, and importantly, this offers the modeller the information necessary to make judgements about the most appropriate form of model. Many explanatory techniques also include a measure of the contribution of the individual independent variables to the overall explanatory power of the model, meaning that the modeller can choose the most useful variables to include.

Regardless of the explanatory technique used, once the system is understood, the relationships are used to predict the outcome of changing one or several of the explanatory variables, making these techniques particularly appropriate for assessing the outcome of events, such as government policy changes, that have wide-ranging consequences. Nevertheless, explanatory analysis is not used to generate a series of future values for a particular variable in the same way as time series forecasting is. The value of this approach lies in both the forecast and the information about the system that is generated from the modelling process itself, such as the knowledge that is gained by gathering appropriate independent variables.

Explanatory modelling does have its problems, particularly because these models can be technically very difficult to implement. They require knowledge of and familiarity with relatively sophisticated mathematical tools, together with some prior knowledge of the system under investigation. This means that the construction of explanatory models is often the outcome of collaboration rather than individual endeavour.

Explanatory models are also very data intensive. Sufficient data need to be gathered not only for the dependent variable but also for each of the explanatory variables. The problem is not just one of quantity but one of quality. It matters very little how sophisticated the model is if data of poor quality are used. Data collection can be an expensive process, and, if external data are sought, there are often problems of availability and reliability.

Unlike time series forecasting, there is no standard approach for the development of explanatory models. The technique chosen depends upon the skill and knowledge of the forecaster, the data that are available, and even prevailing fashion for a certain technique. They are also unlike time series in that they need continuous adjustment and cannot easily be automated, meaning that expertise is generally required to make sure that the model remains a useful tool.

In spite of these issues, explanatory forecasting is well suited to the task of developing a detailed understanding of the interdependencies between the various elements of a system. Consequently, explanatory forecasting is particularly beneficial for forecasting over the long term, when an understanding of a system may be more beneficial in generating accurate forecasts than relying on the continuation of previous behavioural patterns within the data.

Regression is one of the most well known and widely used of the explanatory techniques. This technique assumes that independent variables are determined exogenously. This discussion focuses on the development of a regression model in order to illustrate the general process that must be undertaken.

Linear Regression

The regression technique assumes that independent and dependent variables are related in terms of an equation that is linear in its parameters. For a dependent variable, y (for which there are m observations), and n independent variables, x_i, the linear regression model is given by

$$y_j = \alpha_0 + \sum_{i=1}^{n} \alpha_i x_{ij} + \varepsilon_j \quad \text{for } j = 1, 2, 3, \ldots, m$$

where α_0 and α_i are the model parameters and ε_j are the residual or error terms. These errors represent the difference between the actual value of the observation y_j and the value predicted by the model, i.e. the part of the behaviour of y that is not accounted for by the variables included in the model.

Since this technique requires that the model be linear in its parameters, the following is also an acceptable linear regression model:

$$y_j = \alpha_0 + \sum_i \alpha_i x_{ij}^2 + \varepsilon_j$$

The regression technique uses the available data to estimate the values of the parameters in such a way as to minimise the sum of the squared values[1] of the residuals. This text does not detail the actual mathematical technique used to estimate the parameters, since it is reasonably complex and regression is rarely, if ever, carried out 'by hand' but rather is implemented using suitable software including general spreadsheet packages such as Microsoft Excel or specialist statistical packages such as SAS, SPSS, Minitab, or Genstat. For an explanation of the underlying mathematics, the reader is directed to dedicated statistical texts. This text will explain the regression process using Microsoft Excel and will focus upon the interpretation of the output of the statistical process.

As with all statistical techniques, linear regression is valid for only certain types of data, and the specific requirements for this technique are:[2]

- The data need to be ordinal data (numerical data that have a natural order). Although this technique should be used only with continuous data, it is reasonably robust, and so discrete data can also be used with caution (for example, discrete data that can only assume two values may be very misleading as part of a linear regression model; other types of regression modelling can be used with data of this type).
- The independent variables must be linearly independent, i.e. none of the independent variables can be represented as a linear combination of one or several of the other independent variables. If this is not the case,[3] the model may not give a useful representation of the way in which each of the independent variables affects the dependent variable. A simple way of detecting possible problems of this sort is to divide the dataset into sample groups and create a linear regression model of the same form for each sample. If there are large variations in the parameters between samples, then multicollinearity may be a problem. There are ways of addressing this issue, but they are beyond the scope of this text, and the interested reader is directed towards a more detailed statistical text.

---

[1] Squared values are used in order to avoid negative residuals cancelling with positive ones in the summation and thereby giving an unreliable estimate of the total error.

[2] Methods for testing the validity of these assumptions are presented in many statistical textbooks.

[3] This is known as multicollinearity.

- The residual terms are not related, i.e. the error, ε_i, for a given observation has no impact on the size of the errors for other observations.
- The residual terms have a constant variance.
- The residual terms are normally distributed with a mean of zero.

The latter three assumptions will be explained in more detail at a later point in the chapter, when the reason for their inclusion will become clear.

Example

A local estate agent has collected data relating to recent house sales, including the final sale price of the property, the distance of the property from the city centre, the age the property, and the number of rooms in the property (see Figure 3.1). The agent is interested to know if the final sales price is related to the other variables and whether it is possible to model the sales price based on these variables in order to assist in property pricing strategies.

Sale price	Distance from city centre	Age	Rooms
92 000	11	22	5
133 000	10	15	6
140 000	9	12	6
165 000	12	29	5
165 000	14	5	6
189 000	17	20	8
189 000	12	15	7
194 000	12	16	9
198 000	11	25	5
215 000	16	30	9
220 000	3	4	8
222 000	5	10	8
240 000	28	2	9
243 000	3	46	7
245 000	35	80	12
253 000	33	56	9

Figure 3.1 Property sales data.

270 000	31	46	10
279 000	22	73	8
283 000	4	32	9
284 000	17	47	10
310 000	4	5	6
320 000	5	59	9
334 000	14	103	9
340 000	7	50	9
389 000	5	10	7
397 000	10	80	12
399 000	22	48	11
420 000	36	89	11
445 000	37	60	10
457 000	7	90	9
462 000	28	150	10
620 000	27	80	13

Figure 3.1 (Continued).

The proposed regression model is

$$y_j = \alpha_0 + \alpha_1 x_{1j} + \alpha_2 x_{2j} + \alpha_3 x_{3j} + \varepsilon_j$$

where x_1 is the distance from the city centre, x_2 is the age of the property, and x_3 is the number of rooms. Then, α_1, α_2, and α_3 are the parameters associated with these variables, and α_0 is a constant term. It is these parameters that will be estimated from the data.

Using Microsoft Excel to Determine the Linear Regression Model

In order to carry out a regression analysis in Microsoft Excel, the 'data analysis' tool pack must be added if it has not been used before. In order to add this facility, click the Office button and then select 'Excel Options' from the resulting menu (see Figure 3.2).

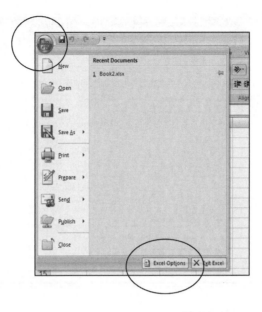

Figure 3.2 Finding Excel Add-Ins.

On the next dialogue box, select 'Add-Ins' from the menu on the left-hand side of the box (see Figure 3.3) and click the 'go' button next to the 'Manage' window at the bottom of the dialogue box, making sure that 'Excel Add-Ins' is selected in the window.

In the resulting dialogue box, tick the 'Analysis ToolPak' box, followed by 'OK' (see Figure 3.4).

Once these steps have been followed, the 'Data Analysis' tool will be available to use via the 'Data' tab (see Figure 3.5).

Now it is possible to formulate the linear regression. Select the Data Analysis tool, and from the resulting menu select 'Regression'. The 'Regression' dialogue box should now be visible (see Figure 3.6).

For this dataset, the dependent variable is the 'Sale price', since the behaviour of this variable is the one that the estate agent wishes to understand in more detail. The other variables are therefore the independent variables, and it these that will be used to describe the variations observed in the sale price of the properties. The layout of the spreadsheet is detailed in Figure 3.7.

The next step is to enter the appropriate cell references in the 'Regression' dialogue box. The 'Input Y Range' window should contain the cell references of the dependent variable, and in this case this will be A1:A33. Note that the cell containing the data label is also included; this will make the results of the regression easier to interpret, as the software will label the output appropriately.

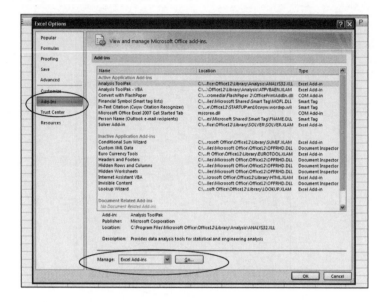

Figure 3.3 Selecting the Add-Ins menu.

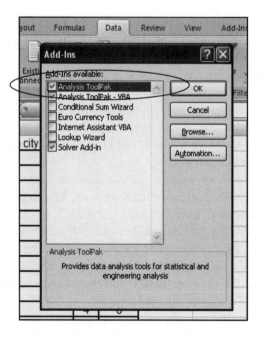

Figure 3.4 Selecting the Analysis TookPak Add-In.

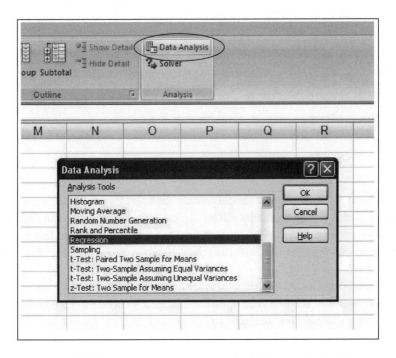

Figure 3.5 Data Analysis tool.

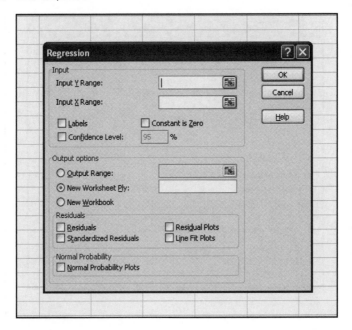

Figure 3.6 Regression dialogue box.

Cells	Description
A2:A33	Sale price – these cells contain the values of the dependent variable.
B2:B33	Distance from city centre – this is an independent variable.
C2:C33	Age of the property – this is an independent variable.
D2:D33	Rooms – this is an independent variable.

Figure 3.7 Layout of the spreadsheet.

The 'Input X̲ Range' window should contain the cell references of the independent variables, and in this example this will be B1:D33. When setting up a spreadsheet for regression analysis, it is usually most efficient to include the independent variables in adjacent columns, as this will ease the data entry process in the 'Regression' dialogue box.

The 'Labels' box must be selected in order to ensure that Excel recognises that the values contained in the first cells of each column are data labels. See Figure 3.8 for the completed 'Regression' dialogue box.

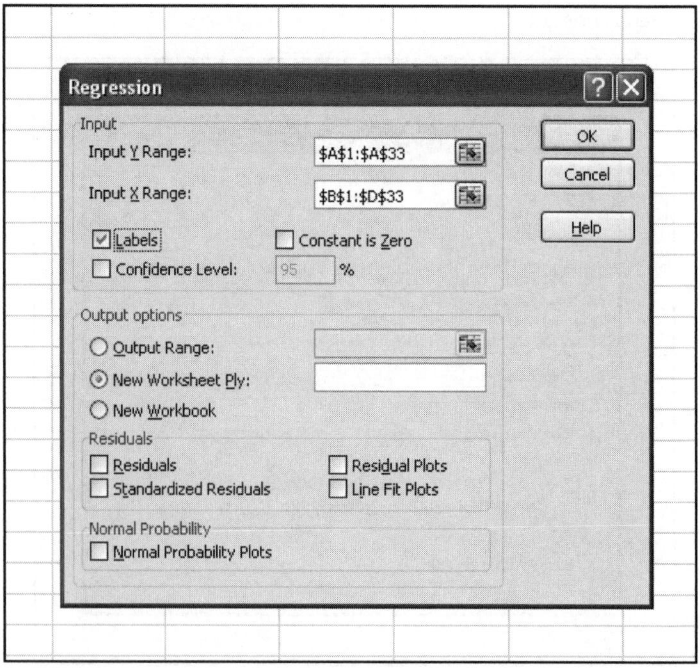

Figure 3.8 Completed 'Regression' dialogue box.

Note that the 'New Worksheet Ply' option under 'Output Options' is selected, ensuring that the software enters the results on a separate worksheet. An output range can also be specified if the results are required on the same page.

Once the dialogue box is complete, clicking 'OK' generates the results of the regression model. These are detailed in Figure 3.9.

Regression Statistics	
Multiple R	0.782724485
R Square	0.61265762
Adjusted R Square	0.571156651
Standard Error	76660.92176
Observations	32

ANOVA

	df	SS	MS	F	Significance F
Regression	3	2.60273E+11	86757628695	14.76248942	5.92531E-06
Residual	28	1.64553E+11	5876896926		
Total	31	4.24826E+11			

	Coefficients	Standard Error	t Stat	P-value	Lower 95%	Upper 95%
Intercept	-7808.164343	61687.00458	-0.126577136	0.900179684	-134168.407	118552.0783
Distance from city centre	-1877.61717	1567.577235	-1.197782877	0.241043018	-5088.657179	1333.422839
Age	1348.263798	503.3298618	2.678688273	0.012230832	317.2381567	2379.289439
Rooms	30934.226	9007.200555	3.4343885	0.001868928	12483.79134	49384.66067

Figure 3.9 Regression results – version 1.

The first of the result tables gives the regression statistics. The values of interest are R^2 and adjusted R^2. Both values measure the explanatory power of the model and can take values between 0 and 1. If the measures are equal to 1, this means that the behaviour of the dependent variable can be explained entirely by the independent variables and does not depend upon any other external factors. If, however, the value of R^2 or adjusted R^2 is equal to 0, this means that there is no relationship (of this form) between the dependent variable and independent variables, and the (likely) conclusion is that the dependent variable is related to other factors external to the regression model. In practice, these extremes are rarely encountered; certainly, if the modeller has done her job correctly, R^2 should not be equal to 0. Models that deliver values close to 1 have greater explanatory power than those with values closer to 0. Nevertheless, models with values close to 0 are rarely dismissed as useless, since discovering which independent variables are not related to the dependent variable has informational value.

The value of adjusted R^2 is generally used when there is more than one independent variable. The way in which R^2 is calculated means that, when an independent variable is added to the regression model, the value of R^2 will increase regardless of whether or not the new variable has any explanatory power. The value of R^2 might therefore be slightly misleading, and hence the adjusted R^2 takes into account the explanatory power of the individual independent variables. This means that the adjusted R^2 is generally lower than the value for R^2, although it is measured on the same scale, between 0 and 1, and values closer to 1 imply that the model has better explanatory power than models where the value is closer to 0. It is possible to have a value of R^2 that is close to 1 and an adjusted R^2 much closer to 0, suggesting that the model consists of a large number of independent variables with little explanatory power.

In this example, the value of R^2 is 0.613 and the value of the adjusted R^2 is 0.571, suggesting that the independent variables are reasonably good predictors of the behaviour of the dependent variable.

The second results table is the ANOVA table which gives an indication of the level of confidence the modeller can have in the model. Since the data values that are used in the regression represent only a sample of all possible values, it is important to know whether the model that has been generated is applicable only to this sample of values or whether it can be applied to the potential future values of the variables, i.e. whether or not it is possible to use the regression model to predict unknown future values of the dependent variable on the basis of known values of the independent variable. This is achieved by using a probability measure that gives an indication of the *statistical significance* of the model.

For regression models, it is convenient to think of statistical significance as a measure of the likelihood that the model will <u>not</u> be useful in predicting further values of the dependent variable.[4] The particular value that indicates the significance of the model is the *significance F* value, which in this case is 5.93E-06 (meaning 0.00000593).[5] This model has a particularly low *significance F* value, but this may not always be the case. There are, however, generally accepted values that act as maximum values above which the model is rejected as a predictive tool. These are often known as *significance levels*, the most common being the 5 % (0.05) level.[6] Hence, when the value of significance F is greater than 0.05, the regression model is rejected as a predictive tool. This means the likelihood that the model will <u>not</u> be useful in predicting future values of the dependent variable is too high, and therefore it is presumed that the regression model is not useful as a predictive tool.

---

[4] This interpretation is not a perfectly accurate interpretation in a statistical sense, but it does help in the understanding of the interpretation of the significance value and is suitable for use when developing regression models. Another useful way of considering this value is as the likelihood that the parameter associated with the independent variable is <u>not</u> significantly different from zero.

[5] This is engineering notation which is commonly used by Microsoft Excel for very large or very small numbers. This translates exactly as $5.93 \times 10^{-6} = 5.93 \times 0.000001 = 0.00000593$.

[6] Other common significance levels are the 10 % (0.1) level and the 1 % (0.01) level. The choice of significance level depends upon the level of confidence that is required. However, for the purposes of regression, the 5 % level normally suffices.

As discussed earlier, a potential disadvantage of explanatory forecasting is that it can be data intensive. Once a useful model has been identified, it is constructive to see whether any independent variables can be removed from the model, consequently removing the necessity to collect further such data. The final table in the regression output contains much of the valuable information resulting from the behaviour of the independent variables. In this table, the first values to consider are those in the P-value column. These are similar to the significance F value for the overall model, but these values indicate the likelihood that each of the independent variables is <u>not</u> a useful predictor in the regression model.[7]

Note from the regression output that the P-value for the 'Rooms' variable is 0.000187, which is less than 0.05 (the same significance level is used), and therefore the 'Rooms' variable is a useful predictor. Similarly, the P value for the 'Age' variable is 0.0122, and so this variable is also a useful predictor.

The P-value for the 'Distance from city centre' variable is 0.241, which is much greater that 0.05. Hence, this variable is rejected as a useful predictor and its removal from the regression model can be considered.

The regression analysis is now run again, but this time with the 'Distance from city centre' variable removed. It is assumed that the new form of the regression model is given by

$$y_j = \alpha_0 + \alpha_1 x_{1j} + \alpha_2 x_{2j} + \varepsilon_j$$

where x_1 is the age of the property and x_2 is the number of rooms. Then, α_1 and α_2 are the parameters for the new model.

The results of the new regression model are shown in Figure 3.10.

Regression Statistics	
Multiple R	0.769942009
R Square	0.592810697
Adjusted R Square	0.564728676
Standard Error	77233.3238
Observations	32

ANOVA

	df	SS	MS	F	Significance F
Regression	2	2.51841E+11	1.25921E+11	21.10997	2.1981E-06
Residual	29	1.72985E+11	5964986305		
Total	31	4.24826E+11			

	Coefficients	Standard Error	t Stat	P-value	Lower 95%	Upper 95%
Intercept	3201.989947	61453.74618	0.052104064	0.958803	-122485.1019	128889.0818
Age	1243.859749	499.4264553	2.490576413	0.018728	222.4174017	2265.302097
Rooms	26679.91888	8339.137571	3.199361883	0.003324	9624.458221	43735.37953

Figure 3.10   Regression results – version 2.

---

[7] Again, this explanation is not a perfectly accurate statistical interpretation but nevertheless is sufficient in developing an understanding.

Note that the results of the new regression show only a small reduction in adjusted R^2, which suggests little loss in explanatory power by excluding the 'Distance from city centre' variable. In addition, the ANOVA table shows that this model is significant and therefore likely to be a useful predictive tool.

The current model contains only those variables that are significant, and so this can now be used as a predictive tool. In order to forecast further values, however, the regression model must be populated with the appropriate values for the parameters, and these are contained in the final output table. These values are listed in the 'Coefficients' column, and the parameters for the 'Age' and the 'Rooms' variables are $\alpha_1 = 1243.860$ and $\alpha_2 = 26679.919$ respectively. These parameters indicate the amount by which the dependent variable increases with every unit increase in the independent variable. Hence, as a property ages by 1 year, its sales price increases by £1244. Similarly, for every additional room in a house, £26 680 is added to the value of the property. Although these relationships would appear to be intuitively clear, care must always be taken when interpreting the values of the parameters in order to provide appropriate information.

The regression model for this particular dataset is given by

$$y_j = 3202 + 1244x_{1j} + 26680x_{2j} + \varepsilon_j$$

Nonetheless, this model cannot yet be used to predict possible future sales price. This equation still includes the residual terms ε_j. Since it is impossible to know much about future values of the residuals, some simplifying assumptions were made at the beginning of the regression process in order that they could be removed from the model. Recall that the last three assumptions stated the following:

- The residual terms are not related, i.e. the error, ε_j, for a given observation has no impact on the size of the errors for other observations.
- The residual terms have a constant variance.
- The residual terms are normally distributed with a mean of zero.

If the residual terms are related, the P-values for the parameters of the model are likely to be unreliable, and hence the final model may not be a useful predictive tool.

By assuming constant variance of residual terms, this implies that all the data points used to estimate the regression model are equally as reliable. In this example, if the sale price of houses with fewer rooms varies much less than that of houses with a greater number of rooms, the sale price data for larger houses are much less reliable than those for smaller houses.

The assumption that the error terms are normally distributed means that information regarding the possible range of values that the parameters may take can be determined. These ranges are known as confidence intervals. Although this text does not engage in a further discussion of confidence intervals, the interested reader is directed to standard statistical texts that present the theory associated with the relevant calculations.

Finally, assuming that the residuals have a mean of zero is important when deriving the final form of the regression model equation. Rather than trying to predict the residuals term, they are removed from the regression equation by taking the expected value (mean) of the dependent variable y:

$$E\left(y_j\right) = E\left(3202 + 1244x_{1j} + 26680x_{2j} + \varepsilon_j\right)$$

Since the expected value operation exhibits the property of distributivity, it follows that

$$E\left(y_j\right) = E(3202) + E\left(1244x_{1j}\right) + E\left(26680x_{2j}\right) + E\left(\varepsilon_j\right)$$

and the expected value of a constant is itself then

$$E\left(y_j\right) = 3202 + 1244E\left(x_{1j}\right) + 26680E\left(x_{2j}\right) + E\left(\varepsilon_j\right)$$

Since it has been assumed that the mean of the residual term is zero, it follows that $E\left(\varepsilon_j\right) = 0$ and so

$$\hat{y} = 3202 + 1244\hat{x}_1 + 26680\hat{x}_2$$

where $^\wedge$ indicates that the variable is an expected value (mean). This is the final form of the linear regression model, and it is this that is used to forecast future values.

Using the Regression Model to Forecast Further Values

Once the most appropriate form for the regression model has been determined, it can then be used to forecast further values.

The estate agent has been asked to value a property that is 11 years old ($\hat{x}_1 = 11$) and has seven rooms ($\hat{x}_2 = 7$). According to the model, the mean final sale price is given by

$$\hat{y} = 3202 + 1244\hat{x}_1 + 26680\hat{x}_2$$

The estate agent therefore estimates that the final sale price is likely to be

$$\hat{y} = 3202 + \left(1244 \times 11\right) + \left(26680 \times 7\right) = £203646$$

The key point to remember is that the parameters in the regression model are interpreted as mean (expected) values. Therefore, these values are the average of all possible values that the parameters could assume. It is possible to calculate prediction limits for the values generated by the regression equation. The formulation of these limits is beyond the scope of this text, but the interested reader is directed to statistical texts for more technical detail.

The linear regression modelling process carried out here has resulted in a numerical model that can explain at least some of the behaviour of the sale price (dependent) variable in terms of the age of the property and the number of rooms (independent variables). The output of the process indicates that the model is a useful predictor of the behaviour of the dependent variable.

Elicitation of an Expert's Probabilities

Eliciting a Probability

Eliciting forecast variables and principally probabilities from the beliefs of experts has recently been substantially reviewed by O'Hagan *et al.* (2006), and their work is largely followed in this section.

An individual expert's probabilities are best surfaced through face-to-face interview rather than by questionnaire. Nevertheless, simply because an individual has expertise in an area does not mean that she has expertise in expressing this in terms of probabilities that represent beliefs or in terms of the variables initially sought for a decision model. For best results, it is important for the elicitation process to include several stages before the elicitation (O'Hagan *et al.*, 2006, pp. 28–31). In a preparatory step, the elicitor needs to prepare for interviewing an expert. This includes recognising the variables of interest and their appropriate form for a decision model, becoming suitably knowledgeable to discuss with an expert, and planning the format of the interview. The second step is to engage an expert or experts. Alongside evidence of expertise in the subject area, in order to take part, an expert clearly needs to be available and ideally to have no potentially biasing pre-existing stake in the decision. A third step is to prepare the expert. As well as buying into the importance of the process, she may need to be trained in expressing beliefs as probabilities, odds, or equivalent, and also to be made aware of well-known cognitive biases. A fourth step taken jointly between elicitor and expert is to agree the structure of the problem, recognising relationships between variables and agreeing appropriate units if relevant. Only after these first four stages should forecast variables such as probabilities be elicited from the expert.

Techniques for eliciting responses (O'Hagan *et al.*, 2006, pp. 87–89) can be direct or indirect. Direct methods include simply asking an expert for a response, using a visual response scale in which lines are drawn or categories selected, or using probability wheels. Care is required with visual scales and probability wheels, as the design and use can have effects on responses obtained. Nonetheless, sometimes they can have specific advantages; for example, logarithmic visual scales are useful for rare events. Indirect methods are associated with bets, an event for which a probability is being elicited being compared with a bet represented by a physical event. Here, probability wheels can be usefully employed (Goodwin & Wright, 2004, pp. 280–281).

Given the difficulties associated with estimating probabilities and the range of approaches available, an important area by which an organization can seek improvement, or by which an expert can be trained, is calibration (O'Hagan et al., 2006, pp. 62–82). Manifestly, if all events that are assigned a probability of, say, 0.3 are considered, then, once the future has unfolded, 30 % of these should have occurred. Similarly, 60 % of events assigned a probability of 0.6 should have occurred. Examining the accuracy for a set of events provides a feedback instrument for learning and improvement. If the percentage of events actually occurring is much greater or smaller than that implied by the elicited probabilities, then the individual or organization is not well calibrated. Commonly observed problems with calibration are overconfidence, underconfidence, and overextremity. Overconfidence is the situation in which the elicited expert probabilities are typically high, that is, the proportion of events occurring is less than would be expected from probability estimates. In contrast, underconfidence is characterised by the proportion of events occurring being greater than would be expected from probability estimates. Overextremity is typified by overconfidence for events with high elicited probabilities and underconfidence for events with low elicited probabilities.

Combining the Responses from Several Experts

If probabilities for an event or other forecast variables have been obtained from several experts, then these can be combined as a mean average. Nevertheless, simple averaging of expert opinion may not always be optimum. Bearing in mind the complexity and uniqueness of situations that call for expert opinion, two concerns immediately surface. Firstly, the situation may be one in which a probabilistic risk-based approach is inappropriate. Quite simply, trying to forecast specific event outcomes is a fruitless task. A divergence in views of experts may indeed be symptomatic of the real complexities present in a problem, and a decision-taker would be better served by capturing rich descriptions of possible futures. This is the approach taken in *scenario analysis*. The second situation is one in which an expert may only be such in some aspects required to estimate a probability or other forecast variable, a second expert being knowledgeable in a different aspect. Rather than average elicited individual variables, the combination of the experts' knowledge base to elicit a group response could provide a better forecast. This is the intent of structured group processes such as the Delphi technique or the nominal group.

Structured Group Processes

The Nominal Group Technique

Group processes may be *interacting* or *nominal*. An interacting group process is one in which all the intragroup communication occurs with little if any control; the communication is not formalised. A nominal group process is one in which group members work within physical proximity of each other but do not verbally interact; any communication that does occur is structured. A *nominal group* is a group in name only. Nominal processes have proved superior to interacting processes in the generation of ideas and for fact-finding, while (possibly structured) interacting processes have proved superior for evaluation. One discussed reason for this distinction is that a nominal process maintains focus on problem identification, while an interacting process shifts focus to evaluation and solution development (Van de Ven & Delbecq, 1971). The *nominal group technique* (NGT) (Delbecq & Van de Ven, 1971; VanGundy, 1988), leverages the advantages of these differing group processes through a structured approach. The NGT includes six clear steps:

1. Silent idea writing.
2. Round-robin idea recording.
3. Serial discussion of recorded ideas.
4. A preliminary anonymous vote.
5. Discussion on the results of the vote.
6. A final anonymous vote.

Adaptation of the NGT to the elicitation of probabilities is transparent, individual estimates being followed by group discussion and then a further round of individual estimates (Gustafson *et al.*, 1973).

The Delphi Technique

The Delphi technique (Dalkey & Helmer, 1963; Linstone & Turoff, 1975) is a structured group process in which a panel of experts iteratively respond to questionnaires combined with structured feedback. It can be considered as a nominal group technique in which the experts do not even share the same physical proximity, summarised results and opinions being shared electronically or by mail. Typically, during 3–5 cycles of questionnaires, expert opinion either converges to a consensus or at least approaches stability.

Using the Delphi approach, even if aided with electronic communication, should be recognised as resource intensive. To begin with, sufficient research has to be carried out to develop appropriate initial questions, typically a small number in open format. These questions are required to be sufficiently broad to obtain apt feedback from experts, but also suitably posed so as not to be open to misinterpretation. Before this first questionnaire is circulated to panel members, these experts have to be identified and recruited. Delphi exercises usually run with between 10 and 100 panel members, often around 20. The panel members are required to possess expertise, to be available, and to be willing to take part over 3–5 rounds of questions that may take from several days to several months to complete. Once the panel experts have been identified and have responded to the first-round questionnaire, the researcher(s) managing the exercise must consider the responses and develop a focused second questionnaire using closed-form questions, for instance: *What is the probability of 50 % of new-build container ships over 80 000 gt being nuclear powered by 2040?* Or, similarly, probabilities may be expressed in the question and dates required in the answer. If this questionnaire is not overly long, and the experts are suitably bought into the process, then brief explanations of the estimates may also be requested. On receiving responses from the second-round questionnaires, the researcher summarises the statistics into a form suitable for the panel experts, such as medians and ranges, or graphical representation of these. Alongside the third-round questionnaire, accompanying statistical summaries and reasons, if given, are distributed. If reasons were not collected during the second round, they may be specifically requested from some respondents during the third round to be distributed in the fourth round. The number of iterations rarely goes above 4, expert opinions usually having settled and/or experts no longer being available. The final-round responses are collated as summary statistics, and reasons for any continuing outliers are captured (Figure 3.11).

By structuring the exchange of information between the panel experts, the Delphi process aims to reduce the deleterious effects of group biases and to separate out the stages of suggesting probability estimates (dates or ideas) and evaluating them. As with the NGT, Delphi has proved superior to simple statistical averaging. Three potential contributions to this improvement have been suggested and, to some extent, evaluated (Rowe & Wright, 1999; Rowe, Wright, & McColl, 2005). These are the process of *iteration*, the role of *statistical* feedback, and the role of *reasoned* feedback. Considering the process of iteration, within a Delphi survey each expert makes and submits estimates, and, owing to the iterative nature, has a period of potential reflection in which to evaluate and further consider her own estimate. This alone could give rise to improvements in estimates. Statistical feedback presents the expert with the opportunity to compare and contrast her own estimates with those of other experts. Under conditions of anonymity, an expert with less expertise or confidence may decide to change her estimate towards the median, while a confident panel member with greater expertise may not be influenced by the suggestions of others. Over several rounds, this process effectively modifies a simple statistical average to a weighted statistical average; those with less confidence or expertise anonymously

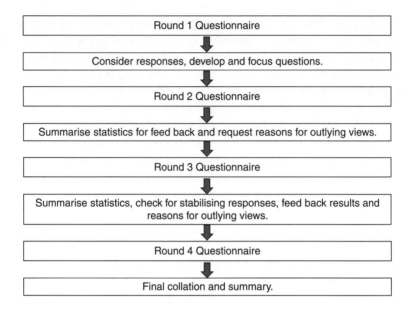

Figure 3.11 An outline Delphi process.

declare themselves. Reasoned feedback allows panel members to see and evaluate the arguments of others, and in so doing a panel member may discount the arguments of others and even submit alternative arguments. Alternatively, she may appreciate that her own initial thinking was limited and consider the reasons of others as rebuttals (see Chapter 1) to or qualifiers of her own reasoned argument.

Literature evaluations of the role of iteration and statistical and reasoned feedback are mixed. This is perhaps unsurprising, given the different applications of Delphi in terms of subject area, panel expertise, and timeframe. Unlike decision-making styles (see Chapter 1), there is limited conclusive advice on how much statistical and reasoned feedback to include. Nevertheless, the researcher should attempt to consider the role of these in obtaining subjective data.

Scenario Analysis

The scenario analysis technique (MacNulty, 1977; Shoemaker, 1995; Moyer, 1996; Coates, 2000) accepts that disagreement with respect to possible futures is an indication of a tangible underlying uncertainty; decision-takers are unable to associate probabilities with futures and, furthermore, may even be unable to order the likelihood of plausible futures. To make progress, a set of credible future scenarios is generated, within which alternative strategies can be considered, for example by using the robustness analysis technique described in Chapter 8. The main features of scenarios are that together they span the range of actual possible futures, although a scenario may never occur itself, and that they need to be captured in compelling pen pictures. Without scenarios being believable to decision-takers, their use becomes restricted.

Many alternative approaches exist to developing scenarios, some rather complex, others much simpler. By pursuing a straightforward approach to scenario generation, the technique becomes accessible to decision-takers and more time can be invested in developing the believability of each scenario. Simple scenario generation approaches have been presented by Mercer (1995) and by Goodwin and Wright (2004, Chapter 15); the key essentials from these will be outlined here.

Firstly, select the issue or system of interest on which to focus the scenario generation. This may be the future existence or profitability of a company or strategic business unit. Next, identify two groups of drivers that could lead to change in the performance of the system. This may require some preliminary broad environmental scanning, and interacting with a range of stakeholders and experts. The first group of drivers are *certainties*. The temptation to overlook these owing to the spotlight falling on uncertainties must be avoided. Certainties are those trends that will have either a positive or negative effect on the company (or other system) but to some extent can be forecast so that the direction of effect is known; for example, changing demographics. The second group of drivers are the *uncertainties*. These are the drivers that could affect the company either positively or negatively, depending on how an uncertainty is resolved. Examples might be political, such as the accession of Turkey to the EU, or technological, such as the success of a development project or choice of a standard. Next, intuitively form clusters of outcomes of uncertainties and to each of these then add the certainties. The simplest approach suggested by Goodwin and Wright (2004) is to make one cluster assuming all uncertainties result in positive outcomes, and to make another cluster assuming the uncertainties result in negative outcomes. For each grouping of uncertainties, a storyline linking the drivers is developed. If 2–4 clusters are being used, then the storylines should paint a convincingly plausible future. If there are more clusters, an alternative is to develop mini-scenarios before reducing these to 2 or 3 (Mercer, 1995).

Summary

This chapter has overviewed several techniques to generate suitable values for use in decision models in situations where time series forecasting and historical frequency data are either unavailable or unsuitable. The simplest explanatory forecasting technique, linear regression, has been demonstrated with the use of MS Excel. Approaches to the use of expert opinion have been developed over several decades, and a number of these have been introduced. Appropriate care is needed in using such techniques to limit the possibilities for bias.

Further Reading

- There are many statistics texts that offer an introduction and more to regression. These include:

  Hinton, P. (2004) *Statistics Explained: A Guide for Social Science Students*. Routledge, London, UK.

  Bradley, T. (2007) *Essential Statistics for Economics, Business and Management*. John Wiley & Sons, Ltd, Chichester, UK.

  Field, A. (2005) *Discovering Statistics Using SPSS*. Sage Publications Ltd, London, UK.

  Tabachnick, BG. & Fidell, LS. (2006) *Using Multivariate Statistics*. Pearson Education, Boston, MA.

  Kline, RB. (2004) *Principles and Practice of Structural Equation Modeling*. Guilford Publications, New York, NY.

- A good early review on the elicitation of subjective probabilities is:

  Chesley, GR. (1975) Elicitation of subjective probabilities: a review. *The Accounting Review* **50**(20), 325–327.

- Two short papers highlighting some issues and applications of Delphi are:

  Keeney, S., Hasson, F., & McKenna, HP. (2001) A critical review of the Delphi technique as a research methodology for nursing. *International Journal of Nursing Studies* **38**, 195–200.

  Landeta, J. (2006) Current validity of the Delphi method in social sciences. *Technological Forecasting and Social Change* **73**, 467–482.

- There are many good volumes on scenario analysis, among these are:

  Van der Heijden, K. (2005) *Scenarios: The Art of the Strategic Conversation*, 2nd edition. John Wiley & Sons, Ltd, Chichester, UK.

  Ringland, G. (1998) *Scenario Planning: Managing for the Future*. John Wiley & Sons, Ltd, Chichester, UK.

Activities

A3.1 For a sport competed between two sides and with many games over a tournament (e.g. tennis) or season (e.g. soccer), predict the probability of one player (or team) winning. Repeat this over many games and record the results. Are your predictions well calibrated?

A3.2 Select a reality TV show that involves viewers, experts, or participants acting to eject other participants from the show. Read the paper below and then write a research proposal to repeat the study but using the reality TV in place of the film used in the paper:

Hall, EJ., Mouton, JS., and Blake RR. (1963) Group problem solving effectiveness under conditions of pooling vs. interaction. *The Journal of Social Pyschology* **59**, 147–157.

A3.3 The *Higher Education Institute of Wherever* (HEIoW) is attempting to visualise its future in order to plan the development of its campus, infrastructure, study programmes, research directions, and other related long-term developments. Considering a 10–20 year time horizon, develop possible future scenarios for HEIoW.

A3.4 Several approaches to combining expert opinion have been introduced in this chapter. Research the topic of *prediction markets*, also known as *information markets*, and write a report comparing these with the NGT and Delphi techniques.

A3.5 Purchase copies of *Time, Fortune, Business Week,* and similar magazines. Read them through, select two or three not obviously related articles from each, and develop a story to show how they could become related.

A3.6 Read Jared Diamond's *Guns, Germs and Steel* and Manuel De Landa's *A Thousand Years of Nonlinear History*.

PART 2

One-off and Repeat Decisions

CHAPTER 4

Inventory Management

Objectives

- *To appreciate the terms 'stock', 'inventory', and 'fixed order quantity'.*
- *To identify contributions to inventory holding costs and reorder costs.*
- *To be able to calculate the economic order quantity.*
- *To be able to calculate the economic order quantity with backorders.*
- *To be able to calculate the economic order quantity with price breaks.*
- *To recognise the relationship between probabilistic demand rate and stock-outs.*
- *To understand the newsvendor model.*

Introduction

Inventory or stock management concerns decisions with respect to the amount of flow units within a transformation process. For example, a small store may carry out the process of changing the ownership of cans of baked beans; a can of baked beans is a flow unit of interest. How many cans should the store purchase? A factory may assemble computers from components; how many components should the factory source?

There are several reasons for inventory or stock being present in a process:

1. There is *pipeline inventory*. Fundamentally, it requires a finite time for a flow unit to pass through a process; for example, it takes time for components to be assembled into a computer.
2. There may be *buffer inventory* in a process. If there are several steps in a process and there is variability in the time of each step, then one step can disrupt the other. Two consecutive steps may each take on average 10 minutes to process a flow unit, but, if for a particular unit the first step takes 11 minutes, without a buffer inventory the second step cannot begin. The buffer acts to decouple the steps.
3. There is *cycle inventory*. In many cases a batch of flow units are simultaneously transformed and then sometime later another batch is transformed, usually to access scale economies. This is often the case in transportation.
4. There is *safety stock*. If there is stochastic demand for a product, then safety stock may be held to meet some of the unpredictable increases.
5. There is *seasonal inventory*. Some transformation processes have rigid capacity, or at least capacity that is expensive to increase and decrease, but supply to a variable demand. In these cases, goods may be produced ahead of demand.

An understanding of inventory management has been developed over the past century. While some of this understanding can be mathematically complicated, the simpler aspects offer a compelling illustration of quantitative models supporting management choice, and moreover are in themselves quite powerful. The inventory management problem is presented both as a means to illustrate the considerations of model building and to introduce features of the theory that underlie many of the issues that surround inventory management. This is achieved by considering two important special cases:

(i)   the fixed order quantity inventory system, and
(ii) the stochastic single period or newsvendor problem.

These two cases contribute to cycle, safety, and seasonal inventory management.

The Fixed Order Quantity Inventory System

There exist many generic approaches to inventory management, but here the focus is on using the fixed order quantity inventory system for independent demand. This is often referred to as the *economic order quantity* (or EOQ) model.

EOQ with Deterministic Demand

Assume a small pet store is selling packets of birdseed and is expected to continue selling birdseed into the distant future. Each year there is a known demand rate, R, for the birdseed, given in packets per year. The store replenishes its stock by ordering a fixed quantity Q, a number of packets, at some time, and then later, when stocks have reduced to a certain level, to the reorder point (ROP), the store repeats the order of Q packets. The pet store therefore places R/Q orders per year. In taking a decision on inventory management, the store manager must decide a quantity Q to order and a reorder point ROP to trigger the order. To begin considering the first decision, that of the order quantity Q, suppose that a supplier offers the store four quantities that it is prepared to supply. The required decision to take is whether to follow strategy S_1 and order quantity Q_1, whether to follow strategy S_2 and order quantity Q_2, and so forth. To aid the store manager to make this decision, it is necessary to associate some measure of value with each of the four strategies, for example profit, revenue, cost, or loss (Figure 4.1).

S_1: Order quantity Q_1	value (Q_1)
S_2: Order quantity Q_2	value (Q_2)
S_3: Order quantity Q_3	value (Q_3)
S_4: Order quantity Q_4	value (Q_4)

Figure 4.1   Outline of the decision-taker's initial model.

Since this situation is one in which there is an outflow of money from the organization, a negative flow, the obvious approach is to associate a total yearly cost with each of the four strategies, and then to select the strategy with the least total yearly cost. Having identified the strategies available, the four order quantities, and the objective, to minimise the total yearly cost associated with ordering, the manager is then ready to build the decision model.

The total cost per year has three components: the cost to purchase the packets of birdseed, the cost of holding birdseed in stock, and the cost associated with placing and receiving an order. The total cost per year is given by

$$TC = (P \times R) + \left(\frac{h \times Q}{2}\right) + \left(\frac{K \times R}{Q}\right) \tag{4.1}$$

where

P is the price at which the pet store purchases one packet of birdseed, i.e. the material cost;

R is the demand rate per year, i.e. the number of packets that flow through the pet store per year;

h is the holding cost per year, i.e. how much it costs the pet store to hold one packet of feed per year; the holding cost includes costs of capital, storage insurance, handling, obsolescence, and shrinkage; only marginal costs should be included;

Q is the fixed quantity of each order, in this case the number of packets of birdseed in each order;

K is the reorder cost, the cost of making and receiving an order; these are fixed costs.

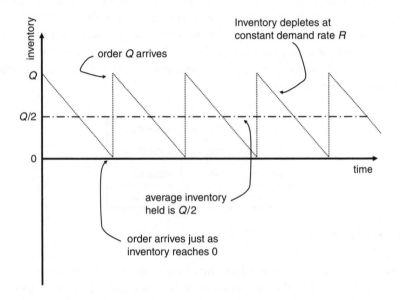

Figure 4.2 Inventory (stock of birdseed packets) in store as a function of time.

What assumptions have been made in constructing equation (4.1) for the total yearly cost? Firstly, the demand rate *R* has been assumed to be constant (Figure 4.2). This has made transparent an appropriate approximation for average inventory held throughout the year. At the beginning of a reorder cycle a quantity *Q* is delivered, by the end of the cycle the stock held is zero, and on average the stock held is *Q*/2. Consequently, the second term in equation (4.1) is the annual stock holding cost. The constant demand rate assumption has also allowed the potential cost to the pet store of stock-outs to be ignored; the store manager knows the demand rate for sure, and so, if the birdseed inventory is well managed, there is no possibility of running out of stock; to be precise, the assumptions made are consistent with the terms in the model. Finally, the combination of a fixed order quantity *Q* and a constant demand rate R makes the number of orders per year obvious, R/Q. Assuming a cost of ordering, K, independent of Q then allows the third term of the equation to be written. Accepting the assumptions means the model can now be populated with appropriate data.

The pet store manager has maintained appropriate records and the following data are available:

$$P = £3.20 \text{ per box}$$

$$R = 900 \text{ packets per year}$$

$$h = £0.80 \text{ per box per year}$$

$$K = £20.00 \text{ per order}$$

The supplier offers four quantities 100, 200, 300, or 400. Substituting into equation (4.1) allows completion of the payoff matrix outlined in Figure 4.1 to give Figure 4.3. The store manager would follow strategy S_2 and order in fixed quantities of 200 packets, placing $R/Q = 4.5$ orders per year. Although this approximates to 80 days between orders, it should be stressed that this is an event-driven process, orders being triggered when the reorder point is reached.

Strategy	Holding cost $= hQ/2$ (£/year)	Ordering cost $= KR/Q$ (£/year)	Holding + ordering cost (£/year)	Cost of goods $= RP$ (£/year)	Total cost (£/year)
S_1: 100 packets	40	180	220	2880	3100
S_2: 200 packets	80	90	_170_	2880	_3050_
S_3: 300 packets	120	60	180	2880	3060
S_4: 400 packets	160	45	205	2880	3085

Figure 4.3 Yearly costs of ordering for four different order quantities.

The payoff matrix of Figure 4.3 has several general characteristics:

1. Each strategy available to the decision-taker is represented by a row of the matrix.
2. A value has been associated with each strategy to enable the decision to be taken, in this case either the total cost per year or the sum of holding and ordering costs per year.
3. A decision rule to choose between the strategies has been defined, here to minimise cost.

The second and third aspects capture the store manager's objective, while the first reflects how she can add value by taking the rational decision.

Examining equation (4.1) and Figure 4.3 further, it is clear why in this case the decision-taker could have used either the total cost per year or the total variable cost per year to take the decision, since, whichever is chosen, the first term, $R \times P$, does not depend upon the variable Q and is hence unaffected by the manager's action.

The second decision to be taken is the reorder point (ROP) decision. How many packets of feed should the store still have in stock when the order is placed? Clearly, until the new order has been received the store has to use existing inventory (Figure 4.4), and so, for a certain lead time from placing to receiving the order (LT), the reorder point is given as

$$ROP = R \times LT \qquad (4.2)$$

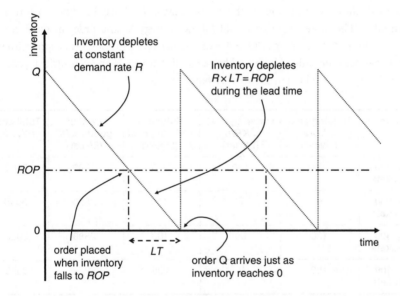

Figure 4.4 Relationship between certain demand rate R, certain lead time LT, and the reorder point ROP.

If the lead time from triggering the order for birdseed to it being available to customers were 1 month, then the pet store's reorder point would be

$$ROP = 900 \times 1/12 = 75$$

The pet store would reorder packets of birdseed once its inventory had depleted to 75 packets.

A simple model has aided the decision-taker with the order quantity and the reorder point decisions and has also encouraged recognition of the assumptions being made.

Suppose there is a pet store in another town that runs a very similar business to the first; the same cost structure, the same suppliers, and so on, the only difference being that the second store has a yearly demand rate twice that of the first, i.e. $R = 1800$. What would be the second store's order quantity? Without a quantitative model, natural intuition might be to say twice the first, suggesting a fixed order quantity Q of 400 rather than 200. Contrary to this suspicion, on substituting the values into equation (4.1), an order quantity of 300 is recommended (Figure 4.5). Building a quantitative model has given an advantage over simple intuition, but is it possible to understand this further and learn why the linear intuition is wrong?

Strategy	Holding cost = $hQ/2$ (£/year)	Ordering cost = KR/Q (£/year)	Holding + ordering cost (£/year)	Cost of goods = RP (£/year)	Total cost (£/year)
S_1: 100 packets	40	360	400	2880	3280
S_2: 200 packets	80	180	260	2880	3140
S_3: 300 packets	120	120	_240_	2880	_3120_
S_4: 400 packets	160	90	250	2880	3130

Figure 4.5 Yearly costs of ordering for four different order quantities with increased demand rate.

It would be unusual, although not unfeasible, for the supplier to restrict order quantities to such a limited range. Suppose now that the pet store is free to order in any quantity it wishes. Since the first term on the right-hand side of equation (4.1) is independent of Q, it is only necessary to consider the final two terms, that is, the total variable cost. Since the total variable cost is not linear in Q, it is appropriate to consider this as an infinite number of strategies, S_i ($i = 1$ to ∞), each with total variable cost (TVC) per year

$$TVC_i = \left(\frac{h \times Q_i}{2}\right) + \left(\frac{K \times R}{Q_i}\right) \tag{4.3}$$

Alternatively, making the further assumption that Q can be approximated by a continuous variable,

$$TVC(Q) = \left(\frac{h \times Q}{2}\right) + \left(\frac{K \times R}{Q}\right) \tag{4.4}$$

permits the optimum to be found by differentiating with respect to Q:

$$\frac{\mathrm{d}\,TVC}{\mathrm{d}\,Q} = \frac{h}{2} - \frac{K \times R}{Q^2} \tag{4.5}$$

Setting equation (4.5) equal to zero, and rearranging for Q, gives an expression for the economic order quantity EOQ (Figure 4.6) (Harris, 1913):

$$EOQ = \sqrt{\frac{2 \times K \times R}{h}} \tag{4.6}$$

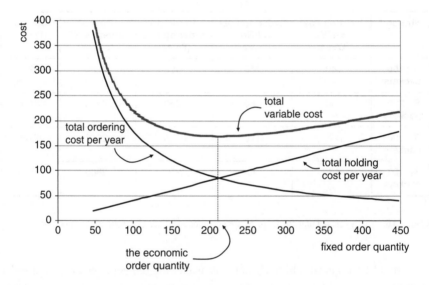

Figure 4.6   The total variable cost per year and economic order quantity.

Returning to the first example with a demand rate per year of $R = 900$ packets, if the pet store were able to order without constraint, the economic order quantity would be

$$EOQ = \sqrt{\frac{2 \times 20 \times 900}{0.8}} = 212.13 \approx 212 \text{ packets of birdseed per order}$$

Equation (4.6) for the economic order quantity not only allows the decision-taker to be more accurate with respect to order quantity, it provides a deep insight for the decision-maker; the economic order quantity formula is square root in the demand rate R, explaining the earlier comparison between the two pet stores in which a doubling of the demand rate did not lead to a doubling of the order quantity. This square root behaviour in demand rate goes further: substituting equation (4.6) back into equation (4.4) gives the total variable cost per year if ordering with the EOQ:

$$TVC(EOQ) = \sqrt{2 \times h \times K \times R} \qquad (4.7)$$

If the pet store were able to quadruple the demand rate for birdseed, only a doubling in total variable cost would result by following an optimum inventory policy.

Having developed a deterministic model of a decision-taking situation, it is possible for the pet store manager to learn more by applying sensitivity analysis, to vary either the variable(s) in the model or the parameter(s) in the model.

Sensitivity of the Total Variable Cost per Year to the Variable Q

Figure 4.6 suggests that the total variable cost curve is rather flat in the neighbourhood of the EOQ. Considering an order quantity that is a multiple of the EOQ

$$Q = \alpha \times EOQ = \alpha \sqrt{\frac{2 \times K \times R}{h}}$$

equation (4.4) leads to a total variable cost

$$TVC(\alpha \times EOQ) = \frac{1}{2}\left(\alpha + \frac{1}{\alpha}\right)\sqrt{2 \times h \times K \times R} = \frac{1}{2}\left(\alpha + \frac{1}{\alpha}\right)TVC\,(EOQ) \quad (4.8)$$

Hence, for example, fixed order quantities 56 % greater or 36 % less than the EOQ, that is, $\alpha = 1.56$ or $\alpha = 0.64$, lead to a 10 % increase in the total variable cost per year.

Sensitivity of the Total Variable Cost per Year to the Parameters h and K

Potential sources of imperfect knowledge in applying the economic order quantity model are inaccuracies in h, the holding cost per unit per year, and in K, the reorder cost. Essentially, EOQ and TVC calculations are actually carried out with estimates of K and h. Suppose

$$K_{estimate} = \alpha_K K \qquad (4.9)$$

and

$$h_{estimate} = \alpha_h h \qquad (4.10)$$

then the estimated economic order quantity

$$EOQ_{\text{estimate}} = \sqrt{\frac{\alpha_k}{\alpha_h}} EOQ \qquad (4.11)$$

results in a relative increase in the total variable cost (Figure 4.7)

$$\frac{TVC(EOQ_{\text{estimate}})}{TVC(EOQ)} = \frac{1}{2}\left(\sqrt{\frac{\alpha_K}{\alpha_h}} + \sqrt{\frac{\alpha_h}{\alpha_K}}\right) \qquad (4.12)$$

Such an understanding may lead the decision-taker to question the suitability of data used to parameterise the model, and to question whether it is worth investing to improve these estimates.

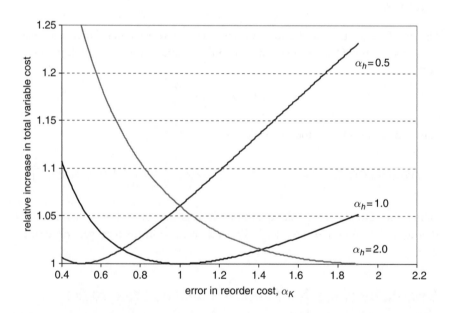

Figure 4.7 The relative increase in the total variable cost as a function of error in the reorder and holding costs.

The EOQ Model with Backorders

The two decisions made so far within the deterministic EOQ model have been the order quantity and the reorder point. It has been assumed that all customer demand will be satisfied from stock. Another decision that might be considered using a deterministic model is whether to satisfy some of the demand from backorders, that is, to fulfil the demand at a later date than initially requested by the customer.

In the pet store example this equates to a customer finding that there are no packets of birdseed in stock and reserving a packet for when the next order is delivered. For the case of outlets with limited storage capacity, a large range (e.g. catalogue shops), or customisable products (furniture showrooms) this may be a reasonable policy. Assuming no customers are lost, a cost per year can be associated with each backorder; this is a similar approach to associating a holding cost per year for each unit in stock. To illustrate this with a slightly artificial example, imagine that the pet store offered a price reduction of 10 pence for each working day that a customer had to wait for a packet of birdseed, then there would be a backorder cost of £30.00 per packet per year.

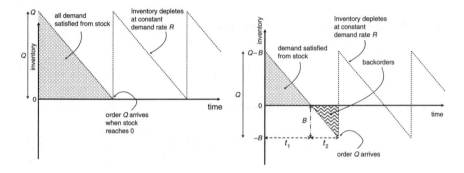

Figure 4.8 Inventory levels without and with a backordering policy.

Figure 4.8 illustrates satisfying all demand from stock and satisfying some demand from backorders. In the case of backorders, the total cost per year, $TC(Q, B)$, is now

$$TC(Q, B) = PR + \frac{K \times R}{Q} + \frac{h \times (Q - B) \times n \times t_1}{2} + \frac{c \times B \times n \times t_2}{2} \qquad (4.13)$$

where

c is the cost of one backorder per year;
n is the number of reorder cycles per year;
B is the number of backorders when a delivery arrives (i.e. the maximum shortage reached);
t_1 is the period within a reorder cycle when demand is satisfied from stock held;
t_2 is the period when demand is satisfied from backorders.

The final two terms of equation (4.13) divide the holding costs between $(Q - B)/2$, the cost of holding an average tangible inventory, and $B/2$, the cost of holding an average number of backorders.

Observing

$$n = R/Q$$

$$t_1 = (Q - B)/R \tag{4.14}$$

$$t_2 = B/R$$

equation (4.13) can be rewritten to give the total cost per year as

$$TC(Q, B) = PR + \frac{K \times R}{Q} + \frac{h \times (Q - B)^2}{2 \times Q} + \frac{c \times B^2}{2 \times Q} \tag{4.15}$$

Taking the partial derivative with respect to B and setting to zero gives

$$B = Q\left(\frac{h}{h+c}\right) \tag{4.16}$$

while minimising with respect to Q leads to

$$Q^2 = \frac{2 \times K \times R}{h} + B^2\left(\frac{h+c}{h}\right) \tag{4.17}$$

Substituting equation (4.16) into equation (4.17) and rearranging gives the economic order quantity with backordering EOQ_B:

$$EOQ_B = \sqrt{\frac{2 \times K \times R}{h}}\sqrt{\frac{h+c}{c}} \tag{4.18}$$

and, before a delivery is received, backorders reach

$$B = \sqrt{\frac{2 \times K \times R}{c}}\sqrt{\frac{h}{h+c}} \tag{4.19}$$

and so the reorder point is modified accordingly:

$$ROP = R \times LT - B \tag{4.20}$$

Reconsidering the earlier pet store example but now allowing backorders with

$$c = £30.00 \text{ per box per year}$$

and maintaining

$$R = 900 \text{ packets per year}$$

$$h = \text{£0.80 per box per year}$$

$$K = \text{£20.00 per order}$$

$$LT = 1 \text{ month}$$

gives

$$EOQ_B = \sqrt{\frac{2 \times K \times R}{h}} \sqrt{\frac{h+c}{c}} = \sqrt{\frac{2 \times 20 \times 900}{0.8}} \sqrt{\frac{30 + 0.8}{30}} = 214.94 \approx 215$$

$$B = \sqrt{\frac{2 \times K \times R}{c}} \sqrt{\frac{h}{h+c}} = \sqrt{\frac{2 \times 20 \times 900}{30}} \sqrt{\frac{0.8}{0.8 + 30}} = 5.58 \approx 6$$

$$ROP = R \times LT - B = (900 \times 1/12) - 6 = 69$$

Furthermore, in this case the resulting policy with backorders leads to little difference in total cost per year to that of the economic order quantity policy without backorders.

The EOQ *Model with Price Breaks*

In the preceding examples it was assumed that P, the purchase price per unit, was constant. This assumption is often invalid, and a supplier's pricing includes quantity discounts (Benton & Park, 1996), i.e. there are ranges over which P takes different values, high for small order quantities, lower for large. Similar non-marginal behaviours can occur for order costs, K, these being set for certain ranges of delivery size, and likewise for holding costs, h. To demonstrate the solution of such problems, a payoff matrix approach will be used for the quantity discount decision alongside a proportional change in holding costs. The method can be adapted for discontinuities in the other parameters.

When quantity discounts are offered, each price, P_i, is available over a feasible range of quantities, $l_i \leq Q \leq u_i$, and it is natural to define the holding cost h_i as an inventory charge r multiplied by the price. So

$$l_1 \leq Q \leq u_1 \Rightarrow P_i = P_1 \quad \text{and} \quad h_i = h_1 = rP_1$$

Under such circumstances, the total cost is given by

$$TC_i = (P_i \times R) + \left(\frac{h_i \times Q}{2}\right) + \left(\frac{K \times R}{Q}\right) = (P_i \times R) + \left(\frac{r \times P_i \times Q}{2}\right)$$

$$+ \left(\frac{K \times R}{Q}\right) \quad \text{for } I_i \leq Q \leq u_i$$

(4.21)

resulting in the economic order quantity

$$EOQ_i = \sqrt{\frac{2 \times K \times R}{r \times P_i}}$$

(4.22)

Three situations can arise: EOQ_i can be within the feasible range (Figure 4.9a), greater than u_i (Figure 4.9b), or less than l_i (Figure 4.9c). If the EOQ_i is not within the feasible range for which P_i is available, then the lowest total cost within that quantity range is that calculated for the quantity at the price break, i.e. at the boundary of the range. Specifically

$$\text{If } EOQ_i > u_i, \text{ then } TC_i = TC_i(u_i)$$

(4.23)

$$\text{If } EOQ_i < l_i, \text{ then } TC_i = TC_i(l_i)$$

(4.24)

Suppose a firm has an annual demand rate of 10 000 units, an annual inventory charge of 30 %, and a marginal reorder cost of £100:

$$R = 10000$$

$$r = 0.3$$

$$K = 100$$

The firm's supplier offers the following order-quantity-dependent pricing:

$$0 \leq Q \leq 499, \text{ then } P = £10.00$$

$$500 \leq Q \leq 3499, \text{ then } P = £9.75$$

$$3500 \leq Q \leq 4999, \text{ then } P = £9.50$$

$$Q \geq 5000, \text{ then } P = £9.25$$

Firstly the firm calculates an EOQ corresponding to each price and determines whether it falls within, below, or above the quantity range for which that price is available. A strategy corresponding to each of the four quantity ranges can then be identified, i.e. the lowest total annual cost within each range (Figure 4.10). Finally, the strategy with the overall minimum is commended (Figure 4.11).

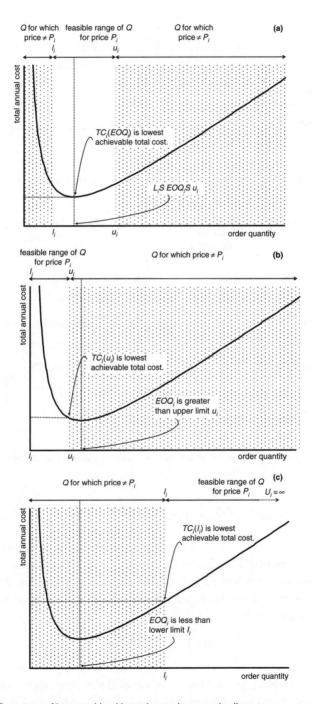

Figure 4.9 Three cases of lowest achievable total cost, given quantity discounts.

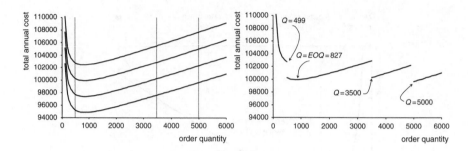

Figure 4.10   Total annual cost curves, valid ranges, and resulting potential strategies.

Range	Economic Order Quantity		Strategy	Total Cost per Year
0–499	817		S_1: $Q=499$	102,753
500–3499	827		S_2: $Q=827$	99,919
3500–4999	838		S_3: $Q=3500$	100,273
≥5000	849		S_4: $Q=5000$	99,638

Figure 4.11   Order quantity choice with price breaks. The quantity with the lowest total cost per year is commended.

The EOQ *Model with Uncertainty but Unknown Stock-out Costs*

Thus far, deterministic inventory management models have been considered, although sensitivity to model parameters has been noted. Often the demand rate is not known with certainty, and so the economic order quantity is calculated using an average demand rate $\overline{R}$:

$$EOQ = \sqrt{\frac{2 \times K \times \overline{R}}{h}} \qquad (4.25)$$

Nevertheless, should all demand have to be satisfied from inventory, backorders not being permitted, once a non-deterministic demand rate is introduced, the possibility of stock-outs is introduced. Considering Figure 4.12, an order is placed once the

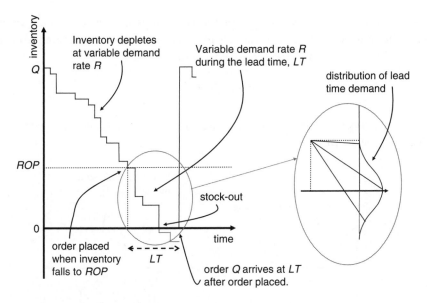

Figure 4.12 Variable demand rate during known lead time, resulting in stock-out.

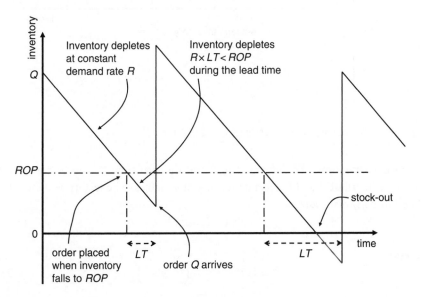

Figure 4.13 Variable lead time with constant demand rate, resulting in stock-out.

ROP is reached, and then subsequent demand is met from existing stock. However, owing to the variability in demand rate R during the lead time, it is possible for the total demand to surpass stock held. Similarly, Figure 4.13 illustrates that, even if the demand rate were constant, variability in the lead time away from the average, $\overline{LT}$, could also give rise to a stock-out. One approach to this issue is to hold an amount of safety inventory or stock, ss, to reduce the likelihood of stock-out during each reorder cycle. This is realised by setting the reorder point to

$$ROP = \bar{R} \times \overline{LT} + ss \tag{4.26}$$

and, as a consequence, increasing the average inventory held throughout the year to $Q/2 + ss$ (Figure 4.14).

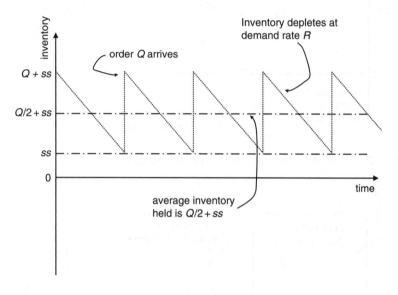

Figure 4.14 Average stock held throughout the year is $Q/2 + ss$.

In many situations the demand rate R and the lead time LT can be considered normally distributed and independent random variables. The lead time demand is then normally distributed as

$$N(\bar{R} \times \overline{LT}, \sigma^2) \tag{4.27}$$

where

$$\sigma^2 = \left(\overline{LT} \times \sigma_R^2\right) + \left(\bar{R}^2 \times \sigma_{LT}^2\right) \tag{4.28}$$

Here

$\bar{R}$ is the mean demand rate;
$\overline{LT}$ is the mean lead time;
σ_R is the standard deviation of the demand rate;
σ_{LT} is the standard deviation of the lead time.

The reorder point is now given as

$$ROP = \overline{R} \times \overline{LT} + ss = \overline{R} \times \overline{LT} + Z \times \sigma = \overline{R} \times \overline{LT} + Z \qquad (4.29)$$

$$\times \sqrt{\left(\overline{LT} \times \sigma_R^2\right) + \left(\overline{R}^2 \times \sigma_{LT}^2\right)}$$

where Z, the number of standard deviations from the mean, is chosen to achieve a particular service level (Nahmias, 2004, p. 256). For example, the service level can be specified in terms of the probability of no stock-out occurring within a reorder cycle (Figure 4.15). Specific values of Z can be read from standard normal distribution tables, or found (Figure 4.16) using the *NORMSINV* function in MS Excel, which returns the inverse cumulative standard normal distribution. Without an explicit knowledge of stock-out costs, the service level chosen can be a matter of tacit judgement; in so doing, it must not be overlooked that the probability of no stock-out per year not only depends upon the probability per reorder cycle but also on the number of reorder cycles, R/Q, per year:

$$\text{Probability of no stock-out in year} = (\text{probability of no stock-out in cycle})^{R/Q}$$
$$(4.30)$$

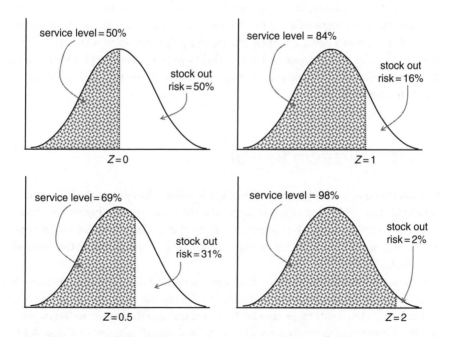

Figure 4.15 Service level risk for increasing Z.

Reorder Cycle Service Level (probability of no shortage expressed as a percentage)	Reorder Cycle Stock-out Risk (probability of shortage expressed as a percentage)	Z
50	50	0.00
60	40	0.25
70	30	0.52
80	20	0.84
90	10	1.28
95	5	1.64
98	2	2.05
99	1	2.33
99.5	0.5	2.58
99.9	0.1	3.09

Figure 4.16   Relationship between service level and the number of standard deviations Z.

Given that the achieved yearly service levels depend upon the order quantity (equation (4.30)), it is natural to criticise the approach of first determining the order quantity and only afterwards the reorder point. An alternative approach would be to decide an optimal order quantity and reorder point simultaneously, and, if the annual stock-out cost per unit is known, this is possible. Before considering this, the simpler problem of single-period stochastic demand, the so-called newsvendor model, is examined.

The Newsvendor Model

The single-period stochastic demand problem is often referred to as the newsvendor model (Khouja, 1999) and is particularly relevant to seasonal or highly perishable products or services. For such products, the demand is available to be satisfied for one period only, and the supplier has to make an inventory decision before the demand is realised.

Suppose a kiosk owner sells a particular daily newspaper for £1.00, purchasing each for £0.50, but if a newspaper is unsold on its publication date then the kiosk owner is only able to achieve a salvage price of £0.25. Using the sales data from previous weeks, the kiosk owner has developed a model of daily demand as given in Figure 4.17. Given that the publisher will supply papers in multiples of 20 copies only, how many

Daily Demand	Probability	Cumulative Probability
100	0.1	0.1
120	0.1	0.2
140	0.1	0.3
160	0.1	0.4
180	0.1	0.5
200	0.1	0.6
220	0.1	0.7
240	0.1	0.8
260	0.1	0.9
280	0.1	1.0
Average = 190		

Figure 4.17 Model of daily demand for newspapers.

newspapers should the kiosk stock each day? Since the average expected demand is 190 newspapers per day, an intuitive response might be to stock 190, but this is not offered. Moreover, on closer inspection, the costs associated with understocking and overstocking are not the same. For every paper understocked the kiosk owner forgoes a potential additional profit of 50 pence (£1.00 − £0.50), while for every paper overstocked the profit is only reduced by 25 pence (£0.50−£0.25). For such an asymmetry, stocking more than 190 newspapers each day seems appropriate. A payoff matrix can be constructed to determine the level. To do this, an expression is first written to describe the daily profit as a function of daily order quantity and daily demand:

$$\pi\,(Q, D) = \left(P_{sa} - P_p\right) \times \min\,[Q, D] + \left(P_{sv} - P_p\right) \times \max\,[Q - D, 0] \qquad (4.31)$$

where

$\pi(Q, D)$ is the daily profit as a function of Q and D;
Q is the order quantity on a particular day;
D is the demand on a particular day;
P_p is the price at which the kiosk owner purchases each newspaper;
P_{sa} is the usual sales price of each newspaper;
P_{sv} is the salvage price of each newspaper.

The expected value of profit for each available order quantity is calculated, and the quantity giving the largest expected profit is selected (Figure 4.18), in this case 220 newspapers.

	Probability	0.1	0.1	0.1	0.1	0.1	0.1	0.1	0.1	0.1	0.1	EV
	Demand	100	120	140	160	180	200	220	240	260	280	
	100	50	50	50	50	50	50	50	50	50	50	50
Q	120	45	60	60	60	60	60	60	60	60	60	58.5
U	140	40	55	70	70	70	70	70	70	70	70	65.5
A	160	35	50	65	80	80	80	80	80	80	80	71
N	180	30	45	60	75	90	90	90	90	90	90	75
T	200	25	40	55	70	85	100	100	100	100	100	77.5
I	220	20	35	50	65	80	95	110	110	110	110	(78.5)
T	240	15	30	45	60	75	90	105	120	120	120	78
Y	260	10	25	40	55	70	85	100	115	130	130	76
	280	5	20	35	50	65	80	95	110	125	140	72.5

Figure 4.18 Newsvendor problem where demand is a discrete probability distribution.

Newsvendor Continuous Probability Distribution

In the above example, the newspaper kiosk, the demand was modelled as a discrete probability distribution. However, in other situations the demand might be considered as a continuous distribution. When this is the case, the expected profit, $\pi(Q)$, can be written in terms of the probability function $f(x)$ of the demand x:

$$\pi (Q) = (P_{sa} - P_p) \int_0^\infty \min [Q, x] \times f(x)\, dx + (P_{sv} - P_p) \int_0^\infty \max [Q - x, 0] \times f(x)\, dx$$

that is

$$\pi (Q) = (P_{sa} - P_p) \int_Q^\infty Q \times f(x)\, dx + (P_{sa} - P_p) \int_0^Q x \times f(x)\, dx \qquad (4.32)$$

$$+ (P_{sv} - P_p) \int_0^Q (Q - x) \times f(x)\, dx$$

and letting $F(x)$ be the cumulative distribution function of demand gives

$$\pi(Q) = \left(P_{sa} - P_p\right) \times Q - \left(P_{sa} - P_{sv}\right) \times \int_0^Q F(x)\,dx \qquad (4.33)$$

Differentiating with respect to Q:

$$\frac{d\pi(Q)}{dQ} = \left(P_{sa} - P_p\right) - \left(P_{sa} - P_{sv}\right) \times F(Q) = 0 \qquad (4.34)$$

and hence

$$F(Q) = \frac{P_{sa} - P_p}{P_{sa} - P_{sv}} = \frac{C_u}{C_u + C_o} \qquad (4.35)$$

where an underage cost, $C_u = P_{sa} - P_p$, and an overage cost, $C_o = P_p - P_{sv}$, have been defined. The underage cost is the profit forgone through understocking by 1 unit, while the overage cost is the profit forgone through overstocking by 1 unit.

Example

Ingrida sells copies of a weekly magazine, the *Peninsula Governance Review*, for £1.60. From past experience, the weekly demand is normally distributed with mean $\mu = 200$ and standard deviation $\sigma = 40$. She purchases the magazine at £0.35 and can salvage £0.10 on unsold copies. How many copies should Ingrida source each week?

$$F(Q) = \frac{P_{sa} - P_p}{P_{sa} - P_{sv}} = \frac{1.60 - 0.35}{1.60 - 0.10} = 0.833$$

Here, Q can be found by using the inverse to the cumulative standard normal distribution curve:

$$Q = \mu + \sigma \times \Phi^{-1}(0.833) = 200 + 40 \times 0.967 = 239$$

or by using *MS Excel*:

$$Q = NORMINV(0.833, 200, 40) = 239$$

Ingrida should purchase 239 copies of the magazine to maximise weekly profits.

Equation (4.35) can be generalised to discrete probabilities by stipulating Q to be the smallest value of demand such that

$$F(Q) \geq \frac{P_{sa} - P_p}{P_{sa} - P_{sv}} \qquad (4.36)$$

Returning to the case of the kiosk owner modelled in Figure 4.17, then the smallest demand such that $F(Q) \geq 0.67$ is 220 with cumulative probability 0.7. This is in agreement with the result of Figure 4.18.

The Economic Order Quantity Model with Known Stock-out Costs

A similar approach to that of the newsvendor problem can be used for jointly optimising the reorder quantity and reorder point. Beginning with the total variable cost equation, (equation (4.4)), the cost of holding safety stock is included in the second term and a third term associated with shortage costs is appended:

$$TC = \frac{K \times \overline{R}}{Q} + h \times \left(\frac{Q}{2} + ROP - \left(\overline{LT} \times \overline{R}\right)\right) + \frac{s \times \overline{R}}{Q} \int_{ROP}^{\infty} (y - ROP) \times f(y)\, dy$$

(4.37)

$$TC = \frac{K \times \overline{R}}{Q} + h \times \left(\frac{Q}{2} + ROP - \left(\overline{LT} \times \overline{R}\right)\right) + \frac{s \times \overline{R}}{Q} \left[\left(\overline{LT} \times \overline{R}\right) - ROP \right.$$
$$\left. + \int_{0}^{ROP} F(y)\, dy \right]$$

(4.38)

where

s is the shortage cost per unit;
$f(y)$ is the probability distribution function of lead time demand;
$F(y)$ is the cumulative distribution function of lead time demand.

Minimising with respect to the order quantity and the reorder point (Nahmias, 2004, p. 286) gives optimum values Q^* and ROP^* which satisfy

$$Q^* = \sqrt{\frac{2 \times \overline{R}}{h} \left(K + s \times \left[\overline{R} \times \overline{LT} - ROP^* + \int_{0}^{ROP^*} F(y)\, dy\right]\right)}$$

(4.39)

$$F(ROP^*) = 1 - \frac{h \times Q^*}{s \times \overline{R}}$$

(4.40)

Solutions are found by iterating between equations (4.40) and (4.39), beginning with an initial value of Q^* equal to the economic order quantity given by equation (4.25).

Summary

This chapter has focused on two important models within inventory management: the continuous-review fixed order quantity inventory system and the newsvendor problem. These two cases aid decision-takers when considering cycle, safety, and seasonal inventory management. Moreover, they provide examples of model use to inform decision-taking.

The case of the EOQ model with deterministic demand illustrates the use of a payoff matrix (Figure 4.3) clearly to associate the value of an objective function (cost) with each of a number of strategies from which to choose. Payoff matrices are further discussed in Chapter 5. If a characteristic variable can distinguish each strategy and it is continuous (e.g. quantity), then it is possible to move from a payoff matrix approach to one of optimisation with calculus. This was illustrated by equations (4.4) and (4.6). Furthermore, such simple models generate powerful understanding; in this case the trade-off between ordering and holding costs is clarified. Identifying the parameters in such models also adds management insight in at least two ways. Firstly, carrying out a sensitivity analysis suggests the parameters of importance in taking a decision. Sensitivity analysis is discussed in later chapters, in particular in Chapter 9. Secondly, parameters to shift the mental model from one of optimisation to one of improvement are highlighted. For example, rather than simply choosing an optimum, the aim may become to decrease the EOQ through a reduction in reorder cost, K.

The EOQ model with deterministic demand also leads to the concept of a reorder point. At the outset there appears to be no management decision to take; once inventory reaches the ROP, an order is placed. Nevertheless, a decision-taker can consider whether to satisfy some demand from backorders, rather than keep products waiting for customers keep customers waiting for products. To do this, the original model is extended and additional data associated with the cost of backordering are required. Another modification is the EOQ model with price breaks. The future demand remains known with certainty, but the purchase price becomes a function of the order quantity. This demonstrates the concept of a feasible range for solutions (Figure 4.9). Moreover, if the total variable price changes monotonically within a feasible range, then the optimum order quantity for a given price falls on a boundary of that price range. The idea of a feasible solution space is extended to more than one decision variable in Chapter 6.

Beyond inventory models with certain futures, this chapter also introduced the concept of decision-making with uncertainty. The case of the *EOQ* model with unknown stock-out costs illustrates decision-taking in which decision variables, i.e. the reorder quantity and the reorder level, are treated independently (equations (4.25) and (4.26)). In contrast, with known stock-out costs the decision variables are jointly optimised. In each of these cases, future uncertainty was described by a continuous probability distribution, whereas the newsvendor model illustrated the use of expected value with either a discrete probability model of future demand (Figure 4.18 and equation 4.17) or a continuous model.

Further Reading

* The *EOQ* formula is sometimes referred to as either the Harris or the Wilson formula; it is given in both Harris (1913) and in Wilson (1934). The latter paper also discusses the reorder point in some detail. The *EOQ* formula history is presented by Erlenkotter (1989, 1990). The possibility of Kelvin's law inspiring the Harris formula has been suggested by Roach (2005). In concluding, the original Harris paper notes: 'It may be objected that interest and depreciation should be figured, not only on original cost, but also on the set-up cost, since that has to be incurred before the parts can be stocked'. Recently, Serrano and Kraiselburd (2007) have questioned the validity of the *EOQ* formula in maximising firm value, one observation being: 'The classic *EOQ* formula takes into account how the purchase payments are financed. However, it does not consider how the ordering and the holding expenses are financed'.

* Alternative presentations to parts of this chapter can be found in other introductory texts. These include:

  Cachon, G. and Terwiesch, C. (2009). *Matching Supply with Demand: An Introduction to Operations Management*, 2nd Edition. McGraw-Hill: New York, NY, Chapter 11.

  Greasley, A. (2005). *Operations Management*. John Wiley & Sons, Ltd, Chichester, UK, Chapter 12.

  Slack, N., Shambers, S., & Johnston, R. (2007) *Operations Management*. Prentice Hall, Harlow, UK, Chapter 12.

  Waters, D. (2003) *Inventory Control and Management*. John Wiley & Sons, Ltd, Chichester, UK.

* More advanced presentations include:

  Axsäter, S. (2006) *Inventory Control*. Springer, Berlin, Germany.

  Lewis, CD. (1970) *Scientific Inventory Control*. Butterworth & Co. Ltd, London, UK.

  Nahmias, S. (2004) *Production and Operations Analysis*. McGraw-Hill: New York, NY. Chapters 4 and 5 discuss inventory control under known and stochastic demand. Each chapter ends with a brief historical note to important early references.

* The following papers provide examples of inventory management:

  Kapuscinski, R., Zhang, RQ., Carbonneau, P., *et al.* (2004) Inventory decisions in Dell's supply chain. *Interfaces* **34**(3), 191–205.

Lewis, T. (1996) Personal operations research: practicing OR on ourselves. *Interfaces* **26**(5), 34–41.

Rosenfield, DB. (1986) Optimal management of tax-sheltered employee reimbursement programs. *Interfaces* **16**(3), 68–72.

Questions

Q4.1 How should the reorder point be interpreted for long lead times? For example, if the lead time were 4 months in the pet store example, equation (4.2), what would be the *ROP*?

Q4.2 Hoi Cheng is an independent mechanic specialising in the servicing of MG Midgets. Hoi operates a 300 day working year and uses 1500 five-litre cans of sports oil annually. The holding cost for one can per year is £3.00, and the reorder cost is £10.00, irrespective of the size of order. What is Hoi's economic order quantity, how many orders are placed per year, and what are the annual holding and ordering costs? Hoi's records show that it typically requires 10 days between placing and receiving an order. How many cans does Hoi have in stock when he places a new order? How would Hoi have to change his reorder point if the lead time were 20 or 30 days?

Q4.3 Recalculate the earlier pet store example with backorders, but, rather than using a backorder cost of £30 per box per year, consider the case of lower backorder costs.

Q4.4 Discount Sports Supplements (DSS) distributes a well-liked protein bar. DSS sells these for £1.25 per bar, experiencing an average demand of 100 bars per day. DSS orders the bars from Nourishing Nutrients Ltd (NNL). NNL sells each bar to DSS for £0.50. Irrespective of the order size, the ordering costs are £4.37 ½ per order. The cost of carrying one bar in stock for a year is £0.14. DSS operates a 250 day working year. Determine the economic order quantity, the number of orders per year, and the time between orders. What is DSS's total order cost per year? What is DSS's total holding cost per year? Suppose NNL offered a discount for orders over 2500 bars or more. At what discount is it worthwhile for DSS to increase its order quantity?

Q4.5 Sheldon is the operations manager of a small, contract research and development company. He is required to make a choice of supplier for a specialist organic compound. Usage of the compound is 500 grams per month, the annual inventory charge is 40 %, and order costs are £30 per order.

Sheldon has identified two potential suppliers that satisfy his company's quality requirements. By considering the data below, advise Sheldon on his choice.

Supplier 1		Supplier 2	
Price per gram		Quantity	Price per gram
£12.00		<500 g	£12.00
A discount of 2.5 % is available on orders over 1 kg.		500–999 g	£11.90
		≥1000 g	£11.80
Conditions: orders supplied in multiples of 10 g only.		Conditions: orders supplied in multiples of 1 g only.	

Q4.6 A surgery operates 365 days per year and has an average yearly demand for hypodermic needles of 4000, with a standard deviation of 500. The average lead time is 10 days, with a standard deviation of 2 days. For a reorder cycle service level of 99 %, calculate the reorder point. Suppose the surgery had an order quantity of 400, what would be the probability of no stock-outs occurring during a year?

Q4.7 When the local football team plays at home, Beckie's Bakers sells pies to fans en route to the stadium. It costs Beckie's 45 pence to produce each pie, and they are sold for £1.20 to fans heading for the match. Any leftover pies are sold off after the match for 25 pence. For a given match, the demand can be considered to be normally distributed with a mean of 400 and a standard deviation of 30. How many pies should Beckie's produce for each game?

Q4.8 When the Hotel Budget is fully booked, the number of last-minute cancellations has a mean of 16 and a standard deviation of 4. Budget's average room rate is £75.20. When overbooked, Budget has a policy of placing clients in the nearby Grand (which always has vacancies), for which it is charged £188. How much should Hotel Budget overbook?

Q4.9 Assuming that the probability distribution of lead time demand is normally distributed with standard deviation σ_{LT}, show that the iterative scheme below can be used to solve equations (4.39) and (4.40) simultaneously:

$$Q_0 = \sqrt{\frac{2K\overline{R}}{h}}$$

$$ROP_i = NORMINV\left(1 - \frac{hQ_{i-1}}{s\overline{R}}, \overline{R} \times \overline{LT}, \sigma_{LT}\right)$$

$$\phi_i = NORMDIST\left(ROP_i, \overline{R} \times \overline{LT}, \sigma_{LT}, FALSE\right)$$

$$Q_i = \sqrt{\frac{2\overline{R}}{h}\left(K + s\sigma_{LT}^2\phi_i\right) - 2Q_{i-1}\left(ROP_i - \overline{R} \times \overline{LT}\right)}$$

where *NORMINV* and *NORMDIST* are MS Excel spreadsheet functions.

Q4.10 The average demand for a product is 120 000 units per year. The ordering cost is £817.00 per order, the holding cost is £0.40 per unit per year, the shortage cost is £5.00 per unit, the average lead time is 2 months, and the standard deviation of demand in the lead time is 5000. Assuming the lead time demand can be approximated as normally distributed, calculate the jointly optimised reorder point and reorder quantity.

Activities

A4.1 In a small group, discuss the recommendation made by Figure 4.11. Is it robust to uncertainties in the model parameters?

A4.2 Noting that the time between orders, T, is given by $T = Q/R$, show that equation (4.8) can be rewritten as

$$TVC(\alpha \times EOQ) = \frac{1}{2}\left(\frac{T(Q)}{T(EOQ)} + \frac{T(EOQ)}{T(Q)}\right)TVC(EOQ)$$

An organization has chosen an order quantity larger than the economic order quantity such that the interval between orders is given by

$$T(Q) = \sqrt{2} \times T(EOQ)$$

Calculate the percentage increase in total variable cost. Carry out a literature search on 'powers-of-two order intervals' and comment on the relevance of your calculation.

A4.3 Read the following novels:

Pollock, D. (1997) *Precipice*. Council of Logistics Management, Oak Brook, IL.
Goldratt, EM., Schragenheim, E., & Ptak, CA. (2000) *Necessary but not Sufficient*. The North River Press Publishing Corp., Great Barrington, MA.

The first is a thriller/whodunit style novel that aims to show the importance of logistics. The second is an ERP novel that recognises the necessity of technology to support the business process but warns that technology alone is insufficient to improve the bottom line.

A4.4 Produce a brief summary of the following paper:

Schwartz, M. & Fish, A. (1998) Just-in-time inventories in old Detroit. *Business History* **40**(3), 48–71.

CHAPTER 5

Payoff Matrices

Objectives

- To appreciate the term 'payoff matrix'.
- To recognise the difference between strict uncertainty and risk.
- To be able to apply the most well-known techniques for decision-taking under strict uncertainty, that is, the dominance, maximax, maximin, Hurwicz, minimax regret, and Laplace criteria.
- To be able to apply expected value decision-making to the case of risk.
- To be able to calculate the expected value of perfect information and understand its relationship with expected opportunity loss.
- To understand the concept of indifference probabilities.

Introduction

The purpose of decision-taking using payoff matrices is to provide a quantitative input into non-sequential decision processes. Such decision-taking might occur for unique situations that only take place once or for similar situations that are repeated

Chance Outcome Strategy	F_1	F_2	$\cdots$	F_{n-1}	F_n
S_1	v_{11}	v_{12}	$\cdots$	v_{1n-1}	v_{1n}
S_2	v_{21}	v_{22}	$\cdots$	v_{2n-1}	v_{2n}
$\vdots$	$\vdots$	$\vdots$	$\ddots$	$\vdots$	$\vdots$
S_{m-1}	v_{m-11}	v_{m-12}	$\cdots$	v_{m-1n-1}	v_{m-1n}
S_m	v_{m1}	v_{m2}	$\cdots$	v_{mn-1}	v_{mn}

Figure 5.1 An $m \times n$ payoff matrix.

many times. A payoff matrix (Figure 5.1), sometimes known as a payoff table, is a simple summary of the decision situation. Typically, the m rows of the matrix summarise the potential strategies, decisions, or actions, S_i, available for the decision-taker, while the n columns summarise possible future states of nature or chance events, F_j, under which the outcomes of the chosen strategy will unfold. The elements of the $m \times n$ payoff matrix, v_{ij}, provide a quantitative summary of the resulting payoff should a given strategy be taken and a state of nature unfold, in other words the matrix summarises the consequences of strategy–chance event pairings.

For the purpose of illustration, Figure 5.2 provides a qualitative example of a payoff matrix. The decision-taker has two possible strategies from which to choose, whether to wear a raincoat over her suit or whether to leave behind her raincoat on departing the office. Each of the strategies has a payoff, here expressed in terms of being *comfortable* or *uncomfortable*, dependent upon the chance outcomes described by the columns, *sunshine* or *cloudy and wet*. In this chapter, the discussion is focused

Chance Outcome Decision	Sunshine	Cloudy and Wet
Wear raincoat.	Uncomfortable with sweaty suit.	Comfortable with dry suit.
Don't take coat.	Comfortable with dry suit.	Uncomfortable with wet suit.

Figure 5.2 A qualitative illustration of a payoff matrix.

upon decision situations in which both the future and the available strategies can be described discretely and the decision-taker can choose exclusively only one of the strategies; in the illustration of Figure 5.2, the decision-taker can only follow one of *wear raincoat* or *don't take coat*, and the future state of nature can only be one of *sunshine* or *cloudy and wet*.

Payoff Matrices with Certainty

Under a decision with certainty there is only one possible future state $(n = 1)$ and the decision-taker simply chooses the strategy with the best outcome under that certain future. In the case of positive flow, such as profits or revenues, the strategy with the maximum payoff is taken (Figure 5.3). In the case of negative flows, such as losses or costs, the strategy that leads to the lowest payoff is chosen.

Decision	Present Value of Payoff (£10k)
Sustain (S_1)	100
Relocate (S_2)	**160**
Expand (S_3)	150

Decision	Cost of Decision as Present Value
S_1	240
S_2	300
S_3	**200**

Figure 5.3 For the case of positive flows, the payoff matrix to the left illustrates taking an optimum decision by choosing a maximum payoff under certainty. For the case of negative flows, the payoff matrix to the right illustrates taking an optimum by choosing a minimum payoff.

Payoff Matrices with Multiple Future States and a Dominant Strategy

For a decision with uncertainty there are several possible future states $(n > 1)$. Nevertheless, if one of the available strategies is superior to the other strategies, irrespective of the future state, then it is termed the *dominant strategy* and is that taken by the decision-taker. Figure 5.4 (left) illustrates the situation in which strategy S_2 has a higher payoff than the alternatives S_1 and S_3 in each of three possible future states. For example, if F_1 were to occur, then the payoff 80 is greater than both 70 and 60. If F_2 were to occur, then the payoff 145 is greater than both 100 and 140. If F_3 were to occur, then the payoff 270 is greater than both 110 and 200. Strategies S_1 and S_3 are dominated by strategy S_2. In contrast, Figure 5.4 (right) illustrates the situation

Chance Outcome	Low (F_1)	Medium (F_2)	High (F_3)	Chance Outcome	Low (F_1)	Medium (F_2)	High (F_3)
Decision	Present Value of Payoff (£10k)			Decision	Present Value of Payoff (£10k)		
Sustain (S_1)	70	100	110	Sustain (S_1)	70	100	110
Relocate (S_2)	80	145	270	Relocate (S_2)	80	110	270
Expand (S_3)	60	140	200	Expand (S_3)	60	140	200

Figure 5.4 Dominant and dominated strategies.

of only one dominated strategy. In this case, S_1 is inferior to S_2 in all future states, and so would never be selected by a rational decision-taker, but S_3 is only inferior in two of the would-be futures.

Payoff Matrices with Strict Uncertainty

In the earlier case of decision-taking under certainty, one number was associated with each possible strategy, and then the strategy that would lead to the optimal value of that number was chosen. Given only one possible future state of nature, the number to associate with each strategy was trivially the payoff of that strategy under the certain future. Conversely, once multiple future states of nature or chance outcomes are introduced, then each strategy has a different payoff under each future state of nature. Under such circumstances, several approaches have been developed to identify a value V_{S_α} with each (undominated) strategy, S_α, defined in terms of the elements of the payoff matrix:

$$V_{S_\alpha} = V_{S_\alpha}\left(v_{ij}\right) \tag{5.1}$$

Following this, the strategy with either the maximum or the minimum value of V_{S_α}, as appropriate, is taken.

In decision-taking situations in which it is not possible to specify a probability distribution over the set of chance outcomes, F_j, the decision situation is described as one with *strict uncertainty* and well-known approaches for defining V_{S_α} are the criteria of *optimism, pessimism, realism, opportunism,* and *insufficient reason*. Each of these will be described in turn.

The Criterion of Optimism

An optimistic decision-taker assumes that, for whichever strategy followed, the future will unfold in the most appropriate manner; it is assumed that the optimal consequences for a strategy will occur. The criterion of optimism is also known as the *maximax* criterion owing to its form when applied to payoff matrices in which the payoffs are expressed as positive flows, such as profit. In this case the criterion of optimism is specified by defining

$$V_{S_\alpha} = \max_{j=1}^{n} \left(v_{\alpha j} \right) \tag{5.2}$$

and choosing S_α such that V_{S_α} is a maximum. Briefly the decision criterion is to identify the maximum possible payoff for each alternative strategy and then choose the strategy with the maximum of these, i.e. the strategy with the value

$$\max_{\alpha=1}^{m} \left(V_{S_\alpha} \right) \tag{5.3}$$

Figure 5.5 demonstrates the criterion of optimism. A value is first associated with each strategy, based upon the maximum payoff that could be achieved through that strategy. For instance, the strategy S_1 has three values associated with different futures: F_1, F_2, and F_3; the largest of these is 110, and so V_{S_1} is 110. Likewise, V_{S_2} and V_{S_3} are 270 and 200. Finally, the strategy that results in the largest of these would be selected; the value $\max_{\alpha}(V_{S_\alpha}) = V_{S_2} = 270$ commends S_2.

Chance Outcome	Low (F_1)	Medium (F_2)	High (F_3)	V_{S_α}
Decision	Present Value of Payoff (£10k)			
Sustain (S_1)	70	100	110	*110*
Relocate (S_2)	10	130	270	**270**
Expand (S_3)	60	140	200	*200*

Figure 5.5 The criterion of optimism applied to the case of positive flows.

In the case of negative flows, such as losses, the criterion of optimism becomes *minimin*, that is

$$V_{S_\alpha} = \min_{j=1}^{n} \left(v_{\alpha j} \right) \tag{5.4}$$

with S_α chosen such that V_{S_α} is a minimum. The decision criterion is to identify the minimum payoff for each alternative strategy and then to choose the strategy with the minimum of these, i.e. the strategy with the value

$$\min_{\alpha=1}^{m} \left(V_{S_\alpha} \right) \tag{5.5}$$

Chance Outcome	F_1	F_2	F_3	V_{S_α}
Decision	Loss			
S_1	50	100	25	**25**
S_2	30	30	120	30
S_3	35	90	80	35

Figure 5.6 The criterion of optimism applied to the case of negative flows.

Figure 5.6 demonstrates the criterion of optimism for negative flows. A value is first associated with each strategy, based upon the minimum payoff that could be achieved by that strategy. For instance, the strategy S_1 has three values associated with different futures: F_1, F_2, and F_3; the smallest of these is 25, and so V_{S_1} is 25. Likewise, V_{S_2} and V_{S_3} are 30 and 35. Finally, the strategy that results in the smallest of these would be selected: $\min_\alpha(V_{S_\alpha}) = V_{S_1}$, i.e. S_1 with a loss of 25.

The Criterion of Pessimism (The Wald Criterion)

Whereas the optimist focuses on the optimum level achievable by each strategy, the pessimist's attention is drawn to the assured return of each strategy, namely the worst that can happen given that a particular strategy has been taken (Wald, 1945).

The criterion of pessimism is also known as the *Wald* criterion, or as the *maximin* criterion owing to its form when applied to payoff matrices in which the payoffs are expressed as positive flows, such as profit. In this case the criterion of pessimism is specified by defining

$$V_{S_\alpha} = \min_{j=1}^{n} (v_{\alpha j}) \tag{5.6}$$

and S_α is chosen such that V_{S_α} is a maximum. The pessimistic decision criterion is to identify the minimum possible payoff for each alternative strategy and then to choose the strategy for which this is the maximum, i.e. the strategy with the value

$$\max_{\alpha=1}^{m} (V_{S_\alpha}) \tag{5.7}$$

Figure 5.7 demonstrates the criterion of pessimism. A value is first associated with each strategy, based upon the minimum payoff that could be achieved by that strategy. For instance, the strategy S_1 has three values associated with different futures: F_1, F_2, and F_3; the smallest of these is 70, and so V_{S_1} is 70. Likewise, V_{S_2} and V_{S_3} are 10 and 60. Finally, the strategy that results in the largest of these would be selected:

Chance Outcome	Low (F_1)	Medium (F_2)	High (F_3)	V_{S_α}
Decision	Present Value of Payoff (£10k)			
Sustain (S_1)	70	100	110	**70**
Relocate (S_2)	10	130	270	10
Expand (S_3)	60	140	200	60

Figure 5.7 The criterion of pessimism applied to positive flows.

$\max\limits_{\alpha}(V_{S_\alpha}) = V_{S_1}$, i.e. S_1 with value 70. By taking S_1, a positive flow payoff of at least 70 is assured.

In the case of negative flows, such as losses, the criterion of pessimism becomes *minimax*, that is

$$V_{S_\alpha} = \max_{j=1}^{n} \left(v_{\alpha j}\right) \tag{5.8}$$

with S_α chosen such that V_{S_α} is a minimum. The decision criterion is to identify the maximum payoff for each alternative strategy and then choose the strategy with the minimum of these, i.e. the strategy with the value

$$\min_{\alpha=1}^{m} \left(V_{S_\alpha}\right) \tag{5.9}$$

Figure 5.8 demonstrates the criterion of pessimism for negative flows. A value is first associated with each strategy, based upon the maximum payoff that could be achieved by that strategy, basically how great a loss could each incur? For instance, the strategy S_1 has three values associated with different futures: F_1, F_2, and F_3; the largest of these is 100, and so V_{S_1} is 100. Likewise, V_{S_2} and V_{S_3} are 120 and 90. Finally,

Chance Outcome	F_1	F_2	F_3	V_{S_α}
Decision	Loss			
S_1	50	100	25	100
S_2	30	30	120	120
S_3	35	90	80	**90**

Figure 5.8 The criterion of pessimism applied to negative payoffs.

the strategy that results in the smallest of these would be selected: $\min_{\alpha} (V_{S_\alpha}) = V_{S_3}$, i.e. S_3 with a worst-case loss of 90.

The Criterion of Realism (The Hurwicz Criterion)

The optimist focuses on the optimum level achievable by each strategy, and the pessimist on the worst case or assured level. However, the realist supposes a compromise between these two, basing the decision taken on a weighting of optimistic and pessimistic criteria (Arrow & Hurwicz, 1972). The criterion of realism is also known as the *Hurwicz* criterion.

For positive flow payoff, such as profit, the Hurwicz criterion is specified by defining

$$V_{S_\alpha} = \theta \max_{j=1}^{n} (v_{\alpha j}) + (1 - \theta) \min_{j=1}^{n} (v_{\alpha j}) \tag{5.10}$$

where θ is called the parameter of optimism and S_α is chosen to maximise V_{S_α}:

$$\max_{\alpha=1}^{m} (V_{S_\alpha}) \tag{5.11}$$

To apply the Hurwicz criterion, it is necessary to identify both the maximum and minimum possible payoffs for each alternative strategy and to take the strategy for which a weighted average is a maximum. This procedure not only requires knowledge of the decision situation but also self-knowledge of the decision-taker. The decision-taker must assess her level of optimism. The decision-taker may characteristically tend towards optimism with $\theta = 1$ or towards pessimism with $\theta = 0$; likewise, she may be somewhere between these.

Figure 5.9 demonstrates the Hurwicz criterion using a moderately pessimistic value for θ of 0.3. A value is first associated with each strategy, based upon the weighted average of the minimum and maximum. For instance, the strategy S_1 has

Chance Outcome	Low (F_1)	Medium (F_2)	High (F_3)	V_{S_α}
Decision	Present Value of Payoff (£10k)			
Sustain (S_1)	⑦⓪	100	⑪⑩⓪	82
Relocate (S_2)	10	130	270	88
Expand (S_3)	60	140	200	*102*

Figure 5.9 The Hurwicz criterion applied to positive payoffs with a parameter of optimism of 0.3.

three values associated with different futures: F_1, F_2, and F_3; the smallest of these is 70 and the largest 110, so

$$V_{S_1} = (0.3 \times 110) + (1 - 0.3) \times 70 = 33 + 49 = 82$$

Similarly

$$V_{S_2} = (0.3 \times 270) + (1 - 0.3) \times 10 = 81 + 7 = 88$$

and

$$V_{S_3} = (0.3 \times 200) + (1 - 0.3) \times 60 = 60 + 42 = 102$$

Finally, the maximum of these is identified: $\max\limits_{\alpha} (V_{S_\alpha}) = V_{S_3} = 102$, and S_3 is suggested to the decision-taker.

For a negative flow payoff such as loss, the Hurwicz criterion is specified by defining

$$V_{S_\alpha} = \theta \min_{j=1}^{n} (v_{\alpha j}) + (1 - \theta) \max_{j=1}^{n} (v_{\alpha j}) \tag{5.12}$$

so θ remains the parameter of optimism, and S_α is now chosen to minimise V_{S_α}:

$$\min_{\alpha=1}^{m} (V_{S_\alpha}) \tag{5.13}$$

Figure 5.10 demonstrates the Hurwicz criterion using a slightly pessimistic value for θ of 0.4. For strategy S_1, the smallest (and hence best) payoff is 25 and the largest (or worst) is 100:

$$V_{S_1} = (0.4 \times 25) + (1 - 0.4) \times 100 = 10 + 60 = 70$$

Similarly

$$V_{S_2} = (0.4 \times 30) + (1 - 0.4) \times 120 = 12 + 72 = 84$$

Chance Outcome	F_1	F_2	F_3	V_{S_α}
Decision		Loss		
S_1	50	⃝100	⃝25	70
S_2	30	30	120	84
S_3	35	90	80	*68*

Figure 5.10 The Hurwicz criterion applied to negative payoff with a parameter of optimism of 0.4.

and

$$V_{S_3} = (0.4 \times 35) + (1 - 0.4) \times 90 = 14 + 54 = 68$$

Finally, the minimum of these is identified: $\min_{\alpha}(V_{S_\alpha}) = V_{S_3} = 68$, and S_3 is suggested to the decision-taker.

The Criterion of Opportunism (The Savage Criterion)

Assuming that the decision-taker is unable to influence the future state of nature that eventually occurs, but only the choice of the strategy followed, each of the optimism, pessimism and Hurwicz criteria might be criticised for the manner in which the future states are treated. Returning to the example application of optimistic decision-taking given in Figure 5.6, it is clear that strategy S_1 is evaluated on the basis of future F_3, while the evaluation of strategy S_3 is considered within future F_1. Although it is not known which, only one of these chance outcomes will occur, and so comparing strategies based upon disparate futures could be considered unreasonable. Alternative procedures that include the step of comparing strategies within the same future are sought (Savage, 1972). The criterion of opportunism is one such method, it is also known as the *minimax regret* or *Savage criterion*.

For the Savage criterion, the payoff matrix is first used to define an opportunity loss or regret matrix, r_{ij}. For positive flow payoffs such as profit

$$r_{ij} = \max_{\gamma=1}^{m} \left(v_{\gamma j} \right) - v_{ij} \tag{5.14}$$

and for negative flow payoffs such as losses

$$r_{ij} = v_{ij} - \min_{\gamma=1}^{m} \left(v_{\gamma j} \right) \tag{5.15}$$

The opportunity loss or regret matrix is then used to associate a value with each strategy:

$$V_{S_\alpha} = \max_{j=1}^{n} \left(r_{\alpha j} \right) \tag{5.16}$$

and then the strategy with the minimum maximum regret is chosen:

$$\min_{\alpha=1}^{m} \left(V_{S_\alpha} \right) \tag{5.17}$$

Thus, the Savage criterion compares each of the strategies within each of the futures and suggests selection based upon minimising the maximum opportunity loss.

Figure 5.11 demonstrates the Savage criterion in the case of positive payoffs. Firstly, the maximum payoff achievable within each future state F_j is identified. If future

Chance Outcome	Low (F_1)	Medium (F_2)	High (F_3)
Decision	Present Value of Payoff(£10k)		
Sustain (S_1)	⑦⓪	100	110
Relocate (S_2)	10	130	②⑦⓪
Expand (S_3)	60	①④⓪	200

Chance Outcome	Low (F_1)	Medium (F_2)	High (F_3)	V_{S_α}
Decision	Present Value of Payoff(£10k)			
Sustain (S1)	0	40	160	160
Relocate (S2)	60	10	0	60
Expand (S3)	10	0	70	70

Figure 5.11 The Savage criterion applied to a positive flow payoff matrix.

F_1 were to occur, then the highest achievable payoff, 70, would have resulted by choosing strategy S_1. Similarly, to realise the maximum payoff under F_2, 140, strategy S_3 would have had to be taken. The next step is to calculate an opportunity loss or regret matrix. Suppose the future state F_1 were to occur; then, if a decision had been taken to follow strategy S_1, the decision-taker would realise the maximum payoff, and there would have been no opportunity loss. Conversely, if either strategy S_2 or S_3 had been pursued, then the decision-taker would have some regret: in the case of S_2 the opportunity loss would be $70 - 10 = 60$, and in the case of S_3 the opportunity loss would be $70 - 60 = 10$. The calculation of the regret matrix is repeated for all remaining future states; this is shown in the matrix to the right in Figure 5.11. A maximum regret value is then associated with each strategy. For instance, strategy S_1 has three regret values associated with different futures: F_1, F_2, and F_3; the largest of these is 160, and so V_{S_1} is 160. Likewise, V_{S_2} and V_{S_3} are 60 and 70. Finally, the strategy that results in the minimum maximum regret would be selected; the value $\min_{\alpha=1}^{m} (V_{S_\alpha}) = V_{S_2} = 60$ commends S_2. If S_2 were to be taken, then the maximum opportunity loss (regret) would be 60.

Figure 5.12 demonstrates the Savage criterion in the case of negative payoffs. The regret matrix is obtained by first identifying the best possible outcome for every future, 30 for F_1 and F_2, 25 for F_3, that is, the smallest losses achievable under the futures are respectively 30, 30, and 25. The regret is then calculated for each strategy under all futures. For example, $r_{11} = 50 - 30 = 20$, $r_{21} = 30 - 30 = 0$, and $r_{31} = 35 - 30 = 5$. Once the regret matrix has been derived, the criterion then suggests the strategy that gives the minimum maximum regret, as in the positive payoff case. In this case (Figure 5.12) the indicated strategy S_3 will not lead to the least loss under any future, but nor can it result in a loss of more than 60 greater than that from the ideal strategy for the eventual future.

Change Outcome	F_1	F_2	F_3		Change Outcome	F_1	F_2	F_3	V_{S_α}
Decision	Loss				Decision	Regret			
S_1	50	100	㉕		S_1	20	70	0	70
S_2	㉚	㉚	120		S_2	0	0	95	95
S_3	35	90	80		S_3	5	60	55	60

Figure 5.12 The Savage criterion applied to a negative flow payoff matrix.

The Criterion of Insufficient Reason (The Laplace Criterion)

Given that for decision situations under strict uncertainty it is not possible to specify a probability distribution over the futures F_j, each of the previously discussed criteria presents an alternative means for defining V_{S_α} without the use of probabilities. Quite the reverse approach is taken by the Laplace criterion. Providing there is insufficient reason to expect one hypothesised future state of nature to be more or less likely than another, the Laplace criterion stipulates a uniform distribution for the probabilities of the future states; in the case of discrete F_j ($j=1$ to n), each is posited to have probability $1/n$.

The Laplace criterion is specified by defining

$$V_{S_\alpha} = \frac{1}{n} \sum_{j=1}^{n} v_{\alpha j} \qquad (5.18)$$

and choosing S_α such that V_{S_α} is a maximum in the case of positive flow payoffs or a minimum in the case of negative flow payoffs, i.e. take the strategy with the value

$$\max_{\alpha=1}^{m} (V_{S_\alpha}) \qquad (5.19)$$

for positive flow payoffs such as profits or revenues, and take the strategy with the value

$$\min_{\alpha=1}^{m} (V_{S_\alpha}) \qquad (5.20)$$

for negative flow payoffs such as losses or costs. In brief, the approach is appropriately to select the strategy with the maximum or minimum mean average payoff.

Chance Outcome	Low	Medium	High	V_{S_α}
Probability	1/3	1/3	1/3	
Decision	Present Value of Payoff (£10k)			
Sustain (S_1)	70	100	110	93.3
Relocate (S_2)	10	130	270	*136.7*
Expand (S_3)	60	140	200	*133.3*

Chance Outcome	F_1	F_2	F_3	V_{S_α}
Probability	1/3	1/3	1/3	
Decision	Loss			
S_1	50	100	25	*58.3*
S_2	30	30	120	60
S_3	35	90	80	68.3

Figure 5.13 The Laplace criterion applied to positive (left) and negative (right) flow payoffs.

Figure 5.13 demonstrates the Laplace criterion applied to both positive and negative flow payoffs. A value is first associated with each strategy, based upon the mean average payoff that could be achieved through that strategy. The strategy with the optimum is then recommended. For the positive flow case, each strategy S_j $(j = 1 - n, n = 3)$ has payoffs associated with each of the three different futures F_1, F_2, and F_3, which lead to

$$V_{S_1} = \frac{1}{3}(70 + 100 + 110) = 93.3$$

$$V_{S_2} = \frac{1}{3}(10 + 130 + 270) = 136.7$$

$$V_{S_3} = \frac{1}{3}(60 + 140 + 200) = 133.3$$

and $\max\limits_{\alpha=1}^{3}(V_{S_\alpha}) = V_{S_2} = 136.7$ commends S_2.

For the negative flow case, each strategy S_j $(j = 1$ to $n, n = 3)$ has associated payoffs which lead to

$$V_{S_1} = \frac{1}{3}(50 + 100 + 25) = 58.3$$

$$V_{S_2} = \frac{1}{3}(30 + 30 + 120) = 60$$

$$V_{S_3} = \frac{1}{3}(35 + 90 + 80) = 68.3$$

and $\min\limits_{\alpha=1}^{3}(V_{S_\alpha}) = V_{S_2} = 58.3$ commends S_1.

Payoff Matrices with Uncertainty or Risk

In decision-taking situations in which it is possible to specify a probability distribution over the set of chance outcomes, F_j, the decision situation is often described
as one with *uncertainty* or *risk*. The well-known approaches for defining V_{S_α} are the
criteria of *expected value* and *expected opportunity loss*. Each will be described in
turn, and their equivalence shown.

Expected Value (Expected Monetary Value)

A probability distribution is specified such that the probability of a future state of
nature F_j occurring is p_j and

$$\sum_{j=1}^{n} p_j = 1 \tag{5.21}$$

The expected value (*EV*) criterion is specified by defining

$$V_{S_\alpha} = \sum_{j=1}^{n} p_j v_{\alpha j} \tag{5.22}$$

and choosing S_α such that the expected value, V_{S_α}, is a maximum in the case of
positive flow payoffs or a minimum in the case of negative flow payoffs, i.e. take the
strategy with the value

$$\max_{\alpha=1}^{m} \left(V_{S_\alpha} \right) \tag{5.23}$$

for positive flow payoffs such as profits or revenues, and take the strategy with the
value

$$\min_{\alpha=1}^{m} \left(V_{S_\alpha} \right) \tag{5.24}$$

for negative flow payoffs such as losses or costs. In brief, the approach is appropriately
to select the strategy with the maximum or minimum expected monetary value.

Figure 5.14 demonstrates the *EV* criterion applied to positive payoffs. For the positive flow case, each strategy $S_j (j = 1 - n, n = 3)$ has payoffs associated with each
of the three different futures F_1, F_2, and F_3 of probabilities p_1, p_2, and p_3. In this
particular case the probabilities of the three future states of nature are 0.1, 0.6, and
0.3, so

$$V_{S_1} = \sum_{j} p_j v_{1j} = (0.1 \times 70) + (0.6 \times 100) + (0.3 \times 110) = 100$$

$$V_{S_2} = \sum_{j} p_j v_{2j} = (0.1 \times 10) + (0.6 \times 130) + (0.3 \times 270) = 160$$

$$V_{S_3} = \sum_j p_j v_{3j} = (0.1 \times 60) + (0.6 \times 140) + (0.3 \times 200) = 150$$

and $\max\limits_{\alpha=1}^{3}\left(V_{S_\alpha}\right) = V_{S_2} = 160$ commends S_2.

Chance Outcome	Low F_1	Medium F_2	High F_3	V_{S_α}
Probability	0.1	0.6	0.3	
Decision	Present Value of Payoff (£10k)			
Sustain (S_1)	70	100	110	100
Relocate (S_2)	10	130	270	**160**
Expand (S_3)	60	140	200	150

Figure 5.14 The expected value criterion applied to positive payoff flows.

Expected Opportunity Loss (Expected Regret)

The expected opportunity loss (*EOL*) or expected regret criterion is specified by defining

$$V_{S_\alpha} = \sum_{j=1}^{n} p_j r_{\alpha j} \tag{5.25}$$

with r_{ij} defined earlier (equation (5.14)), and S_α is chosen such that the expected value, V_{S_α}, is a minimum. In brief, the approach is to calculate a regret matrix and then to choose the strategy with the minimum expected regret.

Figure 5.15 demonstrates the *EOL* criterion. Firstly, a regret matrix is determined as for the Savage criterion, and then the *EOL* for each strategy is calculated. For example

$$r_{11} = 70 - 70 = 0$$

$$r_{12} = 140 - 100 = 40$$

$$r_{13} = 270 - 110 = 160$$

leading to

$$V_{S_1} = \sum_j p_j r_{1j} = (0.1 \times 0) + (0.6 \times 40) + (0.3 \times 160) = 72$$

Chance Outcome	Low (F_1)	Medium (F_2)	High (F_3)
Probability	0.1	0.6	0.3
Decision	Present Value of Payoff (£10k)		
Sustain (S_1)	(70)	100	110
Relocate (S_2)	10	130	(270)
Expand (S_3)	60	(140)	200

Chance Outcome	Low (F_1)	Medium (F_2)	High (F_3)	
Probability	0.1	0.6	0.3	V_{S_α}
Decision	Present Value of Payoff (£10k)			
Sustain (S_1)	0	40	160	72
Relocate (S_2)	60	10	0	12
Expand (S_3)	10	0	70	22

Figure 5.15   The expected opportunity loss criterion applied to positive payoff flows.

Similarly

$$V_{S_2} = \sum_j p_j r_{2j} = 0.1(70 - 10) + 0.6(140 - 130) + 0.3(270 - 270) = 12$$

and

$$V_{S_3} = \sum_j p_j r_{3j} = 0.1(70 - 60) + 0.6(140 - 140) + 0.3(270 - 200) = 22$$

Finally, $\min_{\alpha=1}^{3} (V_{S_\alpha}) = V_{S_2} = 12$ commends S_2.

From Figures 5.14 and 5.15 it is observed that the EV and EOL criteria have resulted in the same preference ordering of the three strategies: S_2 then S_3 then S_1. The equivalence between these two criteria is a general property, and this is clear by substituting equation (5.14) into equation (5.25):

$$EOL_{S_\alpha} = V_{S_\alpha} = \sum_{j=1}^{n} p_j \max_{\gamma=1}^{m} (v_{\gamma j}) - \sum_{j=1}^{n} p_j v_{\alpha j} \tag{5.26}$$

Consequently, the EOL for strategy S_α is simply a constant minus the EV for the strategy; minimising the regret is equivalent to maximising the EV. The analogous result follows for the case of negative flow payoffs.

Choosing a Decision Criterion

For ease of comparison, Figure 5.16 summarises the decision-taking criteria presented in this chapter. Although sometimes the criteria commend the same strategy

Name	Positive Flow		Negative Flow	
	V_{S_α}	Choice Rule	V_{S_α}	Choice Rule
Optimism	$\max\limits_{j=1}^{n}(v_{\alpha j})$	$\max\limits_{\alpha=1}^{m}(V_{S_\alpha})$	$\min\limits_{j=1}^{n}(v_{\alpha j})$	$\min\limits_{\alpha=1}^{m}(V_{S_\alpha})$
Pessimism (Wald)	$\min\limits_{j=1}^{n}(v_{\alpha j})$	$\max\limits_{\alpha=1}^{m}(V_{S_\alpha})$	$\max\limits_{j=1}^{n}(v_{\alpha j})$	$\min\limits_{\alpha=1}^{m}(V_{S_\alpha})$
Realism (Hurwicz)	$\theta \max\limits_{j=1}^{n}(v_{\alpha j}) + (1-\theta)\min\limits_{j=1}^{n}(v_{\alpha j})$	$\max\limits_{\alpha=1}^{m}(V_{S_\alpha})$	$\theta \min\limits_{j=1}^{n}(v_{\alpha j}) + (1-\theta)\max\limits_{j=1}^{n}(v_{\alpha j})$	$\min\limits_{\alpha=1}^{m}(V_{S_\alpha})$
Opportunism/Regret (Savage)	$\max\limits_{j=1}^{n}(r_{\alpha j})$ where $r_{ij} = \max\limits_{\gamma=1}^{m}(v_{\gamma i}) - v_{ij}$	$\min\limits_{\alpha=1}^{m}(V_{S_\alpha})$	$\max\limits_{j=1}^{n}(r_{\alpha j})$ where $r_{ij} = v_{ij} - \min\limits_{\gamma=1}^{m}(v_{\gamma i})$	$\min\limits_{\alpha=1}^{m}(V_{S_\alpha})$
Insufficient Reason (Laplace)	$\frac{1}{n}\sum\limits_{j=1}^{n} v_{\alpha j}$	$\max\limits_{\alpha=1}^{m}(V_{S_\alpha})$	$\frac{1}{n}\sum\limits_{j=1}^{n} v_{\alpha j}$	$\min\limits_{\alpha=1}^{m}(V_{S_\alpha})$
Expected (Monetary) Value	$\sum\limits_{j=1}^{n} p_j v_{\alpha j}$	$\max\limits_{\alpha=1}^{m}(V_{S_\alpha})$	$\sum\limits_{j=1}^{n} p_j v_{\alpha j}$	$\min\limits_{\alpha=1}^{m}(V_{S_\alpha})$
Expected Opportunity Loss (Expected Regret)	$\sum\limits_{j=1}^{n} p_j r_{\alpha j}$ where $r_{ij} = \max\limits_{\gamma=1}^{m}(v_{\gamma i}) - v_{ij}$	$\min\limits_{\alpha=1}^{m}(V_{S_\alpha})$	$\sum\limits_{j=1}^{n} p_j r_{\alpha j}$ where $r_{ij} = v_{ij} - \min\limits_{\gamma=1}^{m}(v_{\gamma i})$	$\min\limits_{\alpha=1}^{m}(V_{S_\alpha})$

Figure 5.16 Summary of decision criteria for considering the $m \times n$ payoff matrix v_{ij}.

choice, as a rule this is not the case, leaving the decision-taker to reflect on the most relevant criterion. If decision models were seen to be wholly normative, then this would suggest a serious criticism to such approaches. However, payoff matrices and models in general are typically used as an aid to structure the decision and to guide the consideration. Having alternative recommendations suggested by each criterion could in effect be helpful to the decision process. Be that as it may, it is worth stressing some aspects of each. Firstly, the criteria of optimism and pessimism (Wald) each focus on extreme cases, the best and the worse, and in some instances a decision-taker may well wish to give significant consideration to these outermost cases: what could be the best or worst consequences of the decision? If both extremes are of interest, then their relative importance from the perspective of the decision-taker can be included using the criterion of realism (Hurwicz). Although consideration of extremes is frequently of interest, with such a focus much information summarised within the payoff matrix is largely ignored, potentially leading to decision-taking by uncharacteristic outcomes. The criterion of regret (Savage) makes further use of the available information by first contrasting strategies within equivalent futures to form a regret matrix and then applying a pessimistic criterion (a criterion of optimism applied to a regret matrix would only discriminate if there were a dominant strategy). A potential difficulty with the Savage criterion is illustrated in Figure 5.17. The lower left-hand payoff matrix illustrates the consequences of four potential strategies in each of four possible futures; to the right is the corresponding regret matrix. The upper matrices duplicate the situation, but in this case the fourth strategy, S_4, is unknown to the decision-taker. For both regret matrices, S_1 and S_2 have greatest

	Profit			
	F_1	F_2	F_3	F_4
S_1	100	80	90	80
S_2	110	140	20	60
S_3	120	60	180	50

	Regret				
	F_1	F_2	F_3	F_4	V_{S_α}
S_1	20	60	90	0	90
S_2	10	0	160	20	160
S_3	0	80	0	30	80

	Profit			
	F_1	F_2	F_3	F_4
S_1	100	80	90	80
S_2	110	140	20	60
S_3	120	60	180	50
S_4	80	160	75	50

	Regret				
	F_1	F_2	F_3	F_4	V_{S_α}
S_1	20	80	90	0	90
S_2	10	20	160	20	160
S_3	0	100	0	30	100
S_4	40	0	105	30	105

Figure 5.17 An irrelevant strategy affecting the recommended strategy under the regret criterion.

regret in future F_3, while strategy S_3 has greatest regret in F_2, although introducing S_4 does change the value of regret associated with electing S_3 should future F_2 occur. The result is that, when only three strategies are known, S_3 is considered preferable to S_1, but, on introducing the alternative S_4, the preference switches to S_1. That the preference ordering of two strategies can depend upon the set of strategies available may cause concern.

When a focus upon extreme outcomes is not of utmost importance, an alternative that utilises more information within the payoff matrix may be sought. Given insufficient reason to associate a greater likelihood with one future than another, the Laplace criterion represents this strict uncertainty by a uniform probability distribution. Aside from criticisms of the continuous case, even in the discrete case there may be concern arising from specification of the chance events. One illustration is to consider Bertrand's box paradox. A desk has two drawers, each containing one coin; the desk might contain two golden coins, two silver coins, or one of each. Taking the identity of a desk as a chance event and applying the Laplace criterion would lead to probabilities of $1/3$ being associated with each. A two-golden-coin desk would have probability $1/3$, a two-silver-coin desk would have probability $1/3$, and a one-of-each desk would have probability $1/3$. In contrast, if the occurrence of a golden or silver coin in a drawer were considered a chance event, then applying the criterion would lead to probabilities of $1/4$, $1/4$, or $1/2$ being associated with each desk type. Strict uncertainty restricts reasoning about the events such that applying a uniform probability distribution does not necessarily follow.

Given the criticisms of applying the strict uncertainty criteria, it is often considered more appropriate to apply the expected value criterion, or, equivalently, the expected opportunity loss criterion. Indeed, this was illustrated in the news-vendor problem in the previous chapter (Figure 4.18). Even so, the decision-taker should remain aware of some possible problems. Are reliable probabilities obtainable? Are there small probability but high payoff strategy–chance event combinations to which special attention ought to be given? Does the organization take a sufficient number of similar decisions such that an expected value approach is justifiable?

The Value of Perfect Information

Should the decision-taker be offered perfect information about the future states of nature, then the question arises as to what the value of such perfect information would be. What is the maximum that the decision-taker would pay? Unsurprisingly, the answer to this depends upon the decision criterion being used. Given that there are initially m strategies under consideration, $S_1, S_2, \ldots, S_m$, the possibility of obtaining perfect information introduces an $(m + 1)$th strategy, which attains the best outcome but for a price π. This is illustrated in Figure 5.18, in which the payoff for S_4 for each future is the best payoff less π. By following S_4, the decision-taker would first purchase perfect information for a fee π and then choose the most appropriate of $S_1, S_2,$ or S_3 for the no longer unknown future. The value of perfect information is that value of π at which the decision-taker is indifferent between the new $(m + 1)$th strategy and the originally preferred strategy. For brevity, each of the decision criteria introduced will now be considered only for the case of positive flow payoffs.

Profit

	F_1	F_2	F_3	F_4
S_1	100	55	90	80
S_2	110	140	20	60
S_3	120	60	180	50
S_4	$120-\pi$	$140-\pi$	$180-\pi$	$80-\pi$

Figure 5.18   Introducing an additional strategy with perfect information obtained for a price π.

The Value of Perfect Information under Strict Uncertainty

There are two straightforward results: that for the opportunist applying the Savage criterion of minimising the maximum opportunity lost, and that for the optimist taking a decision based on the best possible payoffs.

In the case of the opportunist, decisions are taken such that the maximum regret is a minimum. Consequently, if perfect information were accessible, the opportunist would pay any price up to the minimum maximum regret. If there is no dominant strategy, the opportunist will always be prepared to pay for perfect information. To be precise, for the Savage criterion the value of perfect information is equivalent to the minimum maximum regret. Conversely, for the optimist the value of perfect information is always zero. Since the criterion of optimism assumes that the best strategy will be selected, the optimist has nothing to gain by purchasing additional information.

The value of perfect information to the pessimist is less straightforward: on some occasions it is zero, but on others it is greater than zero. Consider the payoff matrices

Profit

	F₁	F₂	F₃	F₄	Vₛₐ
S₁	100	<u>55</u>	90	80	<u>55</u>
S₂	110	140	<u>20</u>	60	20
S₃	120	60	180	<u>50</u>	50
S₄	120 − π	140 − π	180 − π	<u>80 − π</u>	80 − π

Profit

	F₁	F₂	F₃	F₄	Vₛₐ
S₁	100	<u>80</u>	90	80	<u>80</u>
S₂	110	140	<u>20</u>	60	20
S₃	120	60	180	<u>50</u>	50
S₄	120 − π	140 − π	180 − π	<u>80 − π</u>	80 − π

Figure 5.19 Determination of the value of perfect information using the criterion of pessimism.

in Figure 5.19. The only difference is between the payoffs resulting from pursuing strategy S_1 under future F_2. For the first matrix, the pessimist would decide the value of perfect information by equating the payoff with perfect information to the payoff without perfect information:

Payoff with perfect information = payoff without perfect information

$$80 - \pi = 55$$

$$\pi = 80 - 55 = 25$$

giving the value of perfect information as 25. For the second matrix, with $v_{12} = 80$, the same procedure gives $80 - \pi = 80$, and the value of perfect information is zero.

An interesting situation is how the realist, the decision-taker using the Hurwicz criterion, values perfect information as a function of θ. Figure 5.20 provides an illustration. With $\theta = 1.0$ the criterion of optimism is recovered and the

Profit

	F₁	F₂	F₃	F₄	θ = 1.0 Vₛₐ	θ = 0.0 Vₛₐ	θ = 0.3 Vₛₐ
S₁	100	<u>80</u>	90	80	100	80	86
S₂	110	140	<u>20</u>	60	140	20	56
S₃	120	60	180	<u>50</u>	180	50	89
S₄	120 − π	140 − π	180 − π	<u>80 − π</u>	180 − π	80 − π	110 − π

Figure 5.20 Determination of the value of perfect information using the Hurwicz criterion.

value of perfect information is 0. With $\theta = 0.0$ the criterion of pessimism is recovered and, in this case, the value of perfect information is again 0. Perhaps surprisingly for an intermediate level of optimism, $\theta = 0.3$, the value of perfect information is found by rearranging $110 - \pi = 89$ to give $\pi = 21$. Although neither the optimist nor the pessimist would pay for further information in the decision situation of Figure 5.20, the realist would. The explanation becomes clear on noting that the realist with $\theta = 3/11 (\approx 0.3)$ would be indifferent between strategies S_1 and S_3, and would therefore place a value on resolving this indifference.

The Value of Perfect Information under Risk

Proceeding as for the cases of decision-making under strict uncertainty, the value of perfect information can be found for decision-making under risk. This is frequently termed the *expected value of perfect information* (*EVPI*). The *EVPI* is the difference between the expected value with perfect information and the maximum (for positive flow payoffs) expected value without perfect information:

$$EVPI = \sum_{j=1}^{n} p_j \max_{\gamma=1}^{m} (v_{\gamma j}) - \max_{\alpha=1}^{m} \sum_{j=1}^{n} p_j v_{\alpha j} \qquad (5.27)$$

Comparing equation (5.27) with equation (5.26), it is observed that the *EVPI* is equivalent to the expected opportunity loss of the recommended strategy. This conveys very clearly the concept of *EVPI*. For a decision-taker, on average, there is always an opportunity loss, and this represents an upper limit to pay for perfect information. Figure 5.15 illustrates the use of expected opportunity loss to analyse a decision; in that case, strategy S_2 is commended with an expected opportunity loss of 12. Applying equation (5.27) to the payoff matrix gives

$$EVPI = [(0.1 \times 70) + (0.6 \times 140) + (0.3 \times 270)] - [(0.1 \times 10) + (0.6 \times 130)$$

$$+ (0.3 \times 270)]$$

$$EVPI = 172 - 160 = 12.0$$

Sensitivity Analysis

Given that the decision-taker does not have complete knowledge, it is necessary to consider the sensitivity of the decision to the data as captured within the payoff matrix, and also to the data from which this aggregation was assembled. This process is important to identify whether and how:

(i) further information could be sought;
(ii) risk management could be applied.

Each of these responses to sensitivity analysis moves from a static representation of a decision to a sequential one (see Chapter 9). The first approach attempts to reduce uncertainty prior to a major resource commitment, for example through a market or geological survey, while the second has a planned response should a downside begin to unfold, for example an exit strategy.

The positive flow, profit-based, payoff matrices used as examples in this chapter have been straightforward, with each strategy resulting in a positive gain under all chance events. This would be a blissful state of affairs, but it is more likely that the payoffs could change sign. It is important not only to ask what could cause the commended strategy not to be taken but also to identify the statistics to which the outcome of the strategy is sensitive (see Chapter 9). Before committing to a decision, the sensitivity analysis should help the decision-taker understand the robustness of the choice, the need for further data, or the need for a risk response.

Example: Sensitivity to Forecast Payoffs

For the decision described by the payoff matrix of Figure 5.21, assuming that many similar decisions are taken, the expected value criterion commends S_2. Nonetheless, the recommendation is sensitive to the forecast profits of the two strategies in the two potential future states. Figure 5.22 shows the expected values of S_1 and S_2 as a function of the probability of future F_2 occurring. If the probability of F_2 occurring were 0.6 rather than 0.7, then both strategies would have the same expected value. As the difference between the forecast profits of the two strategies changes within the two futures, the indifference probability increases or decreases with respect to the base probability of future F_2. The reliability of the forecast profits of both strategies contributes to the confidence in recommending S_2 over S_1.

	Profit in Future F_1 ($p = 0.3$)	Profit in Future F_2 ($p = 0.7$)	Expected (Monetary) Value
Strategy S_1	2.5	5	4.25
Strategy S_2	−5	10	5.5

Figure 5.21 A simple decision using the expected value criterion.

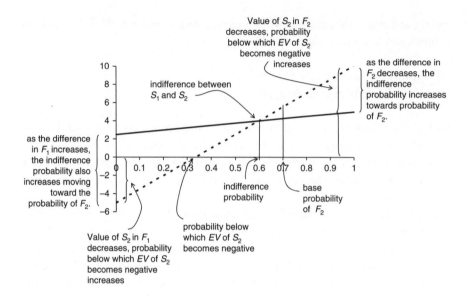

Figure 5.22 Expected value of two strategies as a function of the probability of one of two possible future states.

Summary

This chapter has introduced the concept of payoff matrices to structure decision choices. The approach is firstly to identify potential strategies which a decision-taker may follow. Possible discrete future states or chance events within which the outcomes of these strategies could unfold are then identified, and a value, e.g. present value, profit, or loss, is associated with each strategy–chance event pairing. This information is summarised within a payoff matrix, each row representing a strategy, each column a future. A decision-taking criterion is selected on the basis of the decision context. If it is neither possible nor appropriate to associate probabilities with the future states, then a decision criterion for strict uncertainty is used. These include the criteria of optimism, pessimism, realism, opportunism, and insufficient reason. If it is reasonable to attach a probability distribution to the future states, then the expected value can be used as a decision-taking criterion. In some instances it may be possible to combine criteria (Schenkerman, 1975).

The value of perfect information gives the worth of changing a situation from one of strict uncertainty or risk to one of certainty. The value of perfect information depends upon the decision criterion being used, for example the optimist attaches zero value to perfect information.

Finally, if there is doubt in the parameterisation of a payoff matrix, for example that the probabilities may not be an accurate representation of future uncertainty, then sensitivity analysis might be useful. For instance, changes to payoffs, parameter of optimism, or probabilities can be made, and the resulting effect on the preferential ordering of strategies can be considered.

Further Reading

- Alternative presentations to parts of this chapter can be found in other introductory texts. These include:

    Goodwin, P. & Wright, G. (2003) *Decision Analysis for Management Judgement*, 3rd edition. John Wiley & Sons, Ltd, Chichester, UK.

    Wisniewski, M. (2005) *Quantitative Methods for Decision Makers*, 4th edition. FT/Prentice Hall, Harlow, UK.

    Waters, D. (1998) *A Practical Introduction to Management Science*, 2nd edition. FT/Prentice Hall, Harlow, UK.

- The first two of the following articles aid with an appreciation of payoff matrices. The third to fifth articles are included to highlight the issue of generating potential strategies, although they also include some more general issues:

    Pritchett, J. (2004) Risk decision analysis: MBC Farms' horse hay enterprise. *Review of Agricultural Economics* **26**(4), 579–588.

    Ballestro, E. (2002) Strict uncertainty: a criterion for moderately pessimistic decision makers. *Decision Sciences* **33**(1), 87–107.

    Asch, DA. (1998) Avoidable errors in health policy. *Journal of General Internal Medicine* **13**(11), 26–32.

    Spradlin, CT. & Kutolski, DM. (1999) Action-oriented portfolio management. *Research-Technology Management* **42**(2), 26–32.

    Krumm, FV. & Rolle, CF. (1992) Management and application of decision and risk analysis in Du Pont. *Interfaces* **22**(6), 84–93.

- The next two articles discuss the minimax regret criterion when considering voting. The second of the two papers is a reply to the many responses initiated by the first.

    Ferejohn, JA. & Fiorina, MP. (1974) The paradox of not voting: a decision theoretic analysis. *The American Political Science Review* **69**(3), 920–925.

    Ferejohn, JA. & Fiorina, MP. (1975) Closeness counts only in horseshoes and dancing. *The American Political Science Review* **68**(2), 525–535.

Questions

Q5.1 The following matrix shows the <u>losses</u> from several mutually exclusive strategies under possible future states. Which strategy would be chosen by a decision-maker who is optimistic? Which strategy would be chosen by a decision-maker who is pessimistic? Which strategy would be chosen by a decision-maker who is neither optimistic nor pessimistic? Which strategy would be chosen by a regret-avoiding decision-maker?

	Future 1	Future 2	Future 3
Strategy 1	33	7.5	13.5
Strategy 2	28.5	30	31.5
Strategy 3	10.5	25.5	36

Q5.2 The following matrix shows the <u>gains</u> from several mutually exclusive strategies under possible future states. A decision as to which strategy to follow could be made using the Hurwicz criterion for a given coefficient of optimism θ.

	Future 1	Future 2	Future 3	Future 4
Strategy 1	0	53	20	18
Strategy 2	15.6	19.7	47.4	40
Strategy 3	28.5	31.8	25	21.2
Strategy 4	26.5	26.5	26.5	26.5

(a) To prepare for a decision-taking meeting with colleagues, you have decided to calculate the ranges of θ (from pessimistic to optimistic) over which each strategy would be selected.

(b) You have also decided to calculate the value of perfect information at values of θ defining the endpoints of the ranges over which each strategy would be selected.

Q5.3 For the payoff matrix below, confirm that the criteria of expected value and expected opportunity loss lead to the same ordering of recommended strategies. Calculate the expected value of perfect information and confirm its equivalence to the expected opportunity loss for the preferred strategy.

	Future 1	Future 2	Future 3	Future 4
Probability	0.2	0.1	0.3	0.4
Profit				
Strategy 1	−10	−30	15	50
Strategy 2	5	5	30	10
Strategy 3	10	−15	20	15

Q5.4 For the payoff matrix below, plot a graph showing the expected value of each of the three strategies as p varies from 0 to 1. Calculate indifference probabilities. For the probability $p = 0.5$, which strategy does the expected value criterion suggest? Would reduced confidence in the probability change this recommendation?

	Future 1	Future 2
Probability	p	$1 - p$
Profit		
Strategy 1	10	90
Strategy 2	30	80
Strategy 3	60	40

Q5.5 John and Dagny are discussing a situation for which a decision needs to be taken. This is described by the first payoff matrix below. John is a pessimist and hence prefers S_3; on the other hand, Dagny is an optimist, preferring strategy S_2. During their discussions, an express package is delivered and contains information on a second urgent decision. Coincidentally, this second decision depends on exactly the same future events as the first. Dagny therefore suggests strategy S_5 for the second decision. John, though, does not suggest S_6 but instead changes his earlier recommendation. What are the two possibilities that John might suggest?

Chance Outcome	High Solihull Economy	Low Solihull Economy	Medium Solihull Economy
Decision	Present Value of Payoff (£)		
S_1	10,000	50,000	40,000
S_2	60,000	20,000	30,000
S_3	32,000	32,000	32,000

Chance Outcome	High Solihull Economy	Low Solihull Economy	Medium Solihull Economy
Decision	Present Value of Payoff (£)		
S_4	10,000	50,000	40,000
S_5	60,000	20,000	30,000
S_6	32,000	32,000	32,000

Q5.6 Identify the decision criterion that can be written as $\max_\alpha V_\alpha$ such that $V_\alpha \leq V_{\alpha j} \forall j$.

Q5.7 Several criteria for decision-taking under strict uncertainty have been introduced in this chapter: pessimism, optimism, opportunism. Produce payoff matrices and decision situations for which you do not think particular criteria are suitable.

Activities

A5.1 Studies have been carried out that have used payoff matrices as a means to identify the unstated decision criterion being used by a decision-taker. Essentially, several matrices are shown to the decision-taker, and for each she is asked which strategy she would take. Within each matrix each strategy is compatible only with a restricted number of criteria. Therefore, by using many matrices, the decision-taker's unstated criterion is identified. This chapter has described how the value of perfect information depends on the decision criterion being applied. An alternative approach to identifying an unstated criterion might then be to show many payoff matrices to a decision-taker and ask how much she would pay for perfect information.

Design payoff matrices such that the value of perfect information would be different given different decision criteria. Use these matrices to investigate the possibility of eliciting unstated decision criteria. Approaches that might be considered are whether decisions taken are consistent with the value of perfect information, whether the values are consistent from decision to decision, or, having revealed a decision-taker's criterion, whether later decisions or valuations of perfect information can be predicted.

Useful starting references include:

Seale, DA., Rapoport, A., & Budescu, DV. (1995) Decision making under strict uncertainty: an experimental test of competitive criteria. *Organizational Behavior and Human Decision Processes* **64**(1), 65–75.

Kernan, JB. (1968) Choice criteria, decision behavior and personality. *Journal of Marketing Research* **5**(2), 155–164.

A5.2 Sarah's decision-making under strict uncertainty can be described using the Hurwicz criterion. She is offered the following choice between mutually exclusive strategies:

	Future 1	**Future 2**
Strategy 1	100	−100
Strategy 2	−50	50

She has the opportunity to purchase further information that reduces the situation from one of strict uncertainty to one of risk, i.e. she can invest to attach probabilities to each of the future states. Write an essay that examines how Sarah may consider the purchase of this further information.

A5.3 In this chapter the cases of strict uncertainty, for which probabilities cannot be assigned to chance events, and uncertainty (or risk), for which probabilities can be assigned, have been considered. Some argue that these are only two of several cases. For example, it may only be possible to suggest probability ranges for futures, to be able to order but not evaluate the likelihoods of futures, or to know the probabilities of some but not all future states. Research and discuss this viewpoint. A starting reference is:

Kelsey, D. & Quiggin, J. (1992) Theories of choice under ignorance and uncertainty. *Journal of Economic Surveys* **6**(2), 133–153.

A5.2 Prepare a presentation on Pascal's wager. A brief description is given in:

Priest, G. (2000) *Logic. A Very Short Introduction*. Oxford University Press, Oxford, UK, Chapter 13.

A still brief but fuller introduction can be found in:

Stanford Encyclopedia of Philosophy. Available online: http://plato.stanford.edu/entries/pascal-wager/ [accessed 23 June 2008].

A5.2 Organise a round-table discussion on the suitability of different decision criteria to extreme (i.e. low probability, but high payoff) events:

Bostrom, N. (2002) Existential risks. Analyzing human extinction scenarios and related hazards. *Journal of Evolution & Technology* **9**(1).

Weitzman, M. (2007) *On Modeling and Interpreting the Economics of Catastrophic Climate Change*. REstat Version 6/5/08. Available online: www.economics.harvard.edu/faculty/weitzman/papers_weitzman [accessed 23 June 2008].

Basili, M., Chateauneuf, A., & Fontini, F. (2008) Precautionary principle as a rule of choice with optimism on windfall gains and pessimism on catastrophic losses. *Ecological Ergonomics* **67**(3), 485–491.

Linear Programming

Objectives

- *To be able to structure a linear programming problem.*
- *To formulate a linear programme in Excel.*
- *To interpret the resulting Excel solution output.*
- *To carry out a sensitivity analysis of the solution.*

Introduction

Linear programming (LP) is a numerical optimisation technique frequently used to aid resource planning decisions where scarce resources need to be allocated between two or more activities in such a way as to optimise a particular objective such as maximising profit. The LP approach is primarily used in deterministic situations, and its use in stochastic situations where only expected parameter values are known remains the subject of continuing debate. This chapter therefore focuses on determ- inistic problems, and investigations into ways of dealing with stochastic situations are left as activities for the interested reader.

The LP process involves defining an objective function (e.g. profit maximisation or cost minimisation) and a set of constraint functions representing the availability of the organization's resources, all characterised by linear equations. The technique requires that the objective be optimised subject to the constraints. Consequently, the first step when creating a linear programme is to formulate the problem in mathematical terms. It is important to ensure that this step is performed carefully as the choice of function for each element of the linear programme affects the outcome. A further discussion of this issue is reserved for the latter part of this chapter.

Linear programmes are generally defined in standard form using linear equations or equivalently in matrix notation. This text will use standard form. An example of a simple linear programme expressed in standard form is as follows:

Maximise: $\alpha_1 x_1 + \alpha_2 x_2$ (objective)
Subject to (constraints):

$$\beta_{11} x_1 + \beta_{12} x_2 \leq \theta_1$$
$$\beta_{21} x_1 + \beta_{22} x_2 \leq \theta_2$$
$$x_1 \geq 0$$
$$x_2 \geq 0$$

where x_1 and x_2 represent the competing activities, and the other variables are defined by the availability of resources. A solution to the linear programme will result in values for x_1 and x_2 that maximise the objective function while simultaneously satisfying the constraints. If the objective function represents profit resulting from the output of two processes, with the constraints representing resource limits, the solution of the linear programme projects the output levels of the processes that result in the maximum profit given the limited resources available. If, however, the objective function represents costs, the optimisation process will require the minimisation of the objective, and the solution will specify the production levels that minimise costs.

Simple linear programmes, such as the example described above, can be solved analytically with relative ease, as the following example demonstrates.

Example

A company produces two products A and B and wishes to produce sufficient quantities in order to maximise profit given the available resources. Each unit of A contributes £5 to overall profit, and each unit of B contributes £2 to overall profit, assuming constant returns to scale.

Both A and B are produced using a single material, M, where each unit of A uses 3 units of M, and B uses 1 unit of M. However, the company only has access to a total of 450 units of M.

Finally, each unit of A takes 0.4 working hours to produce, and each unit of B requires 0.2 working hours. The company has 72 working hours available in total.

Objective function

The first step is to define the objective function. For every unit of A produced, profit increases by £5, so the total profit from the production of A is given by $5x_A$, where x_A is the number of units of A produced. Similarly, for every unit of B produced, profit increases by £2, and so the total profit from the production of B is given by $2x_B$, where x_B is the number of units of B produced. Thus, total profit is given by

$$5x_A + 2x_B$$

This is the objective function of the linear programme, since the company aims to maximise profit.

Constraints

In this example, the scarce resources used to produce A and B are the manufacturing material M and labour (i.e. the available working hours). It is these that form the first two constraints.

Since 3 units of M are required to produce every unit of A, the total amount of M required to produce A is given by $3x_A$. Similarly, each unit of B requires x_B units of M. In total, the production of both A and B requires $3x_A + x_B$ units of M.

Since there are only 450 units of M available in total, the production of both A and B cannot use more than this quantity. Consequently, the constraint can be written as follows:

$$3x_A + x_B \leq 450$$

The second constraint results from the availability of working hours. Using the same approach as was followed to generate the materials constraint, the total working hours required for the production of A is given by $0.4x_A$, and, for the production of B, $0.2x_B$ hours are required. Hence, the total number of working hours required is given by $0.4x_A + 0.2x_B$.

The company has a total of 72 working hours available for production, and therefore the constraint is given by

$$0.4x_A + 0.2x_B \leq 72$$

The final two constraints arise from the fact that solutions to linear programmes can result in optimal values that are less than zero. In situations where negative values for solutions are not required or not appropriate, such as production, for example, it is necessary to specify that the solution must be non-negative. The final two constraints are therefore given by

$$x_A \geq 0$$

$$x_B \geq 0$$

The complete linear programme is expressed as follows:

Maximise: $5x_A + 2x_B$
Subject to:

$3x_A + x_B \leq 450$ (materials constraint)
$0.4x_A + 0.2x_B \leq 72$ (labour constraint)
$x_A \geq 0$
$x_B \geq 0$

Solving the Linear Programme

Depending on the complexity of the linear programme, there are several ways in which any existing solutions may be found. One possible approach is to graph the various functions and then plot the feasible area. The feasible area is the set of points that satisfy all constraints and therefore form the set of all possible solutions to the linear programme.

The first step is to graph one of the constraints. By taking the materials constraint $3x_A + x_B \leq 450$, the set of all points that satisfy this constraint can be plotted on suitable axes. Since the constraint is linear, it is only necessary to plot the two points where the constraint boundary line crosses the two axes and then join these with a straight line. Assuming that x_A is plotted on the horizontal axis, by setting $x_B = 0$ and substituting this into the constraint, the horizontal axis intercept point is calculated. Consequently, the constraint boundary line crosses the horizontal axis at the point where $x_A = 450/3 = 150$. Using a similar approach for the vertical axis (i.e. setting $x_A = 0$), the vertical axis intercept point is calculated as 450. For the complete graph, see Figure 6.1.

The shaded area indicates all the points that satisfy the material constraint, and so selecting any point in the shaded area will give values for x_A and x_B that could be produced using the available quantity of manufacturing materials.

Since the final two constraints specify a non-negative solution, the figures therefore only include the positive quadrant, and the shaded areas are bounded by the axes.

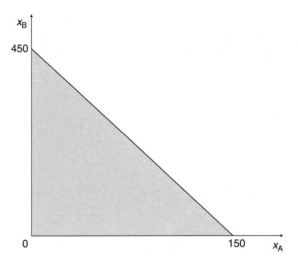

Figure 6.1 Materials constraint.

Should the case arise where the optimal values could be positive or negative, the feasible area would be bounded by the line $x_B = 450 - 3x_A$ but would extend to include both negative axes and the area beyond.

The labour constraint can be treated in a similar manner to the materials constraint. Plotting this function results in the shaded area shown in Figure 6.2.

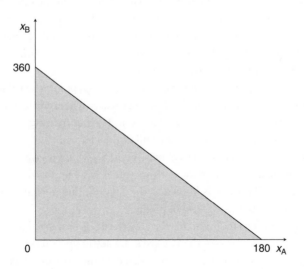

Figure 6.2 Labour constraint.

In order to determine the optimal solution, it is necessary to combine the constraints to indicate the feasible area (see Figure 6.3). The feasible area illustrates all points that are potential solutions to the linear programme.

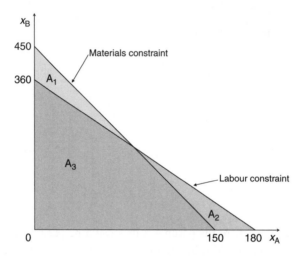

Figure 6.3 All constraints.

The feasible area is represented by the dark-grey shaded area A_3. Although the points in area A_1 satisfy the materials constraint, these points do not satisfy the labour constraint and hence cannot be in the feasible area. Similarly, while the points contained in area A_2 satisfy the labour constraint, they do not satisfy the materials constraint and so cannot form part of the feasible area.

The feasible area (Figure 6.4) will contain the optimal point: the values for x_A and x_B that optimise the objective function. There are cases where constraints are defined in such a way that a feasible area does not exist. Further investigation of this issue is left as an exercise for the reader at the end of the chapter.

In this example, the objective is to maximise profit, which is given by the equation $5x_A + 2x_B$. In order to determine the optimal values of x_A and x_B, the profit function can also be graphed. This line is known as the isoprofit line, meaning that all points on the line represent the same level of profit.

The same approach as that used for the constraints is employed to find the points where the isoprofit line crosses the two axes. By setting $p = 5x_A + 2x_B$, where p is the level of profit, it is clear that the line intercepts the horizontal axis at the point where $x_A = p/5$ and intercepts the vertical axis at the point where $x_B = p/2$ (see Figure 6.5).

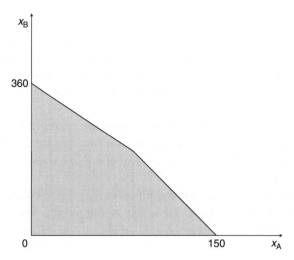

Figure 6.4 Feasible area.

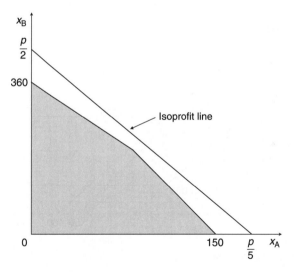

Figure 6.5 The isoprofit line.

It is interesting to note that the isoprofit line is not parallel to either of the constraint boundary lines. This can be confirmed by some simple algebra. To begin, rearrange the isoprofit function $p = 5x_A + 2x_B$ to give x_B in terms of x_A and p. This results in the following equation:

$$x_B = \frac{p}{2} - \frac{5}{2}x_A$$

Note that the gradient of this line is $-5/2$.

Consider the boundary line of the materials constraint represented by the function $3x_A + x_B = 450$ and then rearrange to give $x_B = 450 - 3x_A$. It is clear from this function that the gradient of the line bounding the feasible area of the materials constraint is -3. Hence, the gradient of the isoprofit line is less steep than that of the materials constraint boundary line.

Following the same process for the labour constraint results in the equation $x_B = 360 - 2x_A$. Consequently, the gradient of the line bounding the feasible area of the labour constraint is -2, and hence the gradient of this line is less steep than that of the isoprofit line.

The objective of the company is to maximise the level of profit while still satisfying the constraints by choosing values for x_A and x_B contained in the shaded area. By changing the value of p, the isoprofit line can shift to the left or to the right (see Figure 6.6).

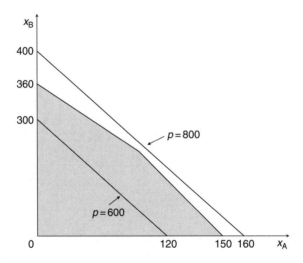

Figure 6.6 Moving the isoprofit line.

As the level of profit increases, the isoprofit line shifts further to the right. Therefore, it is clear that the optimal values of x_A and x_B will be on the isoprofit line that is furthest to the right. Nevertheless, these points will also need to be contained within the feasible area. Therefore, the maximum level of profit is represented by the isoprofit line that just touches the feasible area, since the isoprofit line is not parallel to either of the constraint boundary lines (see Figure 6.7).

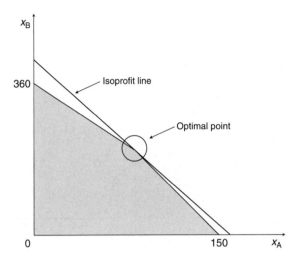

Figure 6.7 Optimal values for x_A and x_B.

Hence, the optimal values of x_A and x_B are given by the point where the isoprofit line meets the boundary of the feasible area. This is the point where the boundary line of the materials constraint crosses the boundary line of the labour constraint, i.e. the point where the two boundary lines are equal. The final task is therefore a simple algebraic exercise.

Let $450 - 3x_A = 360 - 2x_A$, since the optimal values occur at the point where the two constraint boundary lines are equal. Rearranging this equation gives $x_A = 90$ which is the optimal level of production for product A.

In order to find the optimal value of x_B, the value for x_A can be substituted into either of the constraint boundary line equations. Substituting this value into the materials constraint boundary line equation gives $x_B = 180$. Therefore, profit is maximised when the company produces 90 units of A and 180 units of B (see Figure 6.8).

At this optimal point, the company is using all of its material resources and all of its labour resources (this can be verified by substituting the values for production of A and B into the constraint equations). Therefore, the constraints in this case are binding, i.e. all resources are being used. In the case where the constraint is satisfied but the resource is not being used entirely (imagine that the optimal point is $x_A = 0$ and $x_B = 360$, and substitute these values into the constraints), the constraints are known as slack.

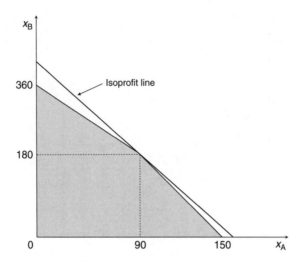

Figure 6.8 Optimal values of x_A and x_B.

Corner Method

A closely related solution method uses the corners of the feasible area and does not require the plotting of graphs, although it remains useful to do so.

It is clear from the figures that the feasible area has four corners:

- the origin of the axes (where $x_A = x_B = 0$);
- the points where the constraint boundary lines meet the axes (where $x_A = 150$ and $x_B = 0$ and where $x_A = 0$ and $x_B = 360$);
- the point where the constraint boundary lines meet (where $x_A = 90$ and $x_B = 180$).

In this example, the gradient of the isoprofit line is such that the maximal point occurs where the isoprofit line touches the corner of the feasible area where the two constraint boundary lines meet.

Since there are only a limited number of possibilities for the value of the gradient of the isoprofit line, a strategy can be devised in order to solve simple linear programmes. In addition to the previous example where the optimal point occurs where the boundary lines of the constraints meet, there are three other possible cases.

Case 1

The first case is where the absolute value of the gradient of the isoprofit line is greater than the gradients of the boundary lines of the constraints (i.e. the isoprofit line is steeper than the constraint boundary lines).

In this circumstance (Figure 6.9), the maximal isoprofit line only touches the feasible area at the corner where the boundary line of the feasible area meets the horizontal axis (i.e. the line where $x_A = 0$).

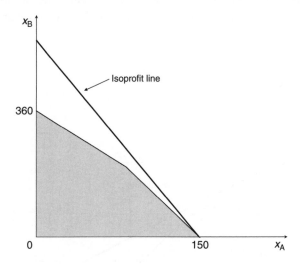

Figure 6.9 Case 1 – example.

Case 2

The absolute value of the gradient of the isoprofit line is less than that of any of the constraint boundary lines (i.e. the constraint boundary lines are steeper than the isoprofit line).

Here (Figure 6.10), the maximal isoprofit line meets the feasible area at the corner where the boundary line of the feasible area meets the vertical axis.

Case 3

The isoprofit line is parallel to one of the constraints (Figures 6.11a and 6.11b).

In either of these cases, the maximal isoprofit line meets the boundary line of the constraint to which it is parallel, leading to multiple maximal points all giving the same level of profit, including both the corner where the constraint boundary lines meet and where the constraint boundary lines meet the axis. The optimal point could be any one of these points, depending on whether the company wishes to make maximum use of all its resources (in which case they would choose the corner where the two constraints meet) or maximum use of one of the resources but partial use of the other (in which case they would choose the corner where the constraint meets the axis).

Consequently, it would make sense that, to find the optimal values for x_A and x_B, it is only necessary to calculate the profit at each of the corner points of the feasible area, since these are the most likely optimal points. The optimal values are then given by whichever corner gives the highest profit. In the case where the isoprofit line is parallel to one of the constraints, it will result in two optimal corner points.

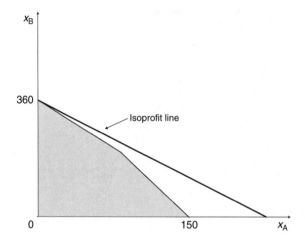

Figure 6.10 Case 2 – example.

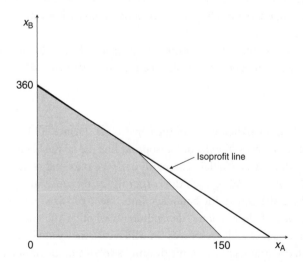

Figure 6.11a Case 3 – example.

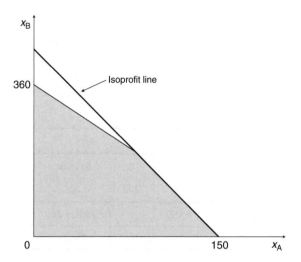

Figure 6.11b   Case 3 – example.

Using the Corner Method – Example

Another company produces goods C and D. In this case, C and D contribute £3 and £4 to profit respectively. These two goods are also produced using manufacturing material M and labour. The production of each unit of C requires 2 units of M and takes 0.12 hours to produce. The production of each unit of D requires 1 unit of M and 0.1 hours to produce. In total, the company has 200 units of M available and 18 working hours.

Consequently, the linear programme is expressed as follows:

Maximise: $3x_C + 4x_D$
Subject to:

$2x_C + x_D \leq 200$
$0.12x_C + 0.1x_D \leq 18$
$x_A \geq 0$
$x_B \geq 0$

In order to solve this programme, the first step is to determine the corner points.

Assuming that x_C is plotted on the horizontal axis, the points where the constraints cross the horizontal axis can be calculated by rearranging the constraint boundary line equation and setting x_D equal to zero.

Taking the materials constraint and rearranging gives

$$x_D \leq 200 - 2x_C \text{ with the boundary line given by } x_D = 200 - 2x_C$$

Hence, if $x_D = 0$, then $x_C = 100$.

A similar process can be followed to find the point where the constraint boundary line crosses the vertical axis. In this case, x_C is set equal to zero. Therefore, the constraint crosses the vertical axis at the point $x_C = 0$ and $x_D = 200$.

Figure 6.12 shows all the points where the constraints cross both axes.

Constraint	x_C	x_D	Axis
Materials	100	0	Horizontal
	0	200	Vertical
Labour	150	0	Horizontal
	0	180	Vertical

Figure 6.12   Axis intercept points.

These points do not all constitute corner points for the feasible area. For example, consider the intercept points on the horizontal axis. Although the point where $x_C = 150$ and $x_D = 0$ satisfies the labour constraint, it does not simultaneously satisfy the materials constraint and hence cannot be part of the feasible area. Consequently, the corner of the feasible area that coincides with the horizontal axis is the point where the materials constraint crosses this axis (i.e. where $x_C = 100$ and $x_D = 0$). Similarly, the corner of the feasible area coinciding with the vertical axis is the point where the labour constraint intercepts this axis (i.e. where $x_C = 0$ and $x_D = 180$).

The final corner point occurs where the two constraints meet. This can be found by setting the two boundary lines as equal and rearranging. This corner point occurs where $x_C = 25$ and $x_D = 150$.

All the corner points are listed in Figure 6.13 and these are illustrated in Figure 6.14.

	x_C	x_D
1	100	0
2	0	180
3	25	150

Figure 6.13   Corner points.

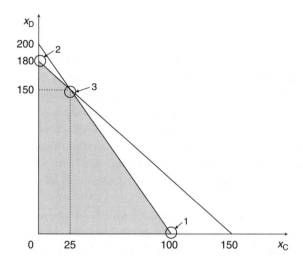

Figure 6.14 Corner points.

To find the optimal point, a graph is not required. It is only necessary to substitute the values of each of the corner points into the objective function in order to determine the maximum level of profit (see Figure 6.15).

Corner	x_C	x_D	Profit
1	100	0	$(3 \times 100) + (4 \times 0) = 300$
2	0	180	$(3 \times 0) + (4 \times 180) = 720$
3	25	150	$(3 \times 25) + (4 \times 150) = 675$

Figure 6.15 Finding the optimal values.

Consequently, the optimal point is corner 2, since the values at this point give the highest level of profit. Therefore, the company should not produce any units of C but should produce 180 units of D.

The optimal level of production in this example uses all of the labour resource but not all of the manufacturing materials available (substitution of the production levels into the constraints confirms this). The labour constraint is binding but the materials constraint is slack. Consequently, this may lead to the question of whether it is worth increasing the quantity of labour in order that more of the material resource is utilised. Using the techniques already described can answer these types of question, and this type of investigation is known as a sensitivity analysis.

Sensitivity Analysis

Sensitivity analyses address two issues: quantifying changes in the optimal solution that result from changes in the levels of resources (changing the right-hand side of the constraints) and changes in the objective function parameters (in the current example, the contribution to profit of each of the production activities). Both these cases have practical applications. By investigating the effects of changing the availability of resources for binding constraints, the maximum value that would feasibly be paid for increasing the availability of resources can be ascertained. Varying the objective function can model situations where, for example, costs or technology are changing.

Sensitivity analysis is useful in stochastic situations where parameter are not known with certainty. The sensitivity analysis gives the domain of the objective function parameters for which the optimal value of the objective function does not change. The sensitivity analysis also gives the changes in the optimal value of the objective function that result from variations in the quantities of resources. Nevertheless, it is important to be aware that the use of LP for decision-making under uncertainty is contested. An investigation of this issue is suggested as part of the further reading for this chapter.

Changing Constraints

Since the labour constraint is binding, it makes sense to ascertain whether it is worth attempting to increase the supply of labour in order to increase profit. It is possible to estimate how much it would be worth paying to relax the labour constraint.

The first step is to increase the right-hand side of the labour constraint by 1 unit, leading to the following linear programme:

Maximise: $3x_C + 4x_D$
Subject to:
$2x_C + x_D \leq 200$
$0.12x_C + 0.1x_D \leq 19$ (the labour resource has increased by 1 unit)
$x_A \geq 0$
$x_B \geq 0$

Following the same solution process as in the main example gives the axis intercept points as shown in Figure 6.16.

Constraint	x_C	x_D	Axis
Materials	100	0	Horizontal
	0	200	Vertical
Labour	158.3	0	Horizontal
	0	190	Vertical

Figure 6.16 Axis intercept points.

The intercept of the materials and labour constraints has also changed. To calculate this point, let $200 - 2x_C = 190 - 1.2x_C$. Rearranging this equation gives $x_C = 12.5$. Hence, $x_D = 175$.

The corner points are listed in Figure 6.17.

	x_C	x_D
1	100	0
2	0	190
3	12.5	175

Figure 6.17 Corner points.

The final step is to calculate the profit at each of the points (shown in Figure 6.18). Point 2 is the optimal point and results in a profit of £760. Consequently, by increasing the amount of labour by 1 unit, profit is increased by £40 (recall the original optimal level of profit was £720). This is known as the *shadow price*, defined as the change in the value of the objective function at the optimal point as the result of a change in the level of a resource by 1 unit. Therefore, in this case, it indicates

	x_C	x_D	Profit
1	100	0	$(3 \times 100) + (4 \times 0) = 300$
2	0	190	$(3 \times 0) + (4 \times 190) = 760$
3	25	175	$(3 \times 12.5) + (4 \times 175) = 737.5$

Figure 6.18 Finding the optimal values.

the maximum amount to pay for an additional unit of labour. The shadow price is based on the assumption that there are no changes in cost associated with increasing resource levels. In this example it therefore makes sense to try to increase the supply of labour, provided the cost of labour does not change. However, there is a limit on the amount by which labour should be increased, and this can be seen in Figure 6.19.

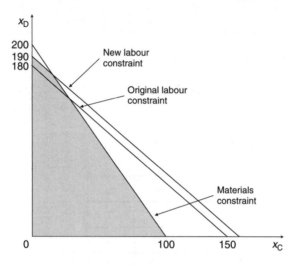

Figure 6.19 Changing the labour constraint.

By increasing the supply of labour, the intercept of the constraint boundary line with the vertical axis moves upwards. It is clear that it only makes sense to increase the supply of labour up to the point where 200 units of x_D can be produced, since, if labour is increased beyond this point, there will not be sufficient quantities of M to produce more units of D (the materials constraint is no longer satisfied), resulting in a surplus of labour.

In order to calculate the maximum quantity of labour that can be used, the labour constraint boundary line equation can be rewritten in the following form:

$$0.12x_C + 0.1x_D = Q$$

At the point of intercept of the horizontal axis, $x_C = 0$. The maximum quantity of D that can be produced is 200, and therefore $x_D = 200$. Hence

$$0.1 \times 200 = Q$$

and so $Q = 20$. Provided the cost of labour does not change, the company should increase the supply of labour to 20 units in order to utilise all of the available resources of manufacturing material M, resulting in an increase in profit of £80.

Changing the Objective Function

So far it has been assumed that resources can be altered without cost. Given that this is not always the case, it is wise to be able to assess the effects changes in the objective function due to costs associated with changing resources.

Changes in the objective function equate to changes in the gradient of the line representing the objective function (in this case the isoprofit line). As has been seen graphically in the previous example, this changes the optimal point, depending upon the magnitude of the gradient of the line of the objective function in relation to the gradients of the constraint boundary lines. This could potentially result in a reduction in the overall level of profit. It is possible to calculate the range of changes to the objective function that do not result in a change in the optimal solution.

In order to do this, it is necessary to consider again the set of corner points. Assuming that the contribution to profit of product D remains the same, let the contribution to profit of C equal p_C. The resulting profit at each of the corner points is given in Figure 6.20.

	x_C	x_D	Profit
1	100	0	$(p_C \times 100) + (4 \times 0) = 100\,p_C$
2	0	180	$(p_C \times 0) + (4 \times 180) = 720$
3	25	150	$(p_C \times 25) + (4 \times 150) = 600 + 25\,p_C$

Figure 6.20   Profit at the corner points.

The previous optimal point was corner 2, which resulted in a level of profit of £720. Looking at both corner 1 and corner 3, it is clear to see that, as p_C increases, the optimal point will eventually change to corner 3. To calculate this value of p_C, set

$$600 + 25\,p_C > 720$$

It follows that, if $p_C > 4.8$, the optimal point will change and will result in a higher level of profit. Remembering that the original optimal solution resulted in a zero level of production of C, only by increasing the contribution to profit of C above 4.8 does it make sense to produce any quantity of that good.

Since in this case the original optimal point is not dependent upon p_C (producing at the optimal point means that the company will not produce good C), it does not matter how small p_C becomes, as it will not affect the level of profit. In order to calculate the changes in the objective function that will result in a reduction in profit, it is therefore necessary to examine changes in the contribution to profit of product D.

Following a similar process, assuming that the contribution to profit of good C remains the same (£3 per unit), let the contribution to profit of product D be equal to p_D. The resulting profit at each of the corner points is given in Figure 6.21.

	x_C	x_D	Profit
1	100	0	$(3 \times 100) + (p_D \times 0) = 100$
2	0	180	$(3 \times 0) + (p_D \times 180) = 180\,p_D$
3	25	150	$(3 \times 25) + (p_D \times 150) = 75 + 150\,p_D$

Figure 6.21   Profit at the corner points.

It is clear that, since the level of profit at points 2 and 3 are dependent on the value of the contribution to profit of product D, any reduction in this value will result in a reduction in the level of profit.

It is possible to calculate a value of p_D which will result in a change in the optimal level of profit. The optimal level of profit will change when

$$75 + 150\,p_D > 180\,p_D$$

So, rearranging this equation leads to $p_D < 2.5$. Hence, if the contribution to profit of product D drops below £2.50 per unit, the optimal point will change, resulting in a change in the level of optimal profit. This also means that, at the new optimal point, a mix of goods C and D will be produced.

A sensitivity analysis can result in useful additional information about the situation to inform decisions about purchasing additional resources, in addition to giving information about the likelihood that the optimal solution is sensitive to small changes in the characteristics of the situation.

The examples presented so far have been simple and therefore readily solved analytically. In most situations, however, there will be multiple activities competing for multiple resources. There are various dedicated software resources[1] that can be used

---

[1] These software packages rely on some manner of algorithm to find solutions to linear programmes, the most common of which is the *simplex algorithm*. This can be implemented 'by hand' for simple examples, although instructions for the implementation of the simplex algorithm are not included in this text. The interested reader is directed to alternative texts listed in the Further Reading section for more details about these algorithms.

for numerical optimisation, although Microsoft Excel has the Solver add-in which can be utilised for many optimisation problems.

Using Excel Solver

A company produces a product P that is assembled of three components, A, B, and C. The company has orders totalling 500 units for P, but has limited resources in terms of the working hours available. Hence, the company must decide whether to outsource any production of the three components in order to meet this demand. The in-house manufacturing costs and outsourcing costs are detailed in Figure 6.22.

Component	Manufacturing cost (£)	Outsource cost (£)
A	0.75	0.90
B	0.4	0.55
C	1.1	1.4

Figure 6.22 Summary of costs.

Each of the three components has to go through two production processes in departments M and N. The production time for each component in each department, together with the total hours available, is shown in Figure 6.23.

	Department	
Component	**M**	**N**
A	0.04	0.05
B	0.03	0.03
C	0.05	0.05
Total time available (h)	50	55

Figure 6.23 Production time (hours).

In order to use Excel Solver to calculate the quantities of each component to manufacture and to purchase, the problem must first be formulated in an Excel spreadsheet (available for download although it is a useful exercise for the reader to recreate the spreadsheet.). Once this has been achieved, the Solver Add-In can be used.

The spreadsheet is set out as detailed in Figure 6.24.

Cells	Description
B3:C5	These cells will contain the optimal production levels, i.e. the quantities of each component manufactured or outsourced that cost the least in total.
D3:D5	The total quantity of each component produced (manufactured plus outsourced).
F3:F5	The cost per unit for each component manufactured.
G3:G5	The cost per unit for each component outsourced.
H3:I5	The total cost for all components manufactured and outsourced.
J3:J5	The total costs (manufactured and outsourced) for each component.
M3:N5	The manufacturing time per unit required in each department for each component.
P3:Q5	The total manufacturing time required for each component in each department.
J7	The total cost. This is the objective function.
M7:N7	The total manufacturing time available in each department.
P7:Q7	The total manufacturing time required in each department.

Figure 6.24   Excel cell references.

It may be necessary to add the Solver facility to Excel if it has not been used before. In order to add the Solver facility, click the 'Office' button and then select 'Excel Options' from the resulting menu (see Figure 6.25).

In the next dialogue box, select 'Add-Ins' from the menu on the left-hand side of the box (see Figure 6.26) and click the 'Go' button next to the 'Manage' window at the bottom of the dialogue box, making sure that 'Excel Add-Ins' is selected in the window.

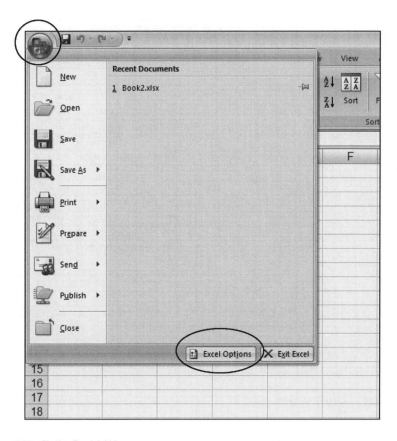

Figure 6.25 Finding Excel Add-Ins.

In the resulting dialogue box, tick the 'Solver Add-In' box, followed by 'OK' (see Figure 6.27).

Check that Solver is now available by selecting the 'Data' tab, where the 'Solver' option should be visible on the right of the main tool bar (see Figure 6.28).

Once the Solver option is available, click the button to reach the main Solver dialogue box, pictured in Figure 6.29.

The next step is to enter the appropriate cell references. The 'Set Target Cell' window should contain the cell reference of the objective function. The objective of this particular problem is to minimise total costs, and therefore the 'Set Target Cell' window is set to cell reference J8 and 'Equal To' is set to 'Min'. The 'By Changing Cells' window should contain the cell references where the optimal resource levels will be stored. In this example, the cell references entered here are B4:C6 (see Figure 6.30).

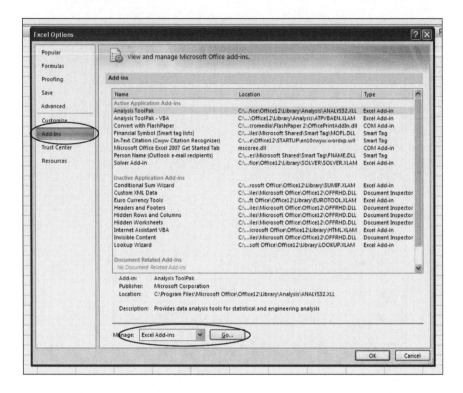

Figure 6.26 Selecting the Add-Ins menu.

The final stage of the process requires the specification of the constraints, and to begin with it is necessary to click the 'Add' button to the right of the 'Subject to the Constraints' window. The cell references of the constraints need to be entered into the relevant windows of the resulting dialogue box (see Figure 6.31).

The first constraint entered is that which requires the production levels to be greater than or equal to 500. The cell references D3:D5 are entered into the 'Cell Reference'box. The sign '>=' should be selected from the drop-down menu of the centre box. The digits 500 must be typed into the 'Constraint' box. The final step requires the 'Add' button to be clicked in order to add the next constraint. See Figure 6.32 for the first constraint.

The cell references for all the constraints are listed in Figure 6.33.

When the final constraint has been specified, the 'OK' button should be clicked to return to the main Solver dialogue box. Once this has been done, the complete linear programme has been specified (see Figure 6.33).

Note that the non-negativity constraint has been omitted from the specification of constraints. This is because there is an option that, when chosen, assumes that all variables are non-negative. To do this, click the 'Options' button on the Solver

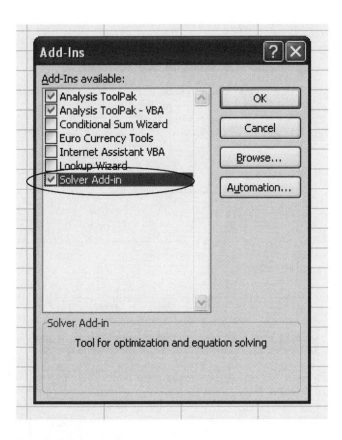

Figure 6.27   Selecting the Solver Add-In.

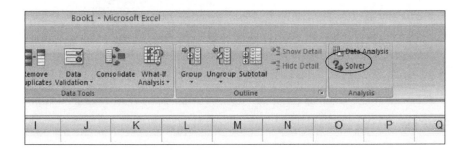

Figure 6.28   Solver option on Data tool bar.

dialogue box and then make sure the 'Assume Non-Negative' box has been selected from the resulting dialogue box (see Figure 6.34).

Once this has been done, click 'OK', and the 'Solve' button should then be clicked to find the optimum solution, which will be stored in the cells B3:C5.

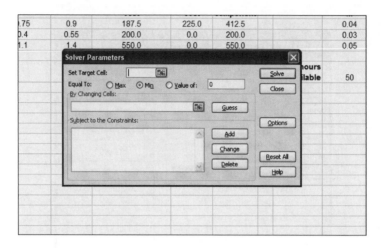

Figure 6.29 Solver dialogue box.

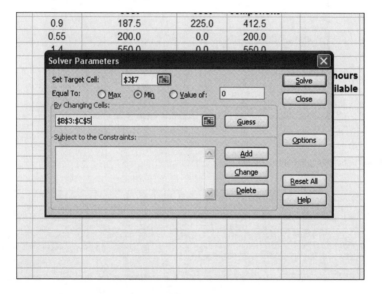

Figure 6.30 Solver specification of objective function and resource variables.

The results show that 250 units of A should be manufactured and 250 units should be outsourced. All 500 units of B and C should be manufactured.

Solver will also perform a sensitivity analysis with ease. In order to generate the appropriate information, it is necessary to click the 'Options' button in the main Solver dialogue box, and 'Assume Linear Model' needs to be selected from the resulting menu (see Figure 6.35).

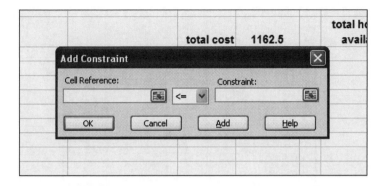

Figure 6.31 Constraints dialogue box.

a)

b)

Cell references	Sign	Constraint	Description
D3:D5	>=	500	Set minimum levels of production to 500 units per component.
P7	<=	M7	Constrains the total production time in department M to the maximum amount of working hours available.
Q7	<=	N7	Constrains the total production time in department N to the maximum amount of working hours available.

Figure 6.32 a) Production levels constraint, b) Specification of constraints.

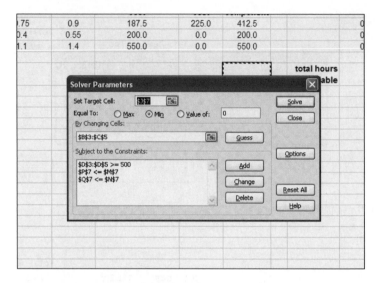

.75	0.9	187.5	225.0	412.5		0
0.4	0.55	200.0	0.0	200.0		0
1.1	1.4	550.0	0.0	550.0		0

Figure 6.33 Solver specification of linear programme.

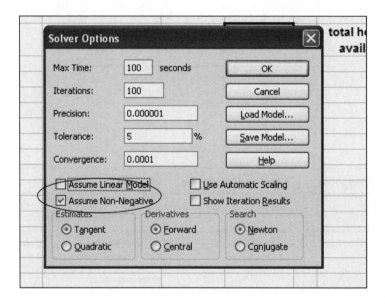

Figure 6.34 Selecting the non-negative option.

Clicking 'OK' returns to the main Solver box, and clicking 'Solve' generates the 'Solver Results' dialogue box. It is necessary at this point to highlight 'Answer' and 'Sensitivity' in the reports box (see Figure 6.36).

The resulting reports are discussed below.

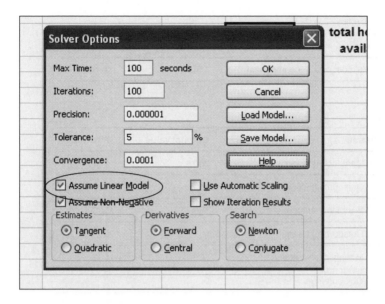

Figure 6.35 Generating a sensitivity analysis.

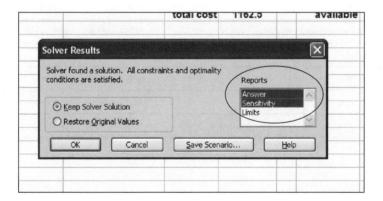

Figure 6.36 Results dialogue box.

The *answer report* (Figure 6.37) details the whole solution and in particular the constraints, indicating those that are slack and those that are binding. In this specific case the manufacturing time is the only resource constraint, and it can be seen that manufacturing time in department M is a binding constraint. The manufacturing time constraint for department N is slack, and as can be seen, there is a slack of 2.5 hours.

The *sensitivity report* (Figure 6.38) indicates a negative shadow price, since the problem is one of minimisation. This result indicates that, if the manufacturing

Target Cell (Min)

Cell	Name	Original Value	Final Value
$J$7	total cost cost per component	1162.5	1162.5

Adjustable Cells

Cell	Name	Original Value	Final Value
$B$3	A Manufacturing levels	250	250
$C$3	A Outsourcing levels	250	250
$B$4	B Manufacturing levels	500	500
$C$4	B Outsourcing levels	0	0
$B$5	C Manufacturing levels	500	500
$C$5	C Outsourcing levels	0	0

Constraints

Cell	Name	Cell Value	Formula	Status	Slack
$Q$7	total hours available department N	52.5	$Q$7<=$N$7	Not Binding	2.5
$D$3	A Total	500	$D$3>=500	Binding	0
$D$4	B Total	500	$D$4>=500	Binding	0
$D$5	C Total	500	$D$5>=500	Binding	0
$P$7	total hours available department M	50.0	$P$7<=$M$7	Binding	0

Figure 6.37 Answer report.

time in department M is increased by 1 hour, the overall costs will be reduced by £3.80. The shadow price, however, is not valid for all changes in the resource. The 'Allowable Increase' and 'Allowable Decrease' indicate the range of possible values for the levels of resource for which the shadow price is valid and also for which the optimal solution will not change. Hence, the working hours in department M could be increased by 2 units to reduce overall costs by £7.60 (2 × 3.60). These values also indicate that the total working hour resource for M could decrease by 10 without changing the optimal solution. Information such as this is useful if there is a possibility of changes in the availability of resources.

The use of Solver allows the user to bypass the relatively complex mathematics required to solve linear programmes analytically. Nevertheless, it is vitally important

Adjustable Cells

Cell	Name	Final Value	Reduced Cost	Objective Coefficient	Allowable Increase	Allowable Decrease
$B$3	A Manufacturing levels	250	0	0.75	0.15	0.05
$C$3	A Outsourcing levels	250	0	0.9	0.05	0.15
$B$4	B Manufacturing levels	500	0	0.4	0.0375	0.5125
$C$4	B Outsourcing levels	0	0	0.55	1E+30	0.0375
$B$5	C Manufacturing levels	500	0	1.1	0.1125	1.2875
$C$5	C Outsourcing levels	0	0	1.4	1E+30	0.1125

Constraints

Cell	Name	Final Value	Shadow Price	Constraint R.H. Side	Allowable Increase	Allowable Decrease
$Q$7	total hours available department N	52.5	0.0	55	1E+30	2.5
$D$3	A Total	500	0.9	500	1E+30	250
$D$4	B Total	500	0.5125	500	333.33	333.33
$D$5	C Total	500	1.2875	500	200	200
$P$7	total hours available department M	50.0	−3.8	50	2	10

Figure 6.38 Sensitivity report.

to ensure that the situation is thoughtfully constructed in mathematical terms and correctly specified in Excel. The benefits of using software such as Excel Solver are completely negated if care is not taken to ensure that the key characteristics of the situation are defined in appropriate mathematical terms. For example, contribution to profit may be defined as a product's sales price minus the cost of the materials, or it could be defined as the sales price minus all variable costs. Using both these definitions may result in very different optimal solutions. The most appropriate choice is dependent upon the characteristics of the situation, including the timescale of the decision. For a discussion of these issues within a theory of constraints[2] approach, see Souren, Ahn, and Schmitz (2005).

Integer Programming

So far the examples presented have resulted in integer solutions. Nevertheless, it is very often the case that the outcome of the optimisation process is a decimal solution. In certain cases a decimal solution makes little sense, such as when the problem relates to a manufacturing process. Since any production process should not result in fractional goods, a decimal solution is not appropriate.

It may be tempting to round the solution to the nearest integer. A rounded solution, however, may not be feasible or optimal. Consider the previous example of a manufacturing company producing goods C and D according to the solution of the following linear programme:

Maximise: $3x_C + 4x_D$
Subject to:
$2x_C + x_D \leq 200$
$0.12x_C + 0.1x_D \leq 18$
$x_C \geq 0$
$x_D \geq 0$

The manufacturing processes for both products have now changed, resulting in a change in the contribution to profit of both goods: good C now contributes £5 per unit and good D contributes £2 per unit. The time needed to produce each good has also changed, meaning that product C requires 0.8 hours per unit to produce and

---

[2] A management technique used to identify constraints in the production process. Although it is not a formal mathematical technique in the way that linear programming is, it is nevertheless a related optimisation technique.

product D requires 0.2 hours per unit to produce. In order to accommodate these changes, more staff have been employed, increasing the number of working hours available to 55. This changes the time constraint to $0.8x_C + 0.2x_D \leq 55$, and the linear programme becomes as follows:

Maximise: $5x_C + 2x_D$
Subject to:

$2x_C + x_D \leq 200$
$0.8x_C + 0.2x_D \leq 55$
$x_C \geq 0$
$x_D \geq 0$

The solution to the linear programme leads to levels of production of 37.5 units of C and 125 units of D. Since it is not feasible to produce fractional units of any good, it would suggest that the solution for the level of production of good C should be rounded. If the value of 38 is chosen, however, neither the materials nor the time constraints are satisfied.

Perhaps the level of 37 should be chosen? Both constraints would be satisfied at this level, and a profit of £435 would result. Nevertheless, a greater level of profit can be achieved by changing the level of production of good D to 126 units. Hence, it is not a simple matter of rounding the non-integer solution to the nearest integer.

In cases where an integer solution is required, an additional constraint needs to be added to the linear programme that constrains the solution to take only integer values. For example:

Maximise: $5x_C + 2x_D$
Subject to:

$2x_C + x_D \leq 200$
$0.8x_C + 0.2x_D \leq 55$
$x_C \geq 0$
$x_D \geq 0$
$x_C, x_D \in Z$ (i.e. both these values must be members of the set of all integers[3])

The feasible area for this linear programme is very different to those already encountered. It is not continuous but is comprised of points indicating the integer values of x_C and x_D (see Figure 6.39).

---

[3] Since the constraints also require that both values be greater than 0, it is not necessary to require that the values be elements of the set of integers greater than or equal to zero.

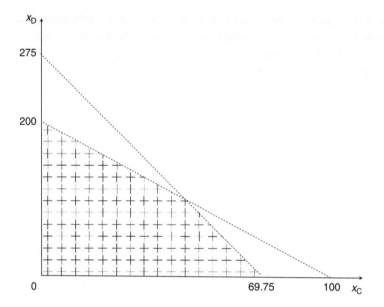

Figure 6.39 Feasible area with integer constraint.

A convenient method of finding a solution to an integer programme is to use Excel Solver, since solutions of integer programmes require non-trivial modifications to the corner method. The constraint selection facility in the Solver dialogue box provides an option for restricting cells to integer values (see Figure 6.40).

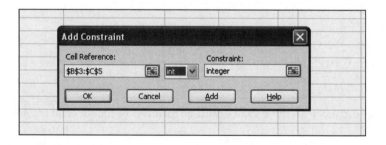

Figure 6.40 Solver specification of integer constraint.

The solution to this integer programme results in a value for x_C of 37 units and a value for x_D of 126 units. This result could have been achieved by trial and error, although with larger linear programmes this approach would be extremely time consuming.

Integer programming has an obvious advantage when allocating resources between activities where solutions in whole units are required. Nevertheless, the process of sensitivity analysis cannot easily be implemented with an integer programme. The key problem arises from the discontinuity of the feasible area. With a standard linear programme, the parameters can take any value and changes to the optimal value of the objective function are continuous. Parameters defining integer programmes can take only whole-number values, and thus changes in the constraints or objective function will cause step changes in the optimal value of the objective function. These step changes are difficult to predict, and an accepted approach to forecasting such occurrences is not currently available.

It should be noted that, if the process under investigation is measured in large integers (at least in thousands), it can be approximated by a standard linear programme rather than an integer programme, meaning that a sensitivity analysis is possible.

Formulating Decision-making Problems as Linear Programmes

Linear programming can be used for many decisions that can be formulated in terms of the maximisation or minimisation of some measure. Minimising costs in a production process is an obvious application of this technique. There are, however, other types of decision that may not immediately appear to lend themselves to such a formulation, but, with some manipulation, a solution of this type can be sought.

The Transportation Problem

A company has three geographically separate production centres, P_1, P_2, and P_3, which can produce a maximum of T_1, T_2, and T_3 units respectively of the same commodity. The company has to transport this commodity to three geographically separate markets, M_1, M_2, and M_3, and each of these markets requires a different quantity, R_1, R_2, and R_3, of the commodity. Linear programming can help to determine optimal levels of the commodity that should be transported between each production centre and each market. Since there is a cost associated with transporting the commodity, the most efficient way to determine the optimal levels is to formulate the situation in terms of a cost minimisation problem.

Figure 6.41 summarises the costs of transporting the commodity between each production centre and each market.

To formulate the problem as a linear programme, the first step is to define the objective function, which in this case is the total transportation costs. The total

		Markets		
		1	**2**	**3**
Production centre	**1**	C_{11}	C_{12}	C_{13}
	2	C_{21}	C_{22}	C_{23}
	3	C_{31}	C_{32}	C_{33}

Figure 6.41 Transportation costs.

cost is dependent upon the amount transported from each production centre to each market. These quantities are detailed in Figure 6.42.

		Markets		
		1	**2**	**3**
Production centre	**A**	Q_{11}	Q_{12}	Q_{13}
	B	Q_{21}	Q_{22}	Q_{23}
	C	Q_{31}	Q_{32}	Q_{33}

Figure 6.42 Quantities shipped.

It is now straightforward to formulate an expression for total cost:

$$\text{Total cost} = C_{11}Q_{11} + C_{12}Q_{12} + C_{13}Q_{13} + C_{21}Q_{21} + \cdots + C_{33}Q_{33}$$

or more succinctly

$$\text{Total cost} = \sum_{i=1}^{3}\sum_{j=1}^{3}\left(C_{ij}Q_{ij}\right)$$

This is the objective function.

The constraints arise primarily from the commodity requirements of each market and production capacity of each production centre. Consequently, the market commodity requirement constraints are as follows:

$$Q_{11} + Q_{21} + Q_{31} = R_1 \text{ (requirement for market } M_1)$$

$$Q_{12} + Q_{22} + Q_{32} = R_2 \text{ (requirement for market } M_2)$$

$$Q_{13} + Q_{23} + Q_{33} = R_3 \text{ (requirement for market } M_3)$$

or

$$\sum_{k=1}^{3} Q_{ki} = R_i \quad \text{for } i = 1, 2, 3$$

Note that these equations specify that the market requirements must be met.

The production capacity constraints are as follows:

$$Q_{11} + Q_{12} + Q_{13} \leq T_1 \text{ (requirement for centre } P_1)$$

$$Q_{21} + Q_{22} + Q_{23} \leq T_2 \text{ (requirement for centre } P_2)$$

$$Q_{31} + Q_{32} + Q_{33} \leq T_3 \text{ (requirement for centre } P_3)$$

or

$$\sum_{k=1}^{3} Q_{jk} \leq T_j \quad \text{for } j = 1, 2, 3$$

Note that the production capacity is an upper limit, but the total supplied from each production centre does not have to meet this limit.

The complete linear programme is given by

Minimise
$$\sum_{i=1}^{3} \sum_{j=1}^{3} (C_{ij} Q_{ij})$$

Subject to:

$$\sum_{k=1}^{3} Q_{ki} = R_i \quad \text{for } i = 1, 2, 3 \text{ (market requirement constraint)}$$

$$\sum_{k=1}^{3} Q_{jk} \leq T_j \quad \text{for } j = 1, 2, 3 \text{ (production capacity constraint)}$$

$Q_{ij} \geq 0$ for all i and j (non-negativity constraint)
$Q_{ij} \in Z$ (integer constraint)

This can then be solved using Excel as before.

Summary

This chapter has introduced the linear programming technique, which is used to optimise an objective according to a set of constraints. For example, linear programming could be used by a manufacturer to determine production levels for different products (variables), given that manufacture of these products draws from the same set of limited resources (constraints) and the goal is to maximise profit (objective). The constraints and objective are formulated as a set of linear mathematical expressions given in terms of the variables. This system of expressions can be solved to find the optimal solution, i.e. the point (a set of values, one for each variable of interest) that results in the maximum or minimum (depending upon the problem) value for the objective function while simultaneously satisfying all constraints.

In simple linear programmes (usually two variables), the optimal solution can be found by using the corner method. This requires the identification of the feasible area, which indicates all possible solutions of the linear programme, i.e. those points that satisfy all of the constraints. The optimal solution will occur at the vertex or corner point of the feasible area, and so, to solve the linear programme, the vertices of the feasible area are identified and the one that optimises the objective function is found.

Complex linear programmes that have three or more variables are solved using suitable software packages such as SAS and Microsoft Excel. This text demonstrates how to formulate a linear programme in Excel and use the Solver add-in to find the optimal solution. The advantage of using software packages is the ease with which a sensitivity analysis can be carried out. A sensitivity analysis will give an indication of how changes in the system, such as the availability of more resources, will affect the optimal solution.

This chapter also discussed the formulation of integer programmes: linear programmes for which the solution values must be integers. These are used when a decimal solution would be inappropriate, such as in transportation problems, when deciding how many units of a product to transport from one location to another.

Further Reading

- Alternative presentations of the standard linear programming technique can be found in the following:

   Hillier, FS. & Lieberman, GJ. (2006) *Introduction to Operations Research*. McGraw-Hill, New York, NY, Chapters 3, 4, 5, 8, and 11.

   Render, B., Stair, RM., & Hanna, ME. (2005) *Quantitative Analysis for Management*. Prentice Hall, Upper Saddle River, NJ, Chapters 7 to 11.

   Waters, CDJ. (1989) *A Practical Introduction to Management Science*. Prentice Hall, Harlow, UK.

- The following references discuss the interpretation of the output from linear programmes including sensitivity analysis:

   Greenberg, HJ. (1993) How to analyze the results of linear programs – Part 1: Preliminaries. *Interfaces* **23**(4), 56–67.

   Greenberg, HJ. (1993) How to analyze the results of linear programs – Part 2: Price interpretation. *Interfaces* **23**(5): 97–114.

Greenberg, HJ. (1993) How to analyze the results of linear programs – Part 3: Infeasibility diagnosis. *Interfaces* **23**(6), 120 –139

Jansen, B., de Jong, JJ., Roos, C., & Terlaky, T. (1997) Sensitivity analysis in linear programming: just be careful!, *European Journal of Operational Research*, **101**(1), 15–28.

Koltai, T. & T. Terlaky (2000) The difference between the managerial and mathematical interpretation of sensitivity analysis results in linear programming. *International Journal of Production Economics* **65**(3), 257–274.

- The following references discuss other optimisation techniques that have been developed to deal with uncertain parameters and multiple objectives:

Inuiguchi, M. & Ramk, J. (2000) Possibilistic linear programming: a brief review of fuzzy mathematical programming and a comparison with stochastic programming in portfolio selection problem. *Fuzzy Sets and Systems* **111**(1), 3–28.

Rommelfanger, H. (1996) Fuzzy linear programming and applications. *European Journal of Operational Research* **92**(3), 512–527.

Sen, S. & Higle, JL. (1999) An introductory tutorial on stochastic linear programming models. *Interfaces* **29**(2), 33–61.

Tamiz, M., Jones, DF., & El-Darzi, E. (1995) A review of goal programming and its applications. *Annals of Operations Research* **58**(1), 39–53.

- Practical applications of linear programming can be found in the following:

Caixeta-Filjo, JV., van Sway-Neto, JM., & de Padua Wagemaker, A. (2002) Optimization of the production planning and trade of lily flowers at Jan de Wit Company. *Interfaces* **32**(1), 35–46.

Farley, AA. (1991) Planning the cutting of photographic color paper rolls for Kodak (Australasia) Pty Ltd. *Interfaces* **21**(1), 92–106.

Koksalan, M. & Sural, H. (1999) Efes Beverage Group makes location and distribution decisions for its malt plants. *Interfaces* **29**(2), 89–103.

Questions

Q6.1 For the linear programme

Maximise: $5x + 8y$
Subject to:
$x + 2y \leq 160$
$5x + 6y \leq 600$
$x, y \geq 0$

(a)   Draw the feasible area and identify the corner points.
(b)   Find the optimal solution.
(c)   Formulate the programme in Excel and use Solver to check the solution.

Q6.2 Consider the linear programme

Minimise: $3x + 2y$

Subject to:

$2x + y \leq 4$

$x \geq 3$

$y \geq 5$

$x, y \geq 0$

(a) Draw the feasible area.

(b) Does this linear programme have a solution? Explain your answer.

Q6.3 A manufacturing company produces two types of detergent, A and B, from two chemicals, C and D, and a carrier fluid, E. The production of 1 L of A requires 0.5 L of C, 0.1 L of D, and 0.4 L of E. Similarly, the production of 1 L of B requires 0.6 L of C, 0.2 L of D, and 0.2 L of E. Each day the company has 600 L of C available, 160 L of D, and 400 L of E. For each litre of detergent A the company receives £0.50 of profit, and for each litre of detergent B the company receives £0.80 of profit.

The company needs to decide how much of each detergent to produce in order to maximise the contribution to profit of this production activity:

(a) Formulate the problem as a linear programme on paper.

(b) Reformulate the programme in Excel and use Solver to find the optimal production levels.

(c) Prepare a brief report on the sensitivity analysis.

Q6.4 The table below represents the costs of transporting detergent from three manufacturing plants, A, B, and C, to the distribution depots, D and E. The values indicate the costs per 100 L of product shipped via each route. The company has to decide exactly how much to send via each transportation route in order to minimise transportation costs. The maximum production capacity of A is 500 L, that of B is 600 L, and that of C is 900 L. Depot D requires 700 L, and E requires 1100 L.

		Depot	
		D	**E**
Plant	**A**	200	100
	B	300	600
	C	500	400

(a) Formulate this problem as a linear programme on paper, assuming that the exact demand must be met.

(b) Transfer the linear programme to Excel.

(c) Use Solver to find the values shipped from each plant to each depot that minimise the transportation costs.

(d) Prepare a brief report on the sensitivity analysis.

Q6.5 Rafael's Chocolate Shop, a manufacturer of organic chocolate, sells boxes of chocolates of three types: basic, standard, and luxury. The contribution to profit and the production time per box for each different type are given in the table below:

Type	Profit (£)	Production time (hours)
Basic	2	0.25
Standard	3.5	0.33
Luxury	5.3	0.67

The company has three employees who make the chocolate and who each work 8 hours per day. The sales manager would like to calculate how many types of each box they should make per day in order to maximise the contribution to profit:

(a) Formulate this problem as a linear programme.

(b) Use Solver to find the values shipped from each plant to each depot that minimise the transportation costs.

(c) Prepare a brief report on the sensitivity analysis.

Activities

Before implementing large linear programmes, there are a number of issues that would need to be considered, including how to deal with programmes that do not have solutions and dealing with uncertainty. These investigations will guide the reader towards thinking about the necessary issues prior to implementing a linear programme.

A6.1 The discussion in this text has been limited to models that have solutions. There are many cases (one is given in **Q6.2**), however, where a solution may not exist. This very often results from constraints that, when taken together, produce no feasible area. With the simple models considered here, it is a relatively simple process to graph the constraints and check that a feasible area does exist. In reality, it is often very difficult to track down sources of infeasibilities. Investigate approaches to detecting infeasibilities in larger linear programmes, including alternative software packages that can be used.

A6.2 In some cases, the actual values of some or all of the parameters that define the situation under investigation may not be known. It may be possible to estimate the distribution of the parameters, and hence expected values may be calculated. In many situations the uncertainty may be resolved. Using any of the analytic examples presented in the text, investigate the sensitivity of the solution to changes in the variables (hint: replace one variable at a time with an unknown value, p say, and then reformulate and solve the LP analytically).

Read the following paper and reflect on the consequences for the analysis you have just carried out:

Higle, JL. & Wallace, SW. (2003) Sensitivity analysis and uncertainty in linear programming. *Interfaces* **33**(4), 53–60 [this is available at the following web address: http://ormstomorrow.informs.org/archive/fall03/ada8701782_article.pdf].

A6.3 The previous activity discussed the problem of uncertain parameters. Investigate the development of alternative programming techniques that can incorporate parameters whose values are not known with certainty. Write a summary of both the stochastic and the fuzzy programming techniques, giving an overview of the issues that lead to their development, how they are implemented, and the types of problem for which the stochastic and fuzzy programming techniques are used to find solutions. See Inuiguchi and Ramk (2000), Rommelfanger (1996), and Sen and Higle (1999) (full references in the Further Reading section).

CHAPTER 7

Simultaneous Move Games

Objectives

- *To introduce the key concepts of game theory, including rational behaviour, zero sum and non-zero sum games, dominant and dominated strategies, and Nash equilibrium.*
- *To be able to find Nash equilibria where they exist by the identification of dominant and dominated strategies.*
- *To be able to calculate mixed strategies when no equilibria are encountered.*

Introduction

Game theory is a branch of mathematics that is used to model strategic interactions between competing agents. It is often used in the field of economics to explain competition within industries, for example, but is also useful to those involved in strategic decision-making. The general principles of game theory supply a framework that allows for a systematic approach to the process of decision-making in a competitive environment.

Historically, game theory has been used in business, economics, and politics and even in the world of entertainment, from the development of nuclear strategies to the development of game shows. The focus in this chapter will be the application of game theory in a business environment.

There are many different ways of classifying games, with one of the most important being whether the competing agents are choosing their actions simultaneously as a one-off or repeated encounter or alternatively are choosing sequentially, in which case their actions have consequences in the future. This chapter will deal with one-off and repeated simultaneous choice games. Unless stated otherwise, the analysis can be used for both one-off and repeated decisions.

Terminology

The term 'game' refers to a competitive situation with a set of players and a set of strategies available to those players. In terms of simultaneous move games, players' strategies are the choices of action available to them. A set of strategies is complete if it covers all possible actions available to a player for every possible contingency in the situation.

A payoff is associated with each outcome resulting from the player's choice of strategy. The payoff is a value denoting the player's rating of the outcome of the strategy. Therefore, the higher the payoff,[1] the greater the value the player places on that outcome. Payoffs are frequently defined in monetary terms, although they can be representative of the player's expected utility[2] from the outcome.

The key assumption for all games is that players prefer better outcomes and will try to achieve the highest outcome. Players are therefore assumed to engage in rational behaviour, meaning that each player has a consistent set of outcomes related to each action and will choose the action with the best outcome. It is important to note that this does not imply that game theory assumes a case of 'every man for himself'. The well-being of others can be valued as the outcome of an action. Rationality implies that players have full knowledge of the outcomes of their actions and a consistent approach to evaluating those outcomes.

Although all players are assumed to be fully aware of their own value system, it is not necessarily the case that players will be aware of their opponent's value

---

[1] Negative payoffs are possible and are usually interpreted as costs to the player.
[2] Expected utility is a concept used largely in economics that attempts to quantify the level of satisfaction an individual derives from the outcome of a particular choice. This is often used to model consumer behaviour, where consumption of goods is modelled by optimising a function representing the consumer utility.

systems. Therefore games are often characterised by asymmetry of information, and attempting to discover opponents' values or conceal their own values becomes an important aspect of the game, dealt with in sequential games (covered in Chapter 10).

Nevertheless, the assumption of rationality is frequently unrealistic. In many types of situation it is difficult to place values on outcomes or for players even to be aware of their own value systems in advance. Hence, serious consideration must be given to the determination of complete strategies and full-value systems, although a degree of uncertainty can be incorporated.

Simultaneous move games are generally depicted as payoff tables when the strategies are pure, that is, when the strategies are discrete. This is known as the normal form of the game. The payoff tables are slightly different from the payoff matrices met in earlier chapters. The rows indicate the various strategies available to one of the players in the game. Unlike the previous forms of payoff matrix, columns indicate the strategies of other players in the game. Each column represents one strategy.

In many types of interaction, the interests of the players are directly opposed. Considering a two-agent game, this implies that a gain made by one of the players would be matched by a loss made by the other player. This is known as a constant-sum game because the payoffs sum to a constant number and represent situations of pure conflict. In certain cases, the gain of one of the agents is exactly matched by a loss made by the other agent. The payoffs then sum to zero, and hence games of this type are known as zero-sum games.

Zero-sum Games

Given that the payoffs are represented in table format, the discussion will be limited to two-player games for simplicity. A brief discussion of multiplayer games is reserved for the latter part of the chapter.

		Agent 2		
		D	E	F
Agent 1	**A**	1	2	3
	B	7	5	2
	C	−1	2	−8

Figure 7.1   Zero-sum game.

In this example (Figure 7.1), agent 1 has three pure strategies (A, B, and C) and agent 2 also has three pure strategies (D, E, and F). With pure conflict games, only the payoffs of the row agent are detailed, as the column agent payoffs can be calculated by subtracting the payoff from the constant sum. In zero-sum games the payoffs will sum to zero, and therefore the payoffs of the column agents are the negatives of the payoffs in the table. Consequently, if agent 1 chooses strategy A and agent 2 chooses strategy D, agent 1 receives a payoff of 1 and agent 2 receives a payoff of -1. The row player's payoffs for choosing a particular strategy are read across rows, while the column player's payoffs for choosing a particular strategy are read down the columns of the table.

Since the primary aim of game theory is to generate understanding of strategic interactions in competitive situations, once a payoff table has been generated, the next step is to ascertain the choice of strategy of each player, taking into account the possible choices of the other player.

Dominant and Dominated Strategies

The easiest way to start this process is to look for dominant or dominated strategies. A dominant strategy is one for which the agent will not achieve a higher payoff by choosing another strategy, regardless of the choice of the other agent. In mathematical terms, if we denote the row player's payoff as p_{ij}, where i denotes the row player's strategy and j denotes the column player's strategy, then a dominant strategy, i, is one for which

$$p_{ij} > p_{kj} \quad \forall\, k \in m,\ i \neq k \text{ and } \forall\, j \in n,$$

where m denotes the total number of strategies available to the row player and n denotes the total number of strategies available to the column player. The row player's payoff from choosing strategy i is greater than the payoff received by choosing any other strategy k, for all possible strategy choices made by the column agent.

By contrast, a dominated strategy, i, is one for which

$$p_{ij} < p_{kj} \quad \forall\, k \in m,\ i \neq k \text{ and } \forall\, j \in n,$$

Hence, the payoff received from choosing strategy i is less than the payoff received by choosing any other strategy k, regardless of the strategy choice of the other agent.

In this example (Figure 7.2), it is clear to see that agent 1 has a dominant strategy, namely strategy B. Regardless of the choice made by agent 2, the best outcome for agent 1 will always be achieved by choosing strategy B. Similarly, agent 2 also has a dominant strategy, and in this case it is strategy F, remembering that the payoffs listed in the table are the negatives of the payoffs received by agent 2. Hence, if agent 1 chooses A and agent 2 chooses F, agent 2 receives a payoff of -0.5.

Both players have a dominant strategy, and hence all other strategies can be eliminated since the rationality assumption implies that the players will always choose

		Agent 2		
		D	E	F
Agent 1	A	1	2	0.5
	B	7	5	3
	C	−1	2	−8

Figure 7.2 Example – dominant strategies.

the best outcome for themselves. The solution to this game is strategy B for agent 1 and strategy F for agent 2. A similar process of reasoning can be applied to games with dominated strategies.

A swift examination of the payoff table shown in Figure 7.3 reveals that neither agent has a dominant strategy. Both agents do have dominated strategies, however. In the case of agent 1, strategy C will never be chosen because it will always be better to choose A or B regardless of the choice of agent 2. Looking at the payoffs of agent 2, it is clear that strategy E will never be chosen because it will always be better to choose D or F regardless of the choice made by agent 1. Consequently, strategies C and E can be eliminated, leaving two strategies for each player (see Figure 7.4).

		Agent 2		
		D	E	F
Agent 1	A	0.5	5	1
	B	2	3	2.5
	C	−1	2	−8

Figure 7.3 Example – dominated strategies.

		Agent 2	
		D	F
Agent 1	A	0.5	1
	B	2	2.5

Figure 7.4 Elimination of dominated strategies.

Both agents are now left with a dominant and a dominated strategy. Strategy B is the dominant strategy for agent 1, and D is the dominant strategy for agent 2. These choices represent the solution of the game, and so agent 1 receives a payoff of 2 and agent 2 receives −2.

From these examples it is clear that rational players will always choose their dominant strategy, if they have one, since they can do no better by choosing another strategy, and they will never choose a dominated strategy since they can always do better by choosing another strategy. The resulting solution is known as a Nash equilibrium. If a Nash equilibrium solution exists, no player can do any better by choosing a different strategy. A Nash equilibrium represents the best choice of strategy for each player, taking into account the choices of the other players. This does not mean that each strategy represents the best possible outcome for each player. Clearly, the best possible outcome for agent 1 results from choosing strategy A if agent 2 chooses strategy E. Agent 1 will know that agent 2 is unlikely ever to choose strategy E, since this represents their worst possible outcome. So, the best agent 1 can do is to choose the strategy that gives the best outcome, regardless of the choice of agent 2, resulting in the Nash equilibrium (provided agent 2 follows the same rationale).

Given that the games being considered are simultaneous move games, it might feel wrong to base decisions upon choices that have yet to be made. Nevertheless, the assumption that all players are rational means that players will always choose dominant strategies and will not choose dominated strategies.

A problem arises if there are no dominant or dominated strategies. Such an example is given in Figure 7.5.

		Agent 2		
		D	E	F
Agent 1	A	0.5	5	1
	B	5	2	2.5
	C	4.5	4	3

Figure 7.5 No dominant or dominated strategies.

A quick inspection of the table should reveal that there are no dominant or dominated strategies for either agent 1 or agent 2. This does not mean, however, that there is no Nash equilibrium. There is another approach to finding solutions to games with no dominant or dominated strategies that is closely related to the methods used to make decisions from payoff matrices.

Minimax Method

Zero-sum games represent situations of pure conflict: one player's gain is another player's loss, and so choosing the best outcome for themselves results in choosing the worst outcome for their opponent. Taking a pessimistic view, the best that players can do is to choose the strategy that results in the best of their worst payoffs. Recall from Chapter 5 that the criterion of pessimism leads to the maximin method (i.e. choose the strategy that will result in the maximum of the minimum payoffs). The maximin method can be used to determine the best strategy for the row player, since the column player will choose the strategy with the lowest payoff for the row player.

Consider the previous example. Agent 1 chooses strategy C because this will result in the best of the minimum payoffs (Figure 7.6). Given the rationality assumption, agent 1 deduces that agent 2 will choose the strategy resulting in the best payoff for agent 2 and hence in the worst payoff for agent 1.

		Agent 2			Minimum
		D	E	F	
Agent 1	A	0.5	5	1	0.5
	B	5	2	2.5	2
	C	4.5	4	3	3

Figure 7.6 Maximin method.

The same process cannot be used for agent 2 without creating a new table detailing the payoffs of agent 2. It is not necessary, however, to resort to this approach. Agent 2 assumes that agent 1 will choose the strategy that results in the highest payoff for agent 1. The best choice that agent 2 can make is to choose the strategy that results in the minimum of Agent 1's maximum payoffs (Figure 7.7). This is simply the minimax method. Agent 2's best choice is therefore strategy F, resulting in a Nash equilibrium of the choice of C for agent 1 and F for agent 2.

This two-stage process is generally known as the minimax method, which is related to, but should not be confused with, the single-stage process used with simple payoff matrices. If players do not have dominated or dominant strategies, then the minimax method is the best approach to finding Nash equilibria if they exist.

		Agent 2		
		D	E	F
Agent 1	A	0.5	5	1
	B	5	2	2.5
	C	4.5	4	3
Maximum		5	5	3

Figure 7.7   Minimax method.

Non-zero-sum Games

The games considered so far have been situations of pure conflict where one player's loss is another player's gain. Competitive situations are not limited to pure conflict, as there may be cases where all players make gains or losses. These games are represented in a slightly different format (see Figure 7.8).

		Agent 2		
		D	E	F
Agent 1	A	0, 1	5, 4	1, 3
	B	2, 5	3, 2	5, 2
	C	4, 2	4, 3	3, 3

Figure 7.8   Non-zero-sum game.

In each cell of this payoff table, the row player's payoff is presented first, followed by the column player's payoff. For example, if agent 1 chooses strategy B and agent 2 chooses strategy E, agent 1 receives 3 and agent 2 receives 2.

The methods used to solve zero-sum games can be used to find solutions of non-zero-sum games, with the exception of the minimax method (since this approach only works because one player receives the negative of the payoff of the other player). The easiest approach is to look for dominant strategies or dominated strategies (Figure 7.9a).

Examining the payoffs (Figure 7.9b) yields a dominated strategy for agent 1 (strategy C) and a dominant strategy for agent 2 (strategy D).

		Agent 2		
		D	**E**	**F**
Agent 1	**A**	3, 2	3, 1	2.5, 1
	B	4, 5	4.5, 1.5	2, 3
	C	2, 4	2, 0.5	1.5, 3.5

Figure 7.9a Non-zero-sum – dominant and dominated strategies.

		Agent 2		
		D	**E**	**F**
Agent 1	**A**	3, 2	3, 1	2.5, 1
	B	4, 5	4.5, 1.5	2, 3
	C	2, 4	2, 0.5	1.5, 3.5

Figure 7.9b Non-zero-sum – dominant and dominated strategies.

It is easy to see the Nash equilibrium: agent 1 chooses strategy B and agent 2 chooses strategy D. Nevertheless, as with zero-sum games, not all non-zero-sum games have dominant or dominated strategies. It is necessary to use alternative approaches when solving games of this type.

Best Response Analysis

When it is not possible to identify dominant strategies or dominated strategies in non-zero-sum games, best response provides a suitable approach for finding Nash equilibrium solutions of the game. Consider the example in Figure 7.10a.

		Agent 2		
		D	**E**	**F**
Agent 1	**A**	0.5, 2	2, 3	2, −2
	B	1, 3	5, 2	1.5, 5
	C	2, 4	4, 2.5	1, 3

Figure 7.10a Best response example.

An examination of the payoff table indicates that neither player has a dominant or dominated strategy. Best response analysis is a step-by-step technique that, as the name suggests, involves finding the best response of each player with regard to the strategy of the other player.

Looking at the game from the point of view of agent 1 (Figure 7.10b), if agent 2 chooses strategy D, then agent 1's best response is strategy C. Similarly, if agent 2 chooses strategy E, then agent 1's best response is strategy B, and if agent 2 chooses F, then agent 1 should choose strategy B.

		Agent 2		
		D	E	F
Agent 1	A	0.5, 2	2, 3	2, −2
	B	1, 3	5, 2	1.5, 5
	C	2, 4	4, 2.5	1, 3

Figure 7.10b Best response example.

The next stage is to consider the game from the point of view of agent 2 (Figure 7.10c). If agent 1 chooses strategy A, then agent 2 should choose strategy E. Likewise, if agent 1 chooses B, then agent 2 should choose F, and if agent 1 chooses C, then agent 2 should choose D.

		Agent 2		
		D	E	F
Agent 1	A	0.5, 2	2, 3	2, −2
	B	1, 3	5, 2	1.5, 5
	C	2, 4	4, 2.5	1, 3

Figure 7.10c Best response example.

So, it is clear that the Nash equilibrium is the choice of strategy C for agent 1 and strategy D for agent 2. Provided a Nash equilibrium of pure strategies exists, best response analysis is guaranteed to find it.

Multiple Nash Equilibria

In some circumstances a game will contain multiple Nash equilibria. Best response analysis will find these equilibria, but it will not determine which of these equilibria represents the most likely solution. In these circumstances, finding and eliminating weakly dominated strategies often reduces the number of equilibria.

For a weakly dominated strategy, i,

$$p_{ij} \leq p_{kj} \quad \forall\, k \in m,\ j \in n,\ i \neq k$$

In other words, a player using this strategy will get a payoff that is either the same as or worse than the payoff the player could receive by choosing another strategy. This differs from the dominated strategy, which always performs worse than the other strategies the player could choose.

It is very often the case that multiple Nash equilibria exist because one or more of the players has a weakly dominated strategy (see the example in Figure 7.11).

		Agent 2		
		D	**E**	**F**
Agent 1	**A**	0.5, 2.5	0.5, 3	2, 2
	B	2, 4	1.5, 5	2, 4
	C	1, 2.5	1, 3	2, 3

Figure 7.11 Weakly dominated strategies.

For agent 1, strategy A is a weakly dominated strategy. If agent 2 chooses strategy D or E, then strategy A is a worse choice than B or C. If agent 2 chooses F, then strategy A results in the same payoff for agent 1 as strategy B or C. Although agent 2 has a dominated strategy (strategy D), an examination of the payoff table shows that strategy F is weakly dominated (Figure 7.12).

Using best response analysis on this game results in two Nash equilibria: (B, E) and (C, F).

		Agent 2		
		D	**E**	**F**
Agent 1	**A**	0.5, 2.5	0.5, <u>3</u>	<u>2</u>, 2
	B	<u>2</u>, 4	<u>1.5</u>, <u>5</u>	<u>2</u>, 4
	C	1, 2.5	1, <u>3</u>	<u>2</u>, <u>3</u>

Figure 7.12 Multiple Nash equilibria – best response analysis.

It is not clear which of the two equilibria is most likely to be reached from simple analysis of the payoffs. Eliminating dominated and weakly dominated strategies, however, results in a single Nash equilibrium (see Figure 7.13).

		Agent 2		
		D	**E**	**F**
Agent 1	**A**	0.5, 2.5	0.5, 3	2, 2
	B	2, 4	1.5, 5	2, 4
	C	1, 2.5	1, 3	2, 3

Figure 7.13 Elimination of dominated and weakly dominated strategies.

In some cases, even iterated elimination of dominated or weakly dominated will not result in a single Nash equilibrium (Dixit & Skeath, 1999). Very often, players may communicate when it is in their interests to reach a particular equilibrium. For example, although cartels are illegal in many countries, competing companies may communicate in order to fix prices.

Where players wish to reach different equilibria, knowledge and reputation can play an important role where players may already have some idea about how their opponents may react. These elements can be incorporated into games, although they are very often formulated as sequential decisions, as prior decisions affect the choices in the game and will be discussed in Chapter 10.

Non-existence of Nash Equilibrium

The examples presented so far have all had at least one Nash equilibrium solution. There are, however, examples where there are no Nash equilibria. Figure 7.14 shows a game where the players only have a choice between two strategies. Best response analysis demonstrates that there are no Nash equilibria.

		Agent 2	
		C	**D**
Agent 1	**A**	1, 3	4, 2
	B	2, 1	3, 2

Figure 7.14 No Nash equilibria.

In cases such as this, the choice made by the players is very much dependent upon their expectation of the other player's choice. This can be represented formally in terms of probabilities.

Considering the previous example, probabilities can be attached to each strategy, describing the likelihood of the player choosing each strategy (see Figure 7.15).

			Agent 2	
			q	$1-q$
			C	D
Agent 1	p	A	1, 3	4, 2
	$1-p$	B	2, 1	3, 2

Figure 7.15 Assigning probabilities.

In these circumstances, p describes the probability that agent 1 chooses strategy A and q describes the probability that agent 2 chooses strategy C. The probabilities for strategies B and D follow from this.

Since the strategy of the players is dependent upon their expectation of the choice of the other player, the probabilities can be used to determine the expected payoff resulting from the choice of each strategy. If strategy A is chosen, agent 1 will receive a payoff of 1 if agent 2 chooses C (with probability q) and a payoff of 4 if D is chosen (with probability $1 - q$). Consequently, agent 1 would expect to receive a payoff of $q + 4(1 - q)$ on average. Applying a similar approach to strategy B results in an expected payoff of $2q + 3(1 - q)$. Agent 1 should choose strategy A if the payoff from choosing A is greater than the payoff from choosing B or

$$q + 4(1 - q) > 2q + 3(1 - q)$$

Rearranging this equation leaves $q < 1/2$. Hence, if the likelihood of agent 2 choosing strategy C is less than a half, agent 1 should choose strategy A. Similarly, if the likelihood of agent 2 choosing C is greater than a half, agent 1 receives a higher payoff by choosing strategy B. If the probability of agent 2 choosing C is exactly a half, then, on average, either strategy will produce the same outcome for agent 1. This is summarised in Figure 7.16. A similar analysis can be performed for agent 2, resulting in the strategy choices shown in Figure 7.17.

Both players are indifferent between their strategies when $p = 0.5$ and $q = 0.5$. This is known as the *mixed strategy equilibrium*: the equilibrium is a mix of the

q	Agent 1's strategy
< 0.5	A
> 0.5	B
= 0.5	A or B

Figure 7.16 Agent 1's strategy mix.

p	Agent 2's strategy
> 0.5	C
< 0.5	D
= 0.5	C or D

Figure 7.17 Agent 2's strategy mix.

available strategies. This can be confirmed by looking at these strategy choices in graphical form when *best response curves* can be drawn.

In order to draw the best response curves, it is helpful to augment the two tables above by adding an extra column. These extra columns indicate the values of the probabilities of strategy choice for each player, given the probabilities of the strategy choice of the other player (Figure 7.18).

Agent 1's Strategies				Agent 2's Strategies		
q	Agent 1's strategy	p		p	Agent 2's strategy	q
< 0.5	A	1		> 0.5	C	1
> 0.5	B	0		< 0.5	D	0
= 0.5	A or B	0.5		= 0.5	C or D	0.5

Figure 7.18 Player's mixed strategies.

The best response curves can be plotted from these tables (Figure 7.19). The lines representing the choices for the two players meet at the point where $p = 0.5$ and $q = 0.5$. At this point, neither player can achieve a better payoff by choosing a different strategy.

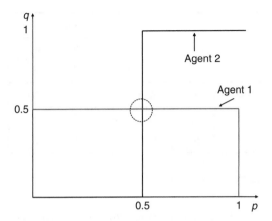

Figure 7.19 Best response curves.

The way in which the players interpret the equilibria depends upon whether the game is a one-off decision or whether it will be repeated. If the game is repeated, the probabilities indicate to the players the proportion of the time that each player should choose each strategy. In this example, each player should choose to play each of their two strategies 50 % of the time. It does not, however, suggest that they should choose to alternate between each strategy. In order to achieve the best outcome, they should randomise between the two strategies but overall should choose each strategy 50 % of the time.

For one-off decisions, the full mixed strategy solution is used. For this particular example, the solution suggests that, if the likelihood that agent 2 will choose strategy C is less than 0.5 (i.e. $q < 0.5$), then agent 1 should choose strategy A. Similarly, if agent 2 believes that the likelihood that agent 1 will choose strategy A is less than 0.5, then agent 2 should choose strategy D.

In one-off games, knowledge will play a key role in mixed strategy equilibria. Knowledge of previous behaviour or reputations may be used to generate these probabilities. In reality, probabilities are very likely to be estimated, and so mixed strategy equilibria are problematic, although there is some experimental evidence that supports the use of mixed strategies in repeated games (Dixit & Skeath, 1999).

Mixed Strategies for Players with Three or More Strategies

If the players have three or more possible strategies in a zero-sum game, the easiest way to find a solution is to formulate the problem in terms of a linear programme.

			Agent 2		
			q_1	q_2	q_3
			D	E	F
Agent 1	p_1	A	2	3	5
	p_2	B	2	3	1
	p_3	C	3	2	2

Figure 7.20   Two-player three-strategy game.

Consider the example illustrated in Figure 7.20. A swift analysis using the minimax approach indicates the non-existence of a Nash equilibrium.

Finding the mixed strategy solution requires a slightly different approach to that used for the 2×2 game. In this case, the expected value of the game for agent 1 is calculated by assuming that agent 2 chooses a single strategy. So, if agent 2 chooses strategy D, agent 1's expected payoff is given by

$$2p_1 + 2p_2 + 3p_3 \tag{7.1}$$

Similarly, if agent 2 chooses E, agent 1's expected payoff is given by

$$3p_1 + 3p_2 + 2p_3 \tag{7.2}$$

Finally, if agent 2 chooses F, agent 1's expected payoff is given by

$$5p_1 + p_2 + 2p_3 \tag{7.3}$$

It is necessary to define a characteristic of zero-sum games known as the *value of the game*. This is the minimum expected payoff that agent 1 would receive if the optimal mix of strategies were chosen regardless of the choice made by agent 2. If the value of the game is denoted by V, then

$$2p_1 + 2p_2 + 3p_3 \geq V \tag{7.4}$$

$$3p_1 + 3p_2 + 2p_3 \geq V \tag{7.5}$$

$$5p_1 + p_2 + 2p_3 \geq V \tag{7.6}$$

The objective of agent 1 is to maximise the expected payoff, and therefore linear programming seems a natural choice for solving this type of problem. It is not possible, however, simply to choose to maximise V, since there are three equations involving V, which would suggest three objective functions. Further manipulation of equations (7.4), (7.5), and (7.6) is therefore required before the linear programme is formulated. Nonetheless, these equations form the basis for the constraints of the linear programming.

The next step requires the definition of new variables x_1, x_2, and x_3, where

$$x_1 = \frac{p_1}{V}, \quad x_2 = \frac{p_2}{V}, \quad x_3 = \frac{p_3}{V}$$

These variables are now used in the programme in place of V on its own.

Dividing through equations (7.4), (7.5), and (7.6) by V, assuming that V is positive, leads to the following:

$$\frac{2p_1}{V} + \frac{2p_2}{V} + \frac{3p_3}{V} \geq 1$$

$$\frac{3p_1}{V} + \frac{3p_2}{V} + \frac{2p_3}{V} \geq 1$$

$$\frac{5p_1}{V} + \frac{p_2}{V} + \frac{2p_3}{V} \geq 1$$

and hence

$$2x_1 + 2x_2 + 3x_3 \geq 1 \qquad (7.7)$$

$$3x_1 + 3x_2 + 2x_3 \geq 1 \qquad (7.8)$$

$$5x_1 + x_2 + 2x_3 \geq 1 \qquad (7.9)$$

These now form a part of the set of constraints for the linear programme. Since V is assumed to be positive in order to divide through the expected payoff equations by V, and since p_1, p_2, and p_3 are probabilities and must therefore be greater than or equal to zero, the final constraint is given by

$$x_1, x_2, x_3 \geq 0 \qquad (7.10)$$

The final step involves defining an objective function. Given that

$$p_1 + p_2 + p_3 = 1$$

and V is positive, it follows that

$$\frac{p_1}{V} + \frac{p_2}{V} + \frac{p_3}{V} = \frac{1}{V}$$

Hence

$$x_1 + x_2 + x_3 = \frac{1}{V}$$

The aim is to maximise the value of the game and therefore to minimise $1/V$. Consequently, the objective of the linear programme is to minimise $x_1 + x_2 + x_3$. The linear programme can now be written in full as follows:

Minimise: $x_1 + x_2 + x_3$
Subject to:
$2x_1 + 2x_2 + 3x_3 \geq 1$
$3x_1 + 2x_2 + 2x_3 \geq 1$
$5x_1 + x_2 + 2x_3 \geq 1$
$x_1, x_2, x_3 \geq 0$

Using Excel Solver to find a solution results in the following values:

$$x_1 = 0.2$$

$$x_2 = 0$$

$$x_3 = 0.2$$

Assuming that $x_1 + x_2 + x_3 = 1/V$, then $1/V = 0.4$, and hence $V = 2.5$. Since $x_1 = p_1/V$, it follows that $p_1 = 0.2 \times 2.5 = 0.5$ and so $p_3 = 0.5$ $(p_2 = 0)$. Consequently, agent 1 should choose strategy A for half of the time and strategy C for half of the time, and should never choose strategy B.

The approach taken to find agent 2's optimal mix is similar, although the payoffs correspond to agent 2's strategies and are therefore read across the rows. Since this is a zero-sum game, the sum of the product of the payoffs and the probabilities has to be less than or equal to the value of the game. Hence

$$2q_1 + 3q_2 + 5q_3 \leq V$$

$$2q_1 + 3q_2 + q_3 \leq V$$

$$3q_1 + 2q_2 + 2q_3 \leq V$$

Following the same process as that used for agent 1, the constraint set is given by

$$2y_1 + 3y_2 + 5y_3 \leq 1$$

$$2y_1 + 3y_2 + y_3 \leq 1$$

$$3y_1 + 2y_2 + 2y_3 \leq 1$$

$$y_1, y_2, y_3 \geq 0$$

where

$$y_i = \frac{q_i}{V}, \quad i = 1, 2, 3$$

The objective function is given by $y_1 + y_2 + y_3$, but in this case it should be maximised because agent 2 will want to minimise V. Consequently, the linear programme is as follows:

Maximise: $y_1 + y_2 + y_3$
Subject to:
$2y_1 + 3y_2 + 5y_3 \leq 1$
$2y_1 + 3y_2 + y_3 \leq 1$
$3y_1 + 2y_2 + 2y_3 \leq 1$
$y_1, y_2, y_3 \leq 0$

Using Excel Solver to find the solution results in the following values:

$$q_1 = 0.5$$

$$q_2 = 0.5$$

$$q_3 = 0$$

Hence, agent 2 should choose strategy D half of the time and strategy E half of the time, and should never choose strategy F.

These probabilities cannot be used in single-round games, as was possible in the previous example where the players had two strategies. This is because the previous example is calculated in a different way: namely that the strategy choice of the player is dependent upon the probabilities of the other player's choices. Games where the players have just two choices can also be solved using linear programming, but in these circumstances it may prove more helpful to use the dual interpretation approach of the previous method.

There is a caveat that must be borne in mind when using linear programming to find mixed strategy solutions. Consider the payoff table in Figure 7.21.

			Agent 2		
			q_1	q_2	q_3
			D	E	F
Agent 1	p_1	A	−2	3	5
	p_2	B	−1	4	1
	p_3	C	−3	1	2

Figure 7.21 A game with a negative value of the game.

The formulation of the linear programme assumed throughout that the value of the game was positive. In this case, the value of the game must be negative because agent 1's payoffs are all negative if agent 2 chooses D. This will then change the sign of the constraints (from greater than or equal to V to less than or equal to V) and will invalidate the constraint that $x_1, x_2, x_3 \geq 0$ (remembering that $x_i = p_i/V$, $i = 1, 2, 3$). Consequently, Excel Solver will not be able to find a solution. The choice is now either to reformulate the linear programme or, more simply, to add a constant to all the payoffs in the game to ensure that the payoffs are all greater than or equal to zero. Adding a constant does not change the overall structure of the game and therefore does not change the overall solution of the game.

In the example shown above, the minimum amount that can be added to make all payoffs non-negative is 3, resulting in the payoff table in Figure 7.22.

			Agent 2		
			q_1	q_2	q_3
			D	E	F
Agent 1	p_1	**A**	1	6	8
	p_2	**B**	2	7	4
	p_3	**C**	0	4	5

Figure 7.22   Adjusted payoff table.

This can then be formulated and solved using Excel Solver as described previously, resulting in the probabilities

$$p_1 = 0$$
$$p_2 = 1$$
$$p_3 = 0$$

Hence, strategy B is a dominant strategy for agent 1.

Continuous Strategies

The strategies considered so far have been discrete: even in the mixed strategy examples, the strategies are discrete even if they are employed in a mix specified by the solution. There are, however, situations in which the strategies are continuous, for example in price-setting situations where the payoff can take any positive value.

Consider two firms, X and Y, manufacturing goods that are close substitutes. Both companies want to choose a price for their product that maximises their revenue. A market research company has estimated that total market demand is equal to 500 units. Company X has determined that demand for their product is linearly related to the prices of their product and their rival's product in the following way:

$$Q_x = 500 - p_x + p_y$$

where Q_x is the quantity demanded of the good produced by X, p_x is the price of that good, and p_y is the price of the good produced by Company Y. Similarly, demand for the good produced by Company Y is represented by

$$Q_y = 500 - p_y + p_x$$

Revenue for each company is simply the price of the good multiplied by the demand for the good. Hence, the revenue for Company X is

$$R_x = p_x Q_x = p_x \left(500 - p_x + p_y\right) = 500 p_x - p_x^2 + p_x p_y$$

and the revenue for Company Y is

$$R_y = p_y Q_y = p_y \left(500 - p_y + p_x\right) = 500 p_y - p_y^2 + p_y p_x$$

Since the revenue functions are not linear, it is necessary to differentiate the functions in order to find the point where the functions are maximised. Since the functions depend upon both prices, it is necessary to use partial differentiation. Hence

$$\frac{\partial R_x}{\partial p_x} = 500 - 2p_x + p_y \tag{7.11}$$

and

$$\frac{\partial R_y}{\partial p_y} = 500 - 2p_y + p_x \tag{7.12}$$

In order to find the maximum revenue, these functions are set to zero. This results in two equations that relate p_x and p_y. These can then be solved simultaneously to determine the point where the maximum revenue for both companies is reached.

Setting equation (7.11) equal to zero and rearranging to give p_y in terms of p_x gives

$$p_y = 2p_x - 500 \tag{7.13}$$

Setting equation (7.12) equal to zero and then substituting (7.13) into the result gives

$$0 = 500 - 2(2p_x - 500) + p_x$$

and hence $p_x = 500$. Substituting this value into equation (7.13) gives $p_y = 500$. Consequently, if each company charges £500 per unit, then neither company can do any better by charging a different price (see Figure 7.23).

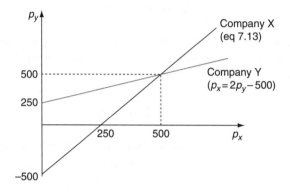

Figure 7.23 Equilibrium for continuous strategies.

With continuous strategies, the important step is to incorporate the influence of the rival company into the function describing the strategies. In this case, the revenue function depended on both the price of the company's own product and the price of their rival's product. It was then a matter of finding the point at which the revenue was at a maximum in terms of the price of the company's own product, solving the resulting equations simultaneously to find the actual prices at which revenue was maximised.

N-Player Games

Although the discussion of games in this chapter has been limited to two players, games can be formulated with multiple players, the details of which depend upon the situation. In cases where multiple players are involved but are essentially acting as a group, such as in the case of trade unions, the group can be treated in the same way as a single player since the individuals are essentially acting as a single entity. These are often referred to as collective action games and will be left as an investigation for the interested reader.

In the case where multiple players are operating as individuals, the resulting games cannot be represented or solved in the same way as those games discussed here. There are many different ways of solving N-player games, but all require the use of more advanced mathematical techniques and computing algorithms beyond the scope of this text. For a survey, see McKelvey and McLennan (1996).

Summary

This chapter has introduced the main concepts of game theory, including the assumption that all players are rational and hence prefer strategies that result in higher outcomes and will choose their strategy accordingly.

In order to find the optimal strategy choices in two-player games, the concepts of dominant and dominated strategies were introduced. A dominant strategy is one for which the player can do no better by choosing another strategy, regardless of the choice of the other player. A dominated strategy is one for which the player can always do better by choosing another strategy, regardless of the choice made by the other player. If both players have dominant strategies, then this set of strategies determines the Nash equilibrium, which is the choice of strategies for which neither player can do better by choosing an alternative strategy. If players have no dominated strategies, a Nash equilibrium may still be found by removing the dominated strategies of both players until a dominant strategy emerges.

If players have neither dominant nor dominated strategies, then other solution methods must be employed. In zero-sum games, the minimax method can be used to find a solution. This results in one player choosing the strategy resulting in the best of the worst payoffs for this player, while the second player chooses the strategy resulting in the minimum of the other player's maximum payoffs. For non-zero-sum games, best response analysis can be used. This involves players determining their best strategy choice for each possible choice of the other player.

Multiple Nash equilibria can be encountered in games and usually arise because one or more of the players has a weakly dominated strategy. This is a strategy for which the payoff is either equal to or worse than the payoff for every other strategy, regardless of the choice of the other player. In many cases of multiple equilibria, a single equilibrium can be reached by elimination of dominated or weakly dominated strategies.

In cases where no Nash equilibrium exists, a solution can be found by incorporating a variable relating to the likelihood of the behaviour of the other player. This is known as a mixed response strategy and gives a player's strategy choice in terms of a variable representing the probabilities associated with the strategy choice of the other player. In games where the players each have three possible strategies, linear programming can be used to reach a mixed strategy solution.

Although the majority of the chapter is devoted to the solution of games with discrete strategies, it is possible to find solutions to games where the players can choose from a continuum of strategies. The most common application of this type of game is in a price-setting scenario. The solution of such games requires that the payoffs of the players are linked both to their strategy and to the strategy of the other player: in the example provided in the text, this meant that the revenue of one player was linked to the price of this player's own product and the price of the rival's product. This meant that the point of maximum payoff for each player was found in terms of the strategy choice of both players, in this case the prices of both products.

Further Reading

- Alternative presentations of the material introduced in this chapter can be found in the following texts:

  Carmichael, F. (2004) *A Guide to Game Theory*. Prentice Hall, Harlow, UK.

  Hillier, FS. & Lieberman, GJ. (2006) *Introduction to Operations Research*. McGraw-Hill, New York, NY, Chapter 14.

  Render, B., Stair, RM., & Hanna, ME. (2005) *Quantitative Analysis for Management*. Prentice Hall, Upper Saddle River, NJ, Chapter 21.

  Straffin, PD. (1996) *Game Theory and Strategy (New Mathematical Library)*. The Mathematical Association of America, Washington, DC.

  Waters, CDJ. (1989) *A Practical Introduction to Management Science*. Prentice Hall, Harlow, UK.

- The following text is less technical but includes many 'real-world' applications of game theory:

  Dixit, AK. & Nalebuff, BJ. (1993) *Thinking Strategically: The Competitive Edge in Business, Politics and Everyday Life*. Norton, New York, NY.

  Dixit, AK. & Nalebuff, BJ. (2008) *The Art of Strategy: A Game Theorist's Guide to Success in Business and Life*. Norton, New York, NY.

  Axelrod, R. (1990) *The Evolution of Cooperation*. Penguin, London, UK.

- The following texts are classic game theory texts and present the theory in its original mathematical formulation:

  Nash, JF. (1951) Non-cooperative games. *Annals of Mathematics* **54**(2), 286–295.

  Maynard Smith, J. (1982) *Evolution and the Theory of Games*. Cambridge University Press, Cambridge, UK.

  von Neumann, J. & Morgenstern, O. (2007) *Theory of Games and Economic Behavior (Princeton Classic Editions)*. Princeton University Press, Princeton, NJ.

- The following references discuss and present arguments both for and against the use of game theory for real business issues:

  Bradenburger, AM. & Nalebuff, BJ. (1995) The right game: using game theory to shape strategy. *Harvard Business Review* **73**(4), 57–71.

Camerer, C.F. (1991) Does strategy research need game theory. *Strategic Management Journal* **12**, 137–152.

Kihn, M. (2005) You got game theory. *Fastcompany* **91**(32).

Economist (1998) Movers and shakers. *Economist* **346**(8052), 63.

Postrel, S. (1991) Burning your britches behind you: can policy scholars bank on game theory?, *Strategic Management Journal* **12**, 153–155.

Questions

Q7.1 Consider the following game, known as the prisoner's dilemma game (this is a non-cooperative game, and so players choose their strategies independently):

		Player B	
		Cooperate	Not cooperate
Player A	Cooperate	5, 5	−1, 7
	Not cooperate	7, −1	0, 0

Looking at the payoffs, what do you think would be the best strategy choice for both players? Explain in words why you think this is the case.

(a) Find the Nash equilibrium of the game.

(b) Does the Nash equilibrium coincide with your reasoning in part (a)?

   (i) If it did coincide with your answer to part (a), explain in terms of the characteristics of non-cooperative games why (cooperate, cooperate) is never chosen, given that it results in a higher payoff for both players than the Nash equilibrium.

   (ii) If it did not coincide with your answer, determine and explain the error in your reasoning that led you to choose a different answer. Hint: think about the characteristics of non-cooperative games.

Q7.2 Consider again the prisoner's dilemma game in question **Q7.1**. Imagine that the players are playing the game twice. The payoffs remain the same for both rounds.

(a) Will repeating the game change the strategy choices of either player? Hint: reason backwards – what will the strategy choices be for the players in round 2? Will this give them any reason to change their choice in the first round?

(b) If the game is repeated 3 times, will this change the strategy choices of the players? Reason backwards, starting at round 3.

(c) If the game is repeated N times, provided the players know how many rounds of the game will be played, will their strategy choices change? Explain in words why this is the case.

(d) If the players do not know how many times the game will be repeated, i.e. if they do not know the endpoint of the game, can backwards reasoning still be applied to determine what strategy choices the players should make?

Q7.3 Consider the following game:

		Agent 2		
		D	**E**	**F**
Agent 1	**A**	2, 8	15, 15	−16, −3
	B	8, 1	8, 0	−12, 3
	C	10, −1	−10, 17	−1, 10

(a) Find the Nash equilibrium.

Consider the following game:

		Agent 2		
		D	**E**	**F**
Agent 1	**A**	5, 6.5	5, 7.5	6.5, 6.5
	B	6.5, 8.5	6, 9.5	6.5, 8.5
	C	7, 7	5, 7.5	7, 7.5

(b) Find the Nash equilibrium.

Q7.4 Consider the following game:

		Agent 2	
		C	D
Agent 1	A	−1, 2	1, −3
	B	1, −1	−1, 5

(a) Does a Nash equilibrium exist?
(b) Determine the equilibrium.
(c) Draw the best response diagrams to show the equilibrium point.
(d) Explain the strategy choices of each player.

Q7.5 Consider the following game:

		Agent 2		
		D	E	F
Agent 1	A	7	3	7
	B	3	7	4
	C	7	1	1

(a) Does this game have any Nash equilibrium?
(b) Find the equilibrium.
(c) Explain the strategy choices of each player.

Q7.6 Two competing supermarket chains, X and Y, have petrol stations at each of their outlets and are currently choosing their fuel price strategy for the next month. They must decide whether to charge a 'high' price or a 'low' price. Company X has estimated the payoffs that each company will receive, and these are given in the table below in £ million.

		Company Y	
		High	**Low**
Company X	**High**	1.5, 1.5	0.25, 2
	Low	2, 0.25	0.75, 0.75

(a) What strategy should Company X choose, given the information it has about the payoffs of Company Y?

(b) Why shouldn't Company X choose the other strategy?

(c) You are part of the executive team working for Company X and you have heard that Company Y is planning to raise its fuel prices. Should this information change the choice of Company X?

Activities

A7.1 The prisoner's dilemma game in question **Q7.1** is a classic game theory example. Research and write a brief history of the prisoner's dilemma and investigate the academic fields in which it has been applied in addition to 'real-life' examples.

A7.2 Consider again two players who are playing the repeated prisoner's dilemma game in question **Q7.2**. Research the use of 'trigger strategies' in repeated prisoner's dilemma games. Find out what trigger strategies are, how they are used, and why they are used.

A7.3 From the Further Reading section, read Chapter 9 'Cooperation and Coordination' of *Thinking Strategically* (Dixit & Nalebuff, 1993). Consider how in situations of collective action, where the problem is one of coordinating group actions, the optimal outcome can be achieved. Find out how norms, conventions (customs), sanctions, and pricing can be used to coordinate the group, and identify the ways in which these were used in the examples in *Thinking Strategically* (Dixit & Nalebuff, 1993).

A7.4 The prisoner's dilemma is often used in economics to analyse collusive agreements in oligopoly markets. Investigate the petroleum cartel OPEC and use your knowledge of the strategy choices of players in prisoner's dilemma type games to explain the choices made by the cartel members. Thinking about what you discovered in activity **A7.2** about trigger strategies, explain how OPEC members could encourage cooperation.

PART 3

Sequential Decisions

CHAPTER 8

Robustness Analysis

Objectives

- *To be able to identify situations in which the robustness analysis framework can be applied.*
- *To appreciate the concepts of exact and superfluous attainability.*
- *To appreciate the concept of a robustness score.*

Introduction

Fred had been ill for a number of days but awoke at eight o'clock on Saturday morning feeling improved. Having been restricted to the house for some time, he decided he needed to escape for some fresh air, but did not wish to drive for much over 3 hours and certainly less than 4. This would then allow him to enjoy the full afternoon. From his house, Fred could manage to reach some moorland within that time and then go walking. Alternatively, he could reach a beach and simply sit, read, and relax. Both of these options seemed satisfactory to Fred. Although Fred's health was improving, he was not sure how well he would be, and so was not sure whether to head for the beach to recuperate further or to head for the moors for some exercise. Nevertheless, Fred needed to set off in order to spend the afternoon outside. Checking his road atlas (Figure 8.1), Fred was able to see that, if he were to follow street 1, he would reach the moorland in about 3 hours. Similarly, if he were to follow street 2, he would reach the beach in about 3 hours. He also noticed that, if he were to follow street 3, he could reach either destination in 3¼ hours, but would not need to decide which for 2 hours after setting off, by which time he would have a good idea of how well he was feeling. By initially committing to take street 3, Fred's drive would take a little longer, but he would maintain the flexibility to choose his final destination until he knew his state of health better.

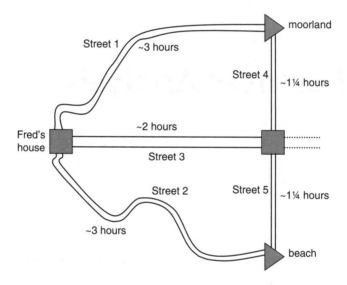

Figure 8.1 Road map of Fred's location with respect to the beach and the moors.

Decisions such as Fred's are made often and seem simple, but it is worth explicitly highlighting some elements of Fred's decision. At the beginning of the morning, Fred was in his house and had a clear planning horizon, that is, to the end of the afternoon of the same day. Of course there was a decision to be made, whether he would be on the beach or on the moorland when the planning horizon was reached. There was also uncertainty in that Fred was at first unaware of how he would later value either of the end states. Nevertheless, both seemed initially satisficing[1]. Fred would spend a period of time making an initial decision and then spend time implementing that decision. It was also possible for the decision to be treated sequentially, the first period

---

[1] To choose a satisficing outcome is to choose an outcome that is 'good enough' rather than optimal.

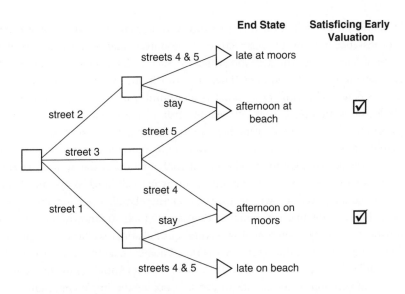

	End State	**Satisficing Early Valuation**
streets 4 & 5	late at moors	
street 2 — stay	afternoon at beach	☑
street 5		
street 3		
street 4	afternoon on moors	☑
street 1 — stay		
streets 4 & 5	late on beach	

Figure 8.2   Fred's initial decision and early valuation of end states.

of implementation being followed by a second decision period, and, in turn, a second implementation period, whether to take street 4 or street 5 (Figure 8.2). Finally, Fred was able to make his decision not by defining one specific objective that attached a valuation to each end state, this he was unable to do beyond his early valuation, but rather by taking an initial decision based on flexibility. Although Fred's choice would overall require a greater resource commitment, 3¼ hours driving rather than 3, the initial commitment to street 3 would keep more (initially satisficing) options open for when Fred's uncertainty had reduced. In this example, the uncertainty originated from the decision-taker's values; equally, uncertainty could have come from future states, in Fred's case a change in weather conditions.

Robustness Analysis

Robustness analysis (RA) was introduced and developed by Rosenhead and colleagues (Gupta & Rosenhead, 1968; Rosenhead, Elton, & Gupta, 1972; Wong & Rosenhead, 2000; Rosenhead, 2001a). Rather than having the concept of optimisation at its foundation, RA has the concept of *robustness*. Some decisions, particularly strategic decisions, have to be made while uncertainty is difficult to characterise clearly, for example objectives and/or probability distributions cannot be clearly specified. Robustness analysis responds to this by accepting such deep uncertainty and offering a framework that aims to keep useful options attainable.

Strategic decisions are applied to a system of interest in an *initial configuration*. The system could be as small as an individual or much larger, such as a supply chain configuration. Whatever the system, it can be characterised in some useful way, for instance in terms of its structure and resources, that is, it can be described in terms of relevance to the decision situation. Such a characterisation defines the initial configuration of the system. There is a timeframe over which the system is being considered. This timeframe consists of a number of *decision periods*, during which decisions are taken, each followed by an *implementation period*. The *planning horizon* falls after the final implementation period. At the planning horizon, the system could take many alternative future configurations that are different from the initial system configuration. The initial configuration of the system, at time zero, exists within its contextual environment, which, although non-controllable, may be reasonably well known. In contrast, at the planning horizon the system exists within a contextual environment that is potentially unknown, and in some circumstances may be represented by several quite distinct scenarios. Taking and implementing a decision during the first periods equates to an initial *set of commitments* that lead to the system being transformed from its initial configuration to an interim configuration. Later periods of decision-taking and implementation transform the interim configuration, moving it towards a future system configuration at the planning horizon (Figure 8.3).

In making commitments to change the initial configuration of the system, some future configurations at the planning horizon remain *attainable* while others become unattainable. More specifically, since it is the choice of the initial commitment set that is of concern, attainability specifies whether a future configuration is attainable from an initial commitment set. Wong and Rosenhead (2000) distinguish between *exact attainability* and *superfluous attainability*. Exact attainability specifies that a future configuration is attainable from an initial commitment set and each of the initial commitments is required by the future configuration. Superfluous attainability indicates that only a subset of the initial commitment set is required by the future configuration, that is, at least one unnecessary commitment has been made. For a given initial set of commitments, a future configuration may be unattainable, exactly attainable, or superfluously attainable.

A slightly short-timeframe but down-to-earth example (Figure 8.4) that clarifies the above concepts is that of a student undertaking a 3 year Bachelor's degree in the disciplinary area of business and management. Suppose the student attends a university or college at which the first year of study is compulsory and covers foundational courses in business, management, economics, and quantitative methods. The system under consideration is the student characterised by her knowledge of business and management, and her academic qualification therein. For the next 2 years the degree is modular, with the student being required to complete at least six but up to eight modules in each of these years. A first decision period exists during which the student becomes aware of the modules available for the second year of study and decides which to follow, subject to the constraints of, among others, the minimum

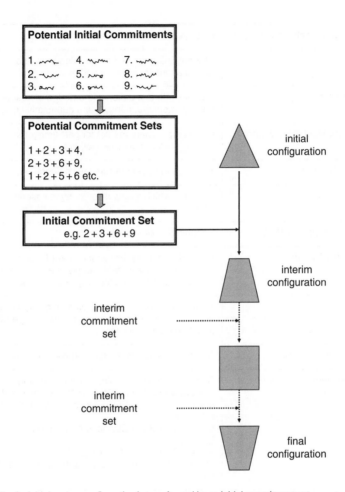

Figure 8.3 An initial system configuration is transformed by an initial commitment set.

and maximum number of modules. An individual module is a commitment, whereas six, seven, or eight modules is a commitment set. The second year of study is then an implementation period. This is followed by a further decision and implementation period before a final configuration is reached. The final configuration of the system, the student at the planning horizon, can be considered in terms of the title of the degree achieved, e.g. BA in Business Administration, BA in Marketing, and so on. In choosing the subject modules to study in the second year, the student ensures the attainability of some degree titles but closes off others. Further, some of the degree titles may be exactly attainable, in that all modules within the commitment set need to be followed to achieve a particular degree title, whereas others may be superfluously attainable.

Robustness Analysis Concept	First-year University Student Example
System	Student characterised by knowledge of and qualifications in business and management.
Initial System Configuration	Student with foundational knowledge of business, management, economics, and quantitative methods.
Initial Contextual Environment	Local employment market for part-time jobs; employers and competitor part-time workers.
Planning Horizon	To end of third year of Bachelor's degree studies.
First Decision Period	Period in which modules for study in second year are chosen.
First Implementation Period	Second year of studies.
Initial Commitments	Available modules for second year of studies, operations management, supply chain management, management accounting, language, and so on.
Constraints	Minimum of six modules, maximum of eight modules, and, for example, at least one module in operations and at least one in finance.
Initial Commitment Sets	Any combination of modules subject to the constraints.
Future System Configuration at Planning Horizon	Student with BA in Business Administration, student with BA in Business Administration with Arabic, student with BA in Business Administration with Mandarin, student with BA in Business Administration with Spanish, student with BA in Marketing, student with BA in Marketing with Statistics, and so on.
Future Contextual Environment	Health of national economy, performance of specific sectors.

Figure 8.4 Example of robustness analysis concepts.

Single Future Contextual Environment Robustness

Each future configuration of a system at the planning horizon has some envisaged level of performance. Here, robustness analysis has only a minimal requirement, to be able to identify whether a future configuration is or is not a *desirable configuration*, i.e. whether it achieves a satisficing level of performance. In some situations, more than such a categorical measure may be possible, and an ordinal or interval scale may be applied. In such cases, a threshold level for satisficing can be adjusted as a form of sensitivity analysis. Figure 8.5 illustrates a choice between commitment set *CS1* and commitment set *CS2*; following some subsequent decisions, any of the system's future configurations *d, e, f,* or *g* could be obtained. An evaluation, in which a higher number is considered preferable, has been carried out, leading to configuration *d* scoring 2, future configurations *f* and *g* scoring 1, and *e* scoring 0. Future configurations *d* and *e* are exactly attainable following *CS1, f* is superfluously attainable following *CS1,* while *f* and *g* are exactly attainable following *CS2.*

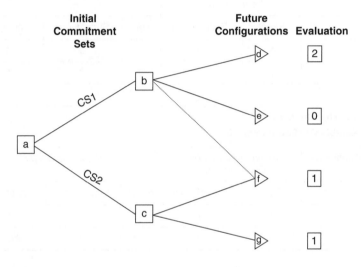

Figure 8.5   The evaluation and attainability of four future configurations from two initial commitment sets. A solid line indicates that the future configuration is exactly attainable; a dashed line indicates superfluous attainability.

Three forms of robustness score can be associated with each initial commitment set. The *exact robustness score* is the proportion of the total number of desirable configurations that are exactly attainable from a commitment set. The *superfluous robustness score* is the proportion of desirable configurations that are superfluously attainable, and the *aggregate robustness score* is the sum of the exact and superfluous scores.

Given a satisficing level of 1, there are three desirable future configurations, *d, f,* and *g.* For the initial commitment set *CS1,* of the three desirable configurations only *d* is exactly attainable, while *f* is superfluously attainable. *CS1* has exact robustness score 1/3, superfluous robustness score 1/3, and aggregate 2/3. A similar reasoning can be carried out both for commitment set *CS2* with a satisficing level of 1 and for both commitment sets with a higher satisficing level (Figure 8.6). In this example, *CS1* appears preferable to *CS2,* having a greater aggregate robustness score at the higher satisficing threshold, and an equivalent aggregate robustness at the lower satisficing threshold. In an actual decision-taking situation, this robustness advantage would be balanced against the feasibility of the next interim configuration.

Satisficing Threshold = 2
Total Desirable Configurations = 1

Commitment Set	Attainable Desirable Configurations		Robustness Scores		
	Exact	Superfluous	Exact	Superfluous	Aggregate
CS1	1	0	1	0	1
CS2	0	0	0	0	0

Satisficing Threshold = 1
Total Desirable Configurations = 3

Commitment Set	Attainable Desirable Configurations		Robustness Scores		
	Exact	Superfluous	Exact	Superfluous	Aggregate
CS1	1	1	1/3	1/3	2/3
CS2	2	0	2/3	0	2/3

Figure 8.6 Calculation of robustness scores for a simple example.

Multiple Futures Robustness

When RA is carried out with clearly delineated future contextual environments (contexts or scenarios), evaluations are assigned to each future system configuration, presuming each future context (Figure 8.7). Robustness scores can then be calculated in turn for each future. To avoid repetition, only aggregate robustness scores are calculated here.

Condensing Figure 8.7 to a table, the upper row of Figure 8.8 lists possible future system configurations, the next three rows indicate the evaluation of each configuration in the alternative futures, and the final four rows record the attainability of a system configuration from a commitment set as a (1, 0) matrix, reminiscent of an incident matrix in graph theory. For example, reading down the second column of the table, configuration b is evaluated at 2 in context 1, at 0 in context 2, and at 1 in context 3. Configuration b is accessible from $CS1$ and $CS2$ but not from

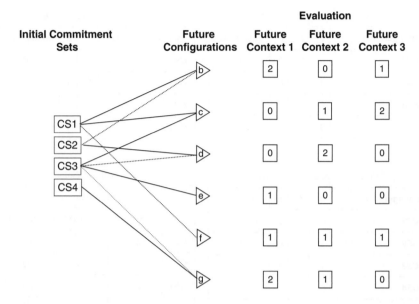

Evaluation

| Initial Commitment Sets | Future Configurations | Future Context 1 | Future Context 2 | Future Context 3 |

Figure 8.7 Future system configurations attainable from initial commitment sets. Each future system configuration is evaluated in three future contextual environments.

Future system configuration	b	c	d	e	f	g
Evaluation in context 1	2	0	0	1	1	2
Evaluation in context 2	0	1	2	0	1	1
Evaluation in context 3	1	2	0	0	1	0
CS1	1	1	0	0	1	0
CS2	1	0	1	0	0	0
CS3	0	1	1	1	0	1
CS4	0	0	0	0	0	1

Figure 8.8 Future system configurations attainable from initial commitment sets. Each future system configuration is evaluated in three future contextual environments.

CS3 or *CS4*. Taking a satisficing level of 1, robustness scores are calculated for the commitment sets in each future context and summarised in a robustness matrix (Figure 8.9). In this example, both *CS1* and *CS3* dominate the other two commitment sets, and so at least *CS1* and *CS3* would be worthy of further, more detailed, consideration.

Robustness Score in Context 1

configuration	b	e	f	g	robustness
CS1	1	0	1	0	2/4
CS2	1	0	0	0	1/4
CS3	0	1	0	1	2/4
CS4	0	0	0	1	1/4

Robustness Score in Context 3

configuration	b	c	f	robustness
CS1	1	1	1	3/3
CS2	1	0	0	1/3
CS3	0	1	0	1/3
CS4	0	0	0	0

Robustness Score in Context 2

configuration	c	d	f	g	robustness
CS1	1	0	1	0	2/4
CS2	0	1	0	0	1/4
CS3	1	1	0	1	3/4
CS4	0	0	0	1	1/4

Robustness Matrix

	robustness score		
	context 1	context 2	context 3
CS1	2/4	2/4	3/3
CS2	1/4	1/4	1/3
CS3	2/4	3/4	1/3
CS4	1/4	1/4	0

Figure 8.9   Calculation of a robustness matrix.

Robustness Analysis as a Framework: Literature Examples

In the preceding account, RA has been largely described as though it were a single method. However, this is not the case, and several approaches to apply RA as a guiding framework have been followed. The four examples below reflect this, having differing levels of participation and using a range of evaluation approaches. In the first example, much of the analysis is backroom and the evaluations of future system configurations are computationally based, using the linear programming technique (see Chapter 6). The second example is participative between a consultant and one individual, RA being used to navigate the individual's own choice problem. In the third example, participatory RA is used with a small company management team to structure a strategic problem, with evaluation being carried out by group scoring. Finally, the fourth example is a paper exercise to illustrate how RA could be used as a means to bridge the gap between thinking flexibly and carrying out complex financial calculations.

Factory Site Location (Gupta & Rosenhead, 1968; Rosenhead, Elton, & Gupta, 1972)

These papers report the application of robustness analysis to the location of new factory sites for the US production of consumer goods sold in the US market. The system considered was that of factories characterised by their location. The initial configuration, in 1966, was the location and capacity of the existing and partially constructed factories. Including the latter, the capacity was 9 million units per year. The initial contextual environment was the demand from various local markets, which aggregated to 6.4 million units. The interim and future contextual environment would be these market demands, which were estimated by quantitative forecasting techniques to be between 7.7 and 8.5 million units in 1971 and between 9.4 and 11.2 million units in 1976, at the 10 year planning horizon. Nevertheless, the company management was more optimistic and felt that higher interim demands of 9.8 million units per year and future demands of 13–15 million units per year were viable. Clearly, there was deep uncertainty, but equally, with a lead time of 4–6 years and a potential interim demand of 0.8 million units greater than the capacity coming on stream, a decision needed to be taken. Even so, the decision could be usefully structured sequentially; the pessimistic quantitative forecast for the planning horizon being less than the optimistic qualitative interim forecast suggested an initial commitment set of one or two factories and a later decision as to whether to add to this once market uncertainty reduced. The initial commitment sets were chosen from the possible initial commitments to build factories in specific locations, and these were subject to constraints of a standard factory capacity and 21 available new locations. Future configurations considered at the planning horizon consisted of the addition of five new factories to those already existing or under construction; that is, any five from the possible 21 new locations (and two potential extensions) could form a future configuration, and hence there were tens of thousands of possible future configurations from which to choose, although only 23 options for the first commitment if this were to be only one factory. Expense apart, given that it was 1966, it was possible to associate a value with each interim or future configuration for a given demand by using linear programming to calculate the transport costs associated with the configuration. Given the computing limitation, a trial and error approach was used to identify good future configurations, and, after the transport costs had been calculated for approximately 300 possible future configurations, reduction in transport costs was not seen. The lowest-cost, five-additional-factories future configuration had annual transport costs of $8.8 million; a further 30 configurations were within $0.52 million dollars of this, which was considered a satisficing level, being of a similar size to other possible variations in the calculation. Nevertheless, the robustness analysis was repeated with a less extreme satisficing level, to ensure that the conclusions drawn were largely insensitive to the satisficing level set. The feasibility of interim systems of one and two additional factories was again character-ised using the criterion of annual transport costs given appropriate demand forecasts. The robustness of each initial commitment set of one additional factory was calcu-lated, leading to a choice between two initial factory locations. In summary, either of the suggested initial factory locations gave low transport costs in the near term but additionally maintained the attainability of many of the future satisficing configura-tions should the optimistic future demand forecasts occur. One of the two had lower short-term costs but with a lower robustness score, while the other had a higher short-term cost but with a higher robustness score, leaving a management choice between these.

High School Subject Choice (Rosenhead, 1978; Rosenhead, 2001b)

These papers report the application of robustness analysis to a 14-year-old girl's choice of school subject to study to examination level. The system considered was that of the girl characterised by her possession and use of externally validated knowledge. The initial commitment sets were combinations taken from available subjects to study and were subject to constraints on number and school time-tabling overlaps. Future configurations were that of the adult girl and the career followed. Subjective valuations were attached to the configurations by the girl's own categorising of careers into definitely attractive, quite attractive, and margin-ally attractive. Notwithstanding the uncertainty that many 14 year olds would have in career, such an ordinal subjective valuation still allows the satisficing level to be varied when considering the robustness of initial commitment sets. Several pos-sible initial commitment sets that gave rise to high robustness scores (in terms of attractive careers left attainable) were identified. Each initial commitment set also led to interim configurations of the pupil undertaking the studies, and these were evaluated on the basis of intrinsic interest. There was a 'management' choice between commitment sets with the highest robustness scores but with a higher interim cost of limited intrinsic value and those with lower robustness scores but lower interim cost.

Online Communication Structure (Wong, 2007)

This paper reports the application of participatory robustness analysis to a small company's choice of online presence. The whole decision process consisted of 3 days of a consultant's time and 1 day participation of the company's senior management team. The system under consideration was the online presence of the company. The initial configuration was that the company had no online presence, its sales to small retail business coming by telephone or in person. The initial and developing future contextual environment was of an eroding profit margin coupled with diminishing retail outlets, brought about by growing online competition. The planning horizon was for 2 years, and the future system configurations were in terms of the company's online presence. The future configurations were participatively identified by the management team and expressed in terms of seven characteristics, for example the target customers, the website topology, and the website brand identity. For each configuration the management team also identified initial commitments and hence commitment sets. Commitments included creating a company brand website, initiating discussions with retailers about microwebsites, and so on. During the same meeting, the team established 14 qualitative evaluation criteria against which each of the future configurations, i.e. the possible online presences at the 2 year horizon, could be scored. Each configuration was quickly scored, the lowest scoring 8, the highest 12. Noting the attainability of each future configuration from each initial commitment set, both exact robustness and superfluous robustness scores were calculated with a satisficing level of 11, and then of 9. At a subsequent meeting between the company CEO and the consultant facilitator, an initial commitment set that could exactly attain the configuration with the highest score and superfluously attain the configuration with the second highest score was actioned.

International Expansion with Embedded Real Options (Driouchi, Leseure, & Benett, 2008)

This paper reports the application of robustness analysis to a multinational's consideration of international expansion. There are three initial commitment sets, to open a new plant in Morocco, in Turkey, or in China. The initial system configuration is the six existing national locations of the company: France, Italy, Russia, Latvia, Japan, and Korea. After an initial implementation period, interim commitments reflect the available real options, for example to expand capacity or to switch production location. Each future configuration is then characterised by a decision sequence, and in this paper it is each sequence that is evaluated to obtain a robustness score. Each of the decision sequences is qualitatively evaluated given the unfolding of each of four future scenarios. Three of the four scenarios are designed in such a way as to modify the preference between the three initially appealing locations: an increase in Chinese labour costs, political upheaval in Morocco, and Turkey joining the EU. The fourth scenario is that of the company going bankrupt. Converting the qualitative evaluation to a numerical score, it is found that Turkey weakly dominates Morocco, and so Morocco is not a preferred initial commitment.

Further Reading

- Jointly the references to this chapter provide an extensive and sufficient presentation of robustness analysis; Rosenhead (2001a) and Rosenhead (2001b) are the ideal starting place.
- An addition to RA of interdependent decision-making, in which one firm's robustness score is reduced by the decisions taken by other organizations, is suggested in:

  Dorward, N. & Wiedermann, P. (1981) Robustness as a corporate objective under uncertainty. *Managerial and Decision Economics* **2**(3), 186–191.

- Other approaches to robust decision-making have been presented within the academic research literature. Lempert and coauthors' papers are worth examining after studying both the current chapter and the sensitivity analysis discussion of Chapter 9:

  Lempert, RJ. & Collins, MT. (2007) Managing the risk of uncertain threshold responses: comparisons of robust, optimum, and precautionary approaches. *Risk Analysis* **27**(4), 1009–1026.

  Lempert, RJ., Groves, DG., Popper, SW., & Bankes, SC. (2006) A general, analytic method for generating robust strategies and narrative scenarios. *Management Science* **52**(4), 514–528.

Activities

A8.1 Prepare a short presentation summarising the concept of robustness analysis. Illustrate your presentation using the following paper:

Best, G., Parston, G., & Rosenhead JV. (1986) Robustness in practice – the regional planning of health services. *Journal of the Operational Research Society* **37**(5), 463–478.

A8.2 Some still pose the question 'Where do you see yourself in 10 years time?' when interviewing candidates for a position. Do you believe such a question reflects well on the interviewer?

A8.3 Where could you see yourself in 5 (or 10) years time? What do you do now?

A8.4 Did Mohammed Ali set out to beat George Foreman with the rope-a-dope strategy, or was it that Ali kept his options open?

A8.5 Read and reflect on the poem *The Road Not Taken* by Robert Frost.

CHAPTER 9

Decision Tree Analysis

Objectives

- *To recognise decision tree notation.*
- *To be able to structure a sequential decision.*
- *To be able to construct a decision tree representation of a sequential decision process.*
- *To be able to populate a decision tree with appropriate quantitative data.*
- *To be able to incorporate the effect of new information into a decision tree.*
- *To be able to roll back a decision tree to use it to inform a current decision.*
- *To be able to carry out sensitivity analysis within a decision tree model.*
- *To appreciate that managers can add value not only by deciding between options but also by creating the opportunity for such options to exist.*

Introduction

The purpose of a decision tree is to provide quantitative support to a sequential decision process. If a decision is taken now, the resulting outcome in the future is dependent on two kinds of occurrence, chance events that are beyond the control of the decision-taker and future decisions that are within the decision-taker's control, i.e. the values considered in taking a decision now are affected by both future chance events and by future decisions. These occurrences can be considered to take place in sequence. An alternative perspective on this is to consider that decisions taken now create value not only in terms of their appropriateness to unknown futures but also by creating the opportunity for future decision-taking. Following a statement of decision tree notation, this chapter will present two core issues:

1. The construction and solution of a decision tree.
2. The application of sensitivity analysis to decision trees.

Decision Tree Notation

Decision trees are drawn from left to right. The leftmost part of the tree represents the present, and reading the tree in this direction characterises the model of the future. A standard notation is used for the *nodes*, which represent chance events, decisions, and the horizon beyond which the model is no longer disaggregated. These three kinds of node are shown in Figure 9.1, together with some of the more commonly used alternative names.

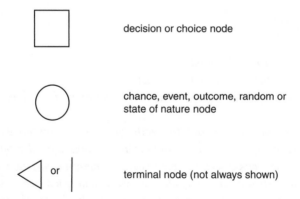

decision or choice node

chance, event, outcome, random or state of nature node

terminal node (not always shown)

Figure 9.1 Commonly used decision tree notation.

Constructing a Decision Tree

Decision trees are helpfully introduced by gradually increasing the complexity from an initially simple example. The simplest decision to structure is one in which there are a number of strategies from which to choose and for each strategy there is an associated known payoff, given, for example, in terms of its present value (PV). A simple model example would be that of a company deciding between three strategies:

1. To pursue a *sustain* (S) strategy of maintaining its current business premises.
2. To pursue a *relocate* (R) strategy of moving its premises.
3. To pursue a *buy land and expand* (BLE) strategy of acquiring neighbouring land and expanding the current premises.

The certain present values of these strategies are £1 000 000, £1 600 000, and £1 500 000 respectively. In Figure 9.2 this is shown as both a payoff table and as a somewhat undemanding decision tree. Nevertheless, it is worth considering this figure further. The payoff table is an immediate and transparent summary of the three strategies; on its reading, the largest payoff and hence optimal decision are easily identified. This is often all that is needed, but, on turning to the tree, the decision structure and the process of choice become apparent. Reading from left to right, the square decision node indicates the necessity for the decision to be taken, and the branches deriving from the decision node indicate distinct forks or pathways that the organization can take; for example, the upper line diagrams the sustain strategy. Following this pathway yields a payoff with a present value of 100 (i.e. £1 000 000). However, not only does this representation illuminate the importance of the decision beyond selecting the largest number, it may also suggest to question the model as to whether the payoffs are really certain and whether there are any other decisions to be taken.

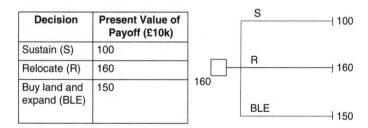

Decision	Present Value of Payoff (£10k)
Sustain (S)	100
Relocate (R)	160
Buy land and expand (BLE)	150

Figure 9.2 A simple business decision (units of £10k).

Rolling Back a Decision Tree 1: Sequential Decision and Event Nodes

The previous example could easily be represented either as a payoff table or a decision tree. The next case also has this property, although it is slightly less simple.

A company is again deciding between the same three strategies, S, R, or BLE, but in each case the payoffs are uncertain and depend upon the demand for the company's output. This uncertainty is often represented as a discrete distribution, and for this example by three probabilities. Suppose low demand has probability 0.1, medium demand has probability 0.6, and high demand has probability 0.3. For each of the demand conditions, each strategy has an associated payoff stated in terms of a present value (Figure 9.3). Although the tree is drawn and read from left to right, it is solved by rolling back from right to left. Starting at any terminal node, the branch is traced backwards from right to left until an event or decision node is reached. If the node does not already have an associated value and a value can be calculated, then this is carried out. If the value cannot be calculated, then another terminal node is chosen and the rollback procedure is repeated. At an event or chance node, the expected value is found; for example, starting at the uppermost terminal node of Figure 9.3, the branch is followed backwards from right to left until event node x is reached. At this event node the expected value is calculated:

$$\text{Expected value at } x = (0.1 \times 70) + (0.6 \times 100) + (0.3 \times 110) = 100$$

Similarly, the expected values at the other events nodes are calculated:

$$\text{Expected value at } y = (0.1 \times 10) + (0.6 \times 130) + (0.3 \times 270) = 160$$

$$\text{Expected value at } z = (0.1 \times 60) + (0.6 \times 140) + (0.3 \times 200) = 150$$

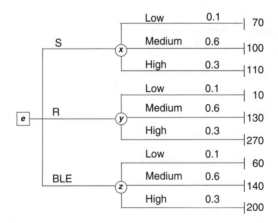

Figure 9.3 A simple business decision with uncertainty.

Continuing to roll back, the initial decision node is reached. At a decision node it is assumed that the rational decision of choosing the optimal strategy is taken.

For positive flows the choice would be the strategy with the maximum present value:

$$\text{Value at } e = \max[100, 160, 150] = 160$$

The completed decision tree together with an equivalent payoff table is given in Figure 9.4.

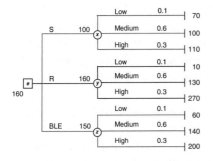

Chance Outcome	Low	Medium	High	Expected Value (£10k)
Probability	0.1	0.6	0.3	
Decision	Present Value of Payoff (£10k)			
Sustain (S)	70	100	110	100
Relocate (R)	10	130	270	**160**
Buy land and expand (BLE)	60	140	200	150

Figure 9.4   Completed decision tree for a simple decision with uncertainty and the equivalent payoff table.

Aside: Uncertainty as a Continuous Distribution in Decision Trees

Within this chapter, chance or event nodes are only modelled as discrete distributions, but the reader should be aware that, on occasions, chance nodes may be shown (Figure 9.5) with associated continuous distributions, such as the normal or beta distributions.

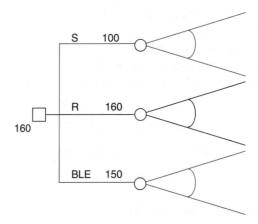

Figure 9.5   Diagramming a chance node with continuous uncertainty.

Rolling Back a Decision Tree 2: Waiting for Uncertainty to Resolve

The decision tree shown in Figure 9.4 highlights that the relocate strategy R would generate a payoff of 270 should the demand be high, the largest of any of the three strategies. However, if the demand actually turned out to be medium, then it would be the BLE strategy that would lead to the largest payoff, while for low demand it would be the sustain strategy S. Observing this, it is not unreasonable to ask whether taking the decision could and should be delayed. Such perception is an example of how the structuring and appraising of a decision tree provides the opportunity for a manager to add value; the use and development of decision trees can be iterative in practice.

A company is again deciding between three strategies, S, R, or BLE, but on this occasion enquiries to the landowner have revealed the additional possibility to purchase an *option to buy the land* (OBL) for £20 000 (i.e. 2 units). By the time the decision as to whether to *exercise* the option (EOBL) has been taken, the demand uncertainty will be largely resolved. Unfortunately, the possibility to relocate, R, will be lost, leaving the choice between maintaining the premises, i.e. *continuing to sustain* (CS), and buying the land to expand (EOBL). In summary, the decision-taker can delay the decision by purchasing an option and consequently also giving up the current best choice to relocate, R. The CS and S strategies are the same, and hence have similar payoffs; however, the EOBL strategy will be somewhat different to that of the BLE strategy owing to the delay in expansion (Figure 9.6).

The tree of Figure 9.6 is now a little more complex, and the advantage over payoff matrices for considering sequential decisions is apparent. The three uppermost event nodes have the same structure as before, but there is an additional strategy, OBL, deriving from the leftmost decision node, e. Associated with this branch is an outflow of 2 units, shown in brackets. Continuing from left to right, the uncertain demand is again shown as an event node, and, following the resolution of this uncertainty, the opportunity to decide between the CS and EOBL strategies is shown. The lower part of the tree has been rolled back from right to left, first evaluating the decision nodes a, b, and c:

$$\text{Value at } a = \max[70, 60] = 70$$

$$\text{Value at } b = \max[100, 165] = 165$$

$$\text{Value at } c = \max[110, 190] = 190$$

The expected value at event node d is then

$$\text{Expected value at } d = (0.1 \times 70) + (0.6 \times 165) + (0.3 \times 190) = 163$$

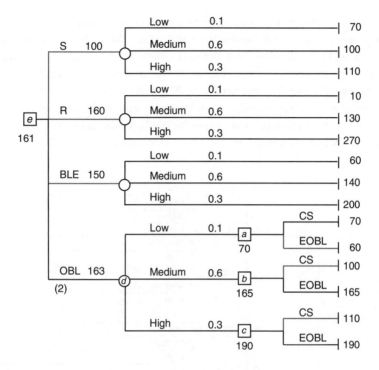

Figure 9.6 Completed decision tree including sequential decision nodes.

and the initial decision to be taken at node **e** has the value

$$\text{Value at } e = \max[100, 160, 150, 163 - 2] = 161$$

which suggests that following the strategy OBL by purchasing the option is optimal.

Undertaking this process may of course suggest other questions for the decision-taker, not least whether strategy BLE could be made sequential by first purchasing the land and later deciding the nature of expansion. Another alternative would be to ask whether the uncertainty in demand could be reduced by purchasing information in the form of a market research survey as an alternative to following the OBL strategy of waiting for the uncertainty to resolve. Such approaches to resolving uncertainty are frequently met in investigative business such as staged R&D or NPD, mining or drilling, test market entry, and any similar exploratory or sampling procedures.

Rolling Back a Decision Tree 3: Exploratory Actions and Posterior Probabilities

Suppose that a *market research survey* (MRS) can be purchased to reduce the uncertainty in future demand and that the MRS can be undertaken very rapidly. Even so, the landowner will not wait this short timescale for a response to the offer of an option to buy the land (OBL) and will withdraw this, although not the offer for the land itself (BLE). Under this short timescale, the PVs of continue to sustain (CS) are approximately equal to those of S, the PVs of continue to buy land and expand (CBLE) are approximately equal to those of BLE, and the possibility of relocating (R) remains viable. The decision under consideration (Figure 9.7) is whether to purchase the option and wait for uncertainty to resolve (OBL) or whether to pay to reduce the uncertainty (MRS). How much would it be worth paying for the MRS?

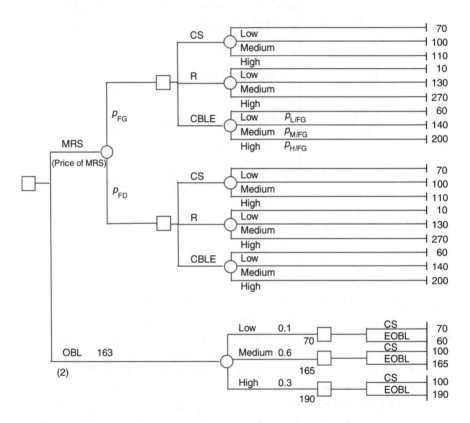

Figure 9.7 Structure of the decision tree to investigate the maximum price worth paying for a market research survey to reduce uncertainty compared with the option to wait for uncertainty to resolve.

Obviously, one input to valuing the MRS will be its usefulness: what will be indicated and how reliably? Given that the MRS, if conducted, will take place over a short timeframe, suppose that it simply suggests whether growth or decline in demand is the more likely. Further, although the survey has good reliability, it is not perfect. Imagine that experience from previous surveys suggests the following:

- If demand were going to be low, then the market research survey would indicate future growth with probability $p_{FG|L} = 0.06$.
- If demand were going to be medium, then the market research survey would indicate future growth with probability $p_{FG|M} = 0.6$.
- If demand were going to be high then the market research survey would indicate future growth with probability, $p_{FG|H} = 0.9$.

The first requirement is to combine the above characteristics of the market research survey with the initial estimates for the probabilities of low, medium, and high demand, $p_L = 0.1$, $p_M = 0.6$, and $p_H = 0.3$, to consider the likelihoods that the survey would result in a forecast growth or a forecast decline in demand (Figure 9.8). To do this, the marginal probabilities of forecast growth and forecast decline are calculated using the *theorem of total probability*:[1]

$$p_{FG} = p_L p_{FG|L} + p_M p_{FG|M} + p_H p_{FG|H} = 0.636$$

$$p_{FD} = p_L p_{FD|L} + p_M p_{FD|M} + p_H p_{FD|H} = 0.364$$

	Forecast Growth	**Forecast Decline**	
Low Demand	0.1 × 0.06 = 0.006	0.1 × 0.94 = 0.094	0. 1
Medium Demand	0.6 × 0.6 = 0.36	0.6 × 0.4 = 0.24	0.6
High Demand	0.3 × 0.9 = 0.27	0.3 × 0.1 = 0.03	0.3
	0.636	**0.364**	**1**

Figure 9.8   Calculation of marginal probabilities using a joint probability table.

Bayes' theorem can then be applied to calculate the posterior probabilities (Figure 9.9).

Using Bayes' theorem, the posterior probabilities of each of low, medium, or high demand, given a forecast of growth, follow:

$$P(\text{low demand}|\text{forecast growth}) = p_{L|FG} = \frac{p_L p_{FG|L}}{p_{FG}} = 0.006/0.636 = 0.009$$

and

$$P(\text{medium demand}|\text{forecast growth}) = p_{M|FG} = 0.36/0.636 = 0.566$$

$$P(\text{high demand}|\text{forecast growth}) = p_{H|FG} = 0.27/0.636 = 0.425$$

---

[1] See the mathematics revision appendix.

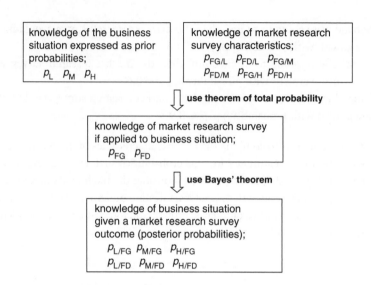

Figure 9.9 Combining knowledge of a business situation with that from a survey.

Similarly, given a forecast of decline:

$$P(\text{low demand|forecast decline}) = p_{\text{L|FD}} = 0.094/0.364 = 0.258$$

$$P(\text{medium demand|forecast decline}) = p_{\text{M|FD}} = 0.24/0.364 = 0.659$$

$$P(\text{high demand|forecast decline}) = p_{\text{H|FD}} = 0.03/0.364 = 0.082$$

The decision tree can now be populated with data and again rolled back (Figure 9.10):

Expected value at f = $(0.009 \times 70) + (0.566 \times 100) + (0.425 \times 110) = 104$

Expected value at g = $(0.009 \times 10) + (0.566 \times 130) + (0.425 \times 270) = 188$

Expected value at h = $(0.009 \times 60) + (0.566 \times 140) + (0.425 \times 200) = 165$

Value at l = max[104, 188, 165] = 188

Expected value at i = $(0.258 \times 70) + (0.659 \times 100) + (0.082 \times 110) = 93$

Expected value at j = $(0.258 \times 10) + (0.659 \times 130) + (0.082 \times 270) = 111$

Expected value at k = $(0.258 \times 60) + (0.659 \times 140) + (0.082 \times 200) = 124$

Value at m = max[93, 111, 124] = 124

Expected value at n = $(0.636 \times 188) + (0.364 \times 124) = 165$

and, as before,

$$\text{Expected value at } \boldsymbol{d} = 163$$

The value at decision node $\boldsymbol{e}$ is

$$\text{Value at node } \boldsymbol{e} = \max[165 - \text{price of MRS}, 163 - 2]$$

The decision-taker would be indifferent between these two if the price of the MRS were 4 units. Hence, if the MRS were less than 4 units (i.e. £40 000), then this strategy would be worth following. The expected value of sample information is 4 units.

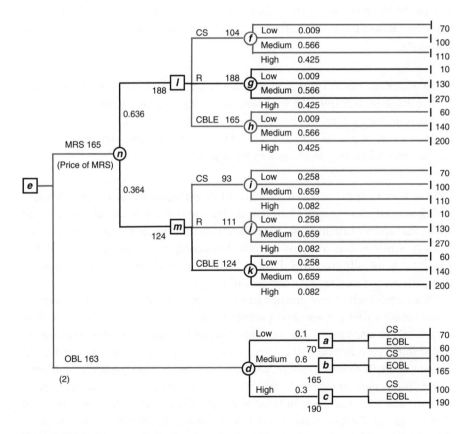

Figure 9.10 Decision tree rolled back to determine the maximum price worth paying for a market research survey.

Introduction to Sensitivity Analysis

The preceding decision models include *first-order uncertainty*, the uncertainty associated with a particular event occurring. For example, in a medical setting there might be a probability p of contracting a disease if exposed, and a probability of $1 - p$ of not being infected. The probability p represents the first-order uncertainty. Quite often in decision-making there is also *second-order uncertainty*, the uncertainty of the parameterisation of the decision model. In the medical case, p may have been given a value of 0.25 to represent the likelihood of contracting the disease, but this may be based on limited information and is itself therefore an estimate.

Sensitivity analysis considers how the output of a decision tree model changes as the component inputs are varied away from the initial or *base values*, the values for which the decision tree is initially solved. The fact that the output of a decision tree model has two aspects, the commended strategy and the expected value of the decision, means that, in carrying out sensitivity analysis, interest lies in the following questions:

- At what value would a change in an input parameter lead to a change in commended strategy away from the *base optimal strategy* (i.e. the commended strategy using the base values)?
- How susceptible is the expected value of the newly solved decision tree and of the base optimal strategy to changes in input parameters?

Sensitivity analysis not only is useful for highlighting the stability of the commended choice but also suggests where further information can be usefully sought and where management attention should be directed during implementation of the taken strategy. Sensitivity analysis may be applied to a completed decision tree model, but equally it is usefully employed during the iterative development of a model so as appropriately to focus any information-gathering efforts.

Even for relatively simple decision tree structures, such an analysis will normally be carried out within a spreadsheet package. Given the facility this affords, particular care should be taken to identify the motivation for the input variations investigated, and with the presentation of the output. Simple sensitivity analyses are carried out by independently changing each independent, or presumed independent, input parameter. Two popular graphical displays for these univariate analyses are the *tornado diagram* and the *spider plot*. In spite of the popularity and, indeed, usefulness of these graphical displays, if the number of inputs being varied is small, consideration should still be given to an easily read numerical summary table. Slightly less simple is bivariate sensitivity analysis, in which two input parameters are changed. Again, interpretation of the results is aided by an appropriate choice of graph or diagram. More complex analysis varies several parameters together, often relying on computational simulation techniques.

Univariate Sensitivity Analysis

Consider the simple decision tree of Figure 9.11. There are essentially two potential strategies, S_1 or S_2, and two future states of nature, F_1 or F_2. A third strategy, S_3, is to buy perfect information concerning which future will occur, and then to take the strategy as appropriate. Purchasing the perfect information costs 9 units. Strategy S_1 would result in payoffs of 40 or -30 in F_1 or F_2 respectively, and S_2 would result in payoffs of 20 or -10. All payoffs are in present value terms. The probability of future F_1 occurring is estimated to be 0.4, and that of F_2 occurring is 0.6. The decision tree has been rolled back and commends S_2 with an expected value of 2 units.

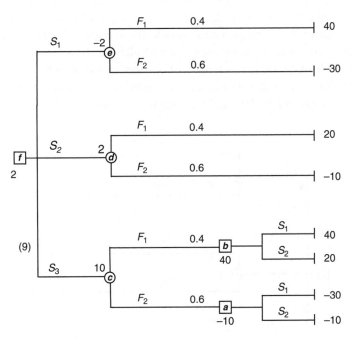

Figure 9.11 A simple decision tree.

Which Input Parameters to Vary

The decision tree of Figure 9.11 has been constructed with six input parameters: specifically, four terminal cash flows, one probability, and one purchasing cost. However, in practice these parameters will already have been aggregated from many other driver inputs. For example, each terminal cash flow may well include sales volume, sales price, labour costs, transport costs, tax rates, etc., some of which will be equivalent between terminal cash flows, and some different. Given this, it is not strictly valid independently to vary each of the terminal flows, and a more realistic univariate analysis would investigate sensitivity to each of these driver inputs. Furthermore, the structuring of a model can lead to correlations between model parameters, for instance terminal payoffs and probabilities are together a model for a probability distribution function for future cash flows. Nonetheless, the same procedure as outlined herein would essentially be carried out, and so in what follows each of these six parameters will be independently varied away from their initial or base values.

Single-parameter Sensitivity Plots

A single-parameter sensitivity plot contrasts the expected value that would result from each of the strategies under consideration, given a change in one of the model parameters away from its base value, with all other parameters held constant. Figure 9.12 illustrates the decision tree with five input parameters held constant and the probability of F_1 taken as a variable, resulting in Figure 9.13, which demonstrates the facility of such a plot. Firstly, the parameter range over which the *base optimal*

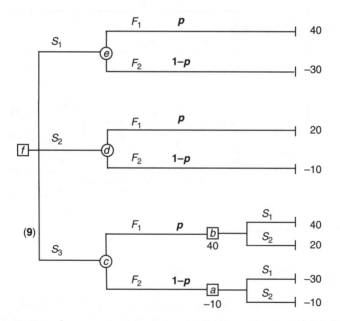

Figure 9.12   A simple decision tree with variable parameter p.

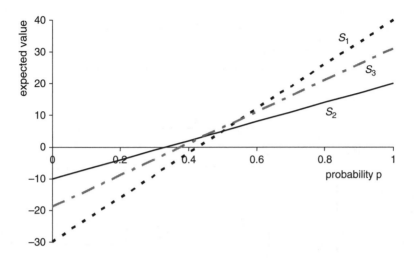

Figure 9.13 Single-parameter sensitivity plot.

strategy remains optimal is clear, S_2 being optimal for low values of p (<0.45) but not optimal for higher values. Further interpretation of the plot is dependent upon the level of second-order uncertainty: is there high confidence in the probability used in the model? For instance, if it is considered that lower values of probability are unlikely but higher values are possible, the model will be somewhat cautious, and consideration may then turn towards the alternative strategies, S_1 or S_3. On the other hand, given the negative expected values, if lower probabilities are considered plausible, then attention might be drawn towards developing risk mitigation strategies or perhaps further researching probability estimates.

Similar plots could be developed for the remaining input parameters, but even in this simple case this would result in six graphs of three strategies each. For a larger number of parameters and strategies, using single-parameter sensitivity plots as a first step may overwhelm the decision-taker. However, for investigating parameters of specific concern, or for communication purposes, the plot remains useful.

Tabular Summary of Strategy Thresholds

One key aspect that is clearly shown in single-parameter sensitivity plots is the range of the parameter over which the base optimal strategy remains optimal. Given a decision tree that is suitably formulated within a spreadsheet, it is a straightforward task to vary each input parameter in turn and to observe the allowable increase and decrease for which the recommended strategy remains optimal. This can be further simplified with tools such as *Goal Seek* in Excel. Let π represent the cost of purchase

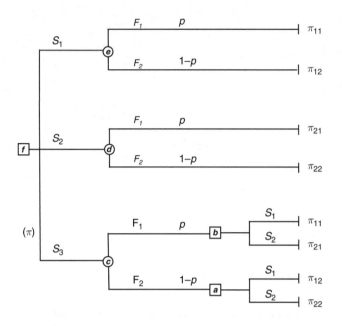

Figure 9.14 A simple decision tree with all input parameters shown as variables.

of perfect information, and further introduce the notation π_{ij} ($i = 1, 2; j = 1, 2$) to represent the payoff resulting from strategy S_i in future F_j, such that the *base value* of $\pi_{12} = -30$, and so on (compare Figure 9.14 with Figures 9.11 and 9.12).

Consideration is first given to π_{11}. With all other parameters held constant (at their base values), it can be seen that increasing π_{11} by 2.5 to 42.5 results in

> Decision node **b** increasing from 40 to 42.5
> Event node **c** increasing from 10 to 11
> Event node **e** decreasing from -2 to -1
> Event node **d** remaining at 2

With this rise in π_{11} there is indifference between strategies S_2 and S_3: the expected value of S_2 has remained at 2, while that of S_3 has increased to $11 - 9 = 2$. In contrast, π_{11} can be decreased indefinitely and S_2 remains the optimal strategy. This process can be repeated for the other three terminal payoffs and the cost π, and the results summarised in a table (Figure 9.15). Although Figure 9.15 does not show the changes in the expected value of the base optimal solution over the parameter ranges for which it remains optimal, it provides a clear indication of the proximity of the base optimal strategy to parameter thresholds beyond which one of the alternative strategies becomes optimum.

Input Parameter Varied	Initial (Base) Value	Allowable Increase	Allowable Decrease
p	0.4	0.05	0.4
π_{11}	40	2.5	∞
π_{12}	-30	6.67	∞
π_{21}	20	∞	2.5
π_{22}	-10	∞	-6.67
π	9	∞	1

Figure 9.15 Stability of strategy 2 to univariate changes in input parameters.

The Tornado Diagram

It is usually the case that an interval or plausible range for each input parameter can be specified, for example a range within which there is a 95 % probability that the parameter can fall. During the development of a decision tree model, univariate sensitivity analysis is carried out using the limits from the plausible ranges, and, should the expected value from the model be more sensitive to particular parameters, then the focus of effort in gathering further information or identifying strategic alternatives is directed towards these parameters. Again, these calculations are simple to undertake in a spreadsheet, but the challenge arises when interpreting a large number of parameters. To alleviate this difficulty, the tornado diagram is used.

A tornado diagram is produced by first calculating the expected value of the decision using the base values of each parameter. Two further calculations are then made per input parameter, one calculation for the lower limit of the parameter and one for the upper limit of the parameter. For example, the decision tree in Figure 9.14 with six parameters would be rolled back 13 times. The input parameters are then ordered by their associated output range and plotted on the tornado diagram. Figure 9.16 shows supposed base, lower, and upper limits for each of the parameters of the example in Figure 9.14. Holding any five parameters at base value allows the decision tree to be rolled back while the remaining parameter is changed to its lower and then upper limit (Figure 9.17). Ordering and plotting these limiting expected values produces a bar graph reminiscent of a tornado (Figure 9.18). Those parameters towards the top of the tornado are often of primary importance to the decision-taker, those towards the base less so. This provides an initial indication for the focus of the information-gathering effort during iterative decision tree development. Figure 9.18 suggests that π_{12} and π are less important than π_{11}, π_{21}, π_{22}, and p. The importance of π_{22} and p is further heightened by the possibility of a negative expected value. Tornado diagrams

Parameter	Initial (Base) Value	Lower Limit (2.5 % chance of parameter being below this value)	Upper Limit (2.5 % chance of parameter exceeding this value)
Probability p	0.4	0.1	0.6
Cash flow π_{11}	40	30	60
Cash flow π_{12}	−30	−40	−20
Cash flow π_{21}	20	0	40
Cash flow π_{22}	−10	−40	0
Cost π	9	6	12

Figure 9.16 Base, lower, and upper values for the input parameters.

Parameter Varied	Expected Value with Parameter at Base Value	Expected Value with Parameter at Lower Limit	Expected Value with Parameter at Upper Limit	Output Range
Probability p	2 (S_2)	−7 (S_2)	12 (S_1)	19
Cash flow π_{11}	2 (S_2)	2 (S_2)	9 (S_3)	7
Cash flow π_{12}	2 (S_2)	2 (S_2)	4 (S_1)	2
Cash flow π_{21}	2 (S_2)	1 (S_3)	10 (S_2)	9
Cash flow π_{22}	2 (S_2)	−2 (S_3)	8 (S_2)	10
Cost π	2 (S_2)	4 (S_3)	2 (S_2)	2

Figure 9.17 Expected values calculated by rollback of the decision tree with one parameter changed to either the lower or upper limit. The corresponding strategy is shown in brackets.

can also be plotted keeping the strategy fixed, which may be useful to communicate the range of possible returns of a commended strategy, i.e. for the base optimal strategy.

The Spider Plot

The tornado diagram is able clearly to illustrate the limits of the output variable when a decision tree is rolled back for an input parameter modified to each of its limiting values. This is the case provided that the relationship between the output

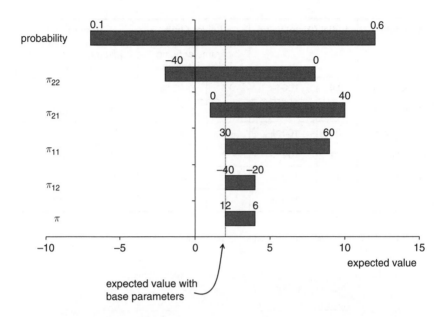

Figure 9.18 A tornado diagram.

variable, namely the expected value, and the explored input parameter is mono-
tonic or zero, i.e. the sign of the relationship does not change. For many models this
is not unreasonable. Nevertheless, this can be confirmed by calculating for input
parameter values between the lower and upper limits. A plot that specifically uses
data from such intermediate calculations is the spider plot. In contrast to the tornado diagram, a spider plot can become cluttered if more than in the order of six
input parameters are considered. Even so, it does allow simultaneous consideration of the range of possible expected values as several input parameters are varied,
with the added advantage of highlighting non-linearities between input and output variables. To produce a spider plot, the input parameters of interest are first
selected, and lower and upper limits are converted to percentages of the base value
(Figure 9.19).

For each input parameter in turn, the decision tree is solved throughout the plausible range of values while holding all other parameters constant, generating the data
for the spider plot (Figure 9.20). As with a tornado diagram, spider plots can be created for a fixed strategy, which may be useful to communicate the range of possible
returns of the base optimal strategy.

Spider plots are conventionally produced with the abscissa shown as a percentage
of the input parameter base values (Figure 9.20). This has the advantage of being
readily understood and facilitates quick mental conversion of limiting values back

Parameter	Initial (Base) Value		Lower Limit (2.5 % chance of parameter being below this value)		Upper Limit (2.5 % chance of parameter exceeding this value)	
Probability p	0.4	100 %	0.1	25 %	0.6	150 %
Cash flow π_{11}	40	100 %	30	75 %	60	150 %
Cash flow π_{12}	−30	100 %	−40	125 %	−20	50 %
Cash flow π_{21}	20	100 %	0	0 %	40	200 %
Cash flow π_{22}	−10	100 %	−40	400 %	0	0 %
Cost π	9	100 %	6	67 %	12	133 %

Figure 9.19   Base, lower, and upper values for input parameters.

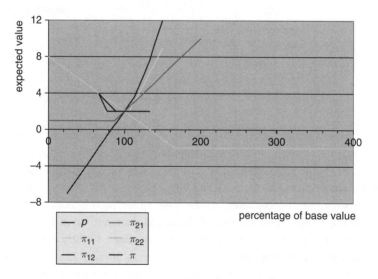

Figure 9.20   Spider plot showing the change in the expected value of the optimal strategy for plausible changes in input variables (as a percentage).

to those estimated in absolute terms. In some instances, an alternative of using a range-normalised deviation from the base value may be preferred (Figure 9.21):

$$(\text{Parameter value} - \text{base value})/(\text{upper limit} - \text{lower limit})$$

Figure 9.22 illustrates such spider plots: Figure 9.22a has allowed the optimal strategy to change during the sensitivity analysis; Figure 9.22b has fixed the strategy as the base optimal strategy, S_2; Figure 9.22c shows the difference in expected values

Parameter	Initial (Base) Value			Lower Limit (2.5 % chance of parameter being below this value)			Upper Limit (2.5 % chance of parameter exceeding this value)		
Probability p	0.4	100 %	0	0.1	25 %	−0.6	0.6	150 %	0.4
Cash flow π_{11}	40	100 %	0	30	75 %	−0.33	60	150 %	0.67
Cash flow π_{12}	−30	100 %	0	−40	125 %	−0.5	−20	50 %	0.5
Cash flow π_{21}	20	100 %	0	0	0 %	−0.5	40	200 %	0.5
Cash flow π_{22}	−10	100 %	0	−40	400 %	−0.75	0	0 %	0.25
Cost π	9	100 %	0	6	67 %	−0.5	12	133 %	0.5

Figure 9.21   Base, lower, and upper values for input parameters.

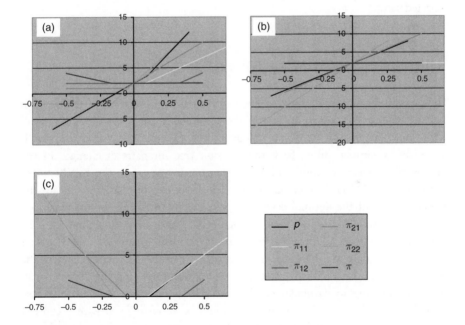

Figure 9.22   Spider plots using range-normalised deviation for the abscissa, and for the ordinate: (a) expected value of the optimal strategy, (b) expected value of the base optimal strategy, and (c) value of perfect information.

between the optimal strategy and the base optimal strategy (Figure 9.22b subtracted from Figure 9.22a).

Figure 9.22c illustrates that, given a normalised deviation of −0.06 to +0.08 of any individual parameter, the base optimal strategy would remain optimal; that is, no additional value could be gained by knowing a parameter exactly if it were in this interval (assuming all other parameters are at base value). Even so, considering Figure 9.22b across similar deviations indicates the corresponding change in the expected value of S_2 given changes in p, π_{21}, and π_{22}. Returning attention to Figure 9.22c and to more negative parameter deviations, it is evident that precognition of π_{21}, π_{22}, and π would be valuable, since a strategy other than S_2 would be commended from decision tree analysis. Consequently, it may be worth investing to reduce uncertainty here. While for negative deviations first sight indicates that it is not worth investing to increase knowledge of π_{11}, π_{12}, and p, scrutiny of Figure 9.22b leads to a question with respect to parameter p. There it can be seen that, although changes in p leave S_2 optimal, the expected value becomes increasingly negative. Either improved knowledge of the deviation or a new alternative strategy might be sought. Lastly, greater positive deviations (Figure 9.22c) of p, π_{11}, and π_{12} would lead to S_2 no longer being optimal. An alternative strategy could yield a greater positive expected value.

Bivariate Sensitivity Analysis

The preceding univariate analyses have highlighted the sensitivity of the decision in particular to the probability p and the terminal cash flow π_{22}. Assuming all other input parameters remain constant, these two can be considered simultaneously by simply rolling back the decision tree for pairs of changes in the parameters. For ease of communication, such an investigation can be illustrated as in Figure 9.23. Here, contours or shaded areas can be used to indicate the expected value of the optimal decision, given the input parameter values shown on the two axes. Additional lines, in Figure 9.23 the solid white lines, can be included to designate indifference between neighbouring strategies, and a marker added to designate the base optimal strategy. Figure 9.23 usefully shows the proximity of the base optimal strategy to the alternatives and the expected values corresponding to particular combinations of parameters. As with the case of spider plots (Figure 9.22), Figure 9.23 could be supplemented with a contour plot showing the expected value for a fixed strategy, or showing the value of information.

N-Way (Multivariate) Sensitivity Analysis

Exploring more than two concurrently changing variables becomes a progressively more difficult task to both implement and to appraise. In Figure 9.22c the difference

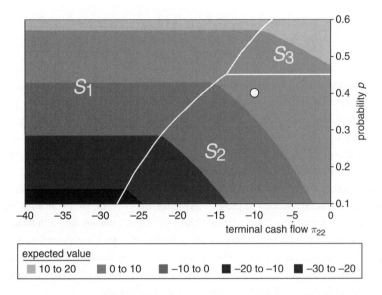

Figure 9.23 Bivariate sensitivity plot. Shading shows the resulting value from decision tree rollback, the white lines indicate the strategy threshold, and the white circle indicates the base (initial) values for the two variables. All other input parameters are at base value.

in expected values between the optimal strategy and the base optimal strategy was calculated to define a value of perfect information as one parameter is varied from its base value. Further progress is possible if a probability distribution (or mass) function can be associated with each input parameter. In this situation, an expected value for perfect information over a parameter can be calculated as the expectation of the difference in expected values between the optimal strategy and the base optimal strategy. This can be generalised to taking the expectation over any parameter set, including all of the parameters. It is then possible to compare the expected value of perfect information for each parameter with that for all parameters in order to determine the focus of further investigation. This approach can be facilitated by using Monte Carlo simulation. A draw is taken from the appropriate probability distribution for a parameter, and the tree is rolled back, making optimum choices to achieve maximum value. The difference is found between this maximum and the value obtained, assuming the base optimal strategy is followed, that is, following the decisions that would be taken using the base values of the parameters. This process is repeated many times and averaged to determine the expected value of perfect information over the chosen parameter. The Monte Carlo approach is individually repeated for each parameter, and jointly for all parameters.

Summary of the Decision Tree Analysis Method

The decision tree analysis method is appropriate to sequential decision-taking situations. In practice, the development and use of a decision tree is an iterative process. Nonetheless there are several important phases. It is necessary to structure a tree to represent the decision sequence and to capture any uncertainty associated with decision outcomes. In developing the tree, opportunities for adding value through creating flexibility are sought. This may involve contributions from more than one individual. Once the structure of a decision tree has been developed, it is often populated with monetary values in present value terms. (In some applications, such as medical decision-making, the outcome values might be expressed in different terms, e.g. disease cases prevented). Uncertainties within the tree are described by probabilities, and, if required, Bayes' theorem is used. The tree is then rolled back to inform the decision-taker. Sensitivity analysis may be used during the construction, population with data, and interpretation of the decision tree.

Chapter Appendix. A Brief Introduction to Monte Carlo Simulation

If the payoff from a decision is determined by many variables and none of these is known with certainty, then it is not always easy to calculate an expected payoff. It can be even trickier to determine the distribution of possible payoffs. Under such circumstances an approach called Monte Carlo simulation is used.

Beginning with a simple case, suppose a business has forecast revenues of either £100 000 or £50 000, each with probability 0.5, and forecast costs of either £75 000 or £25 000, each again with probability 0.5. Then the expected profit can be simply calculated:

Expected profit = expected revenues − expected costs

Expected profit = [(0.5 × £100k) + (0.5 × £50k)] − [(0.5 × £75k) + (0.5 × £25k)]

Expected profit = £75k − £50k = £25k

Equally, the probability distribution of profits can be easily calculated:

Probability (revenues = £100k and costs = £75k) = 0.5 × 0.5 = 0.25

Probability (revenues = £100k and costs = £25k) = 0.5 × 0.5 = 0.25

$$\text{Probability (revenues} = £50k \text{ and costs} = £75k) = 0.5 \times 0.5 = 0.25$$

$$\text{Probability (revenues} = £50k \text{ and costs} = £25k) = 0.5 \times 0.5 = 0.25$$

So

$$\text{Probability (profit} = -£25k) = 0.25$$

$$\text{Probability (profit} = £25k) = 0.50$$

$$\text{Probability (profit} = £75k) = 0.25$$

In the above case there were only two variables, each with only two distinct values. Nevertheless, four probabilities had to be calculated to determine the distribution of possible payoffs. As the number of variables increases and the models of their probability distributions become more complicated, the number of calculations required increases very rapidly. On account of this, the Monte Carlo simulation approach is used.

Returning to the simple case above, the obtained revenues and profits could be simulated with the toss of two fair coins. For example, if the first coin showed heads, then the revenues would be £100 000, but if it showed tails the revenues would be £50 000. By tossing the two coins many times and recording the proportion of occurrences for the resulting profits, the probability distribution is simulated. Figure 9.24 shows the case for 20 simulations, leading to a profit of −£25 000 with proportion 0.3, £25 000 with proportion 0.5, and £75 000 with proportion 0.2. The average profit is £20 000. If many more simulations were to be carried out, then the simulated proportions would approximate the required probability distribution.

It is clear that a decision model with more variables can be readily simulated; the toss of a fair coin would be required for each variable. However, in most situations a variable cannot be modelled by a 50–50 probability distribution. To develop a more flexible simulation, a method of obtaining general randomisers is required. Fortunately, several algorithms have been developed to produce numbers drawn from a standard uniform distribution. In Excel the function RAND() does this. Imagine that a business has forecast revenues of £100 000 with probability 0.2, £60 000 with probability 0.5, and £20 000 with probability 0.3. Such a situation can be simulated by drawing X from a standard uniform distribution and specifying the following:

$$\text{If } 0 < X \leq 0.3, \text{ then revenues} = £20\,000$$

$$\text{If } 0.3 < X \leq 0.8, \text{ then revenues} = £60\,000$$

$$\text{If } 0.8 < X \leq 1, \text{ then revenues} = £100\,000$$

First Coin	Second Coin	Revenues	Costs	Profit
T	H	50 000	25 000	25 000
H	H	100 000	25 000	75 000
H	H	100 000	25 000	75 000
T	H	50 000	25 000	25 000
T	T	50 000	75 000	−25 000
T	H	50 000	25 000	25 000
T	H	50 000	25 000	25 000
T	H	50 000	25 000	25 000
H	T	100 000	75 000	25 000
T	T	50 000	75 000	−25 000
T	T	50 000	75 000	−25 000
T	T	50 000	75 000	−25 000
H	H	100 000	25 000	75 000
H	T	100 000	75 000	25 000
T	T	50 000	75 000	−25 000
T	T	50 000	75 000	−25 000
H	H	100 000	25 000	75 000
T	H	50 000	25 000	25 000
T	H	50 000	25 000	25 000
H	T	100 000	75 000	25 000

Figure 9.24 Simple coin tossing simulation of revenues and costs.

Essentially, the inverse of the cumulative distribution function for the revenues has been used to determine the revenue level in each simulation (Figure 9.25). As long as a distribution function can be associated with each variable to be simulated, this approach can be used. Figure 9.26 illustrates the case for the variable *costs* with a continuous distribution. Activity **A9.7** gives some practice of this.

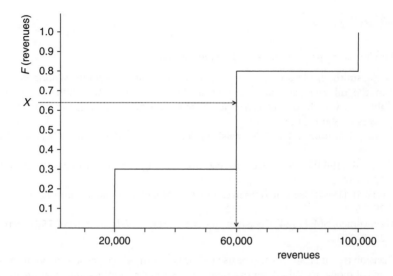

Figure 9.25 Simulation with a discrete distribution. X is drawn from a standard uniform distribution.

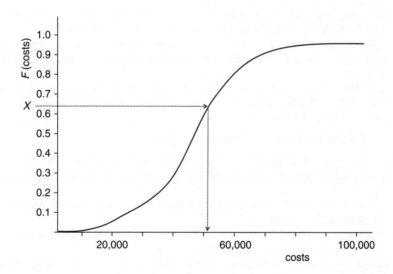

Figure 9.26 Simulation with a continuous distribution. X is drawn from a standard uniform distribution.

Further Reading

- For alternative presentations on decision tree analysis:

  Coopersmith, E., Dean, G., McVean, J., & Storaune, E. (2000) Making decisions in the oil and gas industry. *Oilfield Review* **Winter 2000/2001**, 2–9. Available at www.slb.com/media/services/resources/oilfieldreview/ors00/win00/p2_9.pdf [accessed 9 July 2008].

  Cowles, S. & Rowley, J. (1995) Revisiting decision trees. *Management Decision* **33**(8), 46–50.

  Magee, JF. (1964) Decision trees for decision making. *Harvard Business Review* **42**(4), 126–137.

  Magee, JF. (1964) Decision trees in capital investment. *Harvard Business Review* **42**(5), 79–96.

  Malinconico, SM. (1984) Decisions under uncertainty. *Library Journal* **15**(November) 2129–2131.

- Decision tree analysis can also be used in situations in which payoffs are not framed in terms of monetary values; for example, in medical decision-making, quality-adjusted life years might be used instead. Applying DTA in the medical field is presented in the following series of papers:

  Detsky, AS., Naglie, G., Krahn, MD., *et al.* (1997) Primer on medical decision analysis: Part 1 – Getting started. *Medical Decision Making* **17**(2), 123–125.

  Detsky, AS., Naglie, G., Krahn, MD., *et al.* (1997) Primer on medical decision analysis: Part 2 – Building a tree. *Medical Decision Making* **17**(2), 126–135.

  Naglie, G., Krahn, MD., Naimark, D., *et al.* (1997) Primer on medical decision analysis: Part 3 – Estimating probabilities and utilities. *Medical Decision Making* **17**(2), 136–141.

  Krahn, MD., Naglie, G., Naimark, D., *et al.* (1997) Primer on medical decision analysis: Part 4 – Analyzing the model and interpreting the results. *Medical Decision Making* **17**(2), 142–151.

- For use of and discussions on sensitivity analysis:

  Von Wintefeldt, D. & O'Sullivan, TM. (2006) Should we protect commercial airplanes against surface-to-air missile attacks by terrorists?, *Decision Analysis* **3**(2), 63–75.

  Eschenbach, TG. (1992) Spider plots versus tornado diagrams for sensitivity analysis. *Interfaces* **22**(6), 40–46.

  Eschenbach, TG. (2006) Technical note: Constructing tornado diagrams with spreadsheets. *The Engineering Economist* **51**, 195–204.

  Vrijland, MSA. (2003) Visual display of sensitivity and risk. *47th Annual Meeting AACE – International Transactions*, pp. RISK 11.1–11.8.

  Eschenbach, TG. & Gimpel, RJ. (1990) Stochastic sensitivity analysis. *The Engineering Economist* **35**(4), 195–204.

  Felli, JC. & Hazen, GB. (1998) Sensitivity analysis and the expected value of perfect information. *Medical Decision Making* **18**(1), 95–109.

Felli, JC. & Hazen, GB. (2004) Javelin diagrams: a graphical tool for probabilistic sensitivity analysis. *Decision Science* **1**(2), 93–107.

Detilleux, JC. (2004) Javelin diagrams: applications in veterinary medical decision analysis. *Veterinary Research* **35**, 617–624.

- For an introduction to simulation:

Hertz, DB. (1964) Risk analysis in capital investment. *Harvard Business Review* **42**(1), 95–106.

Denardo, EV. (2002) *The Science of Decision Making: A Problem-Based Approach Using Excel.* John Wiley & Sons, Chapter 15.

Goodwin, P. & Wright, G. (2004) *Decision Analysis for Management Judgement.* John Wiley & Sons, Ltd, Chichester, UK, Chapter 7.

Murtha, J. (2000) Decision Trees vs. Monte Carlo simulation, in *Risk Analysis for the Oil Industry.* Supplement to *Hart's E&P*, August 2000. Available at www.crystalball.com/articles/download/trees_vs_mcs.pdf [accessed 9 July 2008].

Bailey, W., Couët, B., Lamb, F., *et al.* (2000) Taking a calculated risk. *Oilfield Review* **Autumn 2000**, 20–35. Available at www.slb.com/media/services/resources/oilfieldreview/ors00/aut00/p20_35.pdf [accessed 9 July 2008].

- For examples of decision trees:

Collins, I. (2003) Scale management and risk assessment for deepwater developments. *World Oil Magazine* **224**(5). Available at www.worldoil.com/magazine/MAGAZINE_DETAIL.asp?ART_ID=2036&MONTH_YEAR=May-2003 [accessed 9 July 2008].

Feinstein, CD. (1990) Deciding whether to test student athletes for drug use. *Interfaces* **20**(3), 80–87.

Millet, I. (1994) A novena to Saint Anthony, or how to find inventory by not looking. *Interfaces* **24**(2), 69–75.

Ulvila, JW. & Brown, RV. (1982) Decision analysis comes of age. *Harvard Business Review* **60**(5), 130–141.

Willoughby, KA. & Kostuk, KJ. (2005) An analysis of a strategic decision in the sport of curling. *Decision Analysis* **2**(1), 58–63.

Yue, Y. & Scutter, M. (2000) Quantitative decision making for cued land reconnaissance: a defence case study. *International Transactions in Operational Research* **7**, 449–463.

Questions

Q9.1 Roll back the following decision tree, assuming the payoffs represent positive cash flows. Repeat the rollback, assuming the payoffs represent negative cash flows.

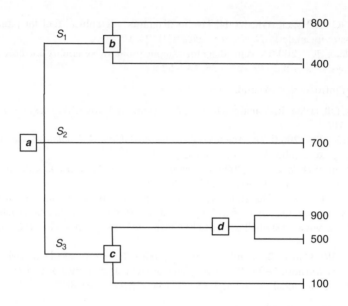

Q9.2 Assuming the payoffs represent positive cash flows, investigate the sensitivity of the following decision tree to the probability p. Repeat the investigation, assuming the payoffs represent negative cash flows.

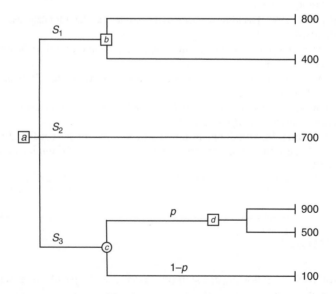

Q9.3 Proto Pharm is deciding whether to fund the penultimate stage of a drug development project. This would require an investment of £50 million. Alternatively, Proto can sell the intellectual property from its existing results to another company for £40 million. Proto and the other company do not compete in the same market, and the executives at Proto do not believe there is any additional organizational learning to be gained from continuing the drug development. The decision is considered to be purely financial. If Proto fund the penultimate stage there is a 0.6 chance of a poor result and a 0.4 chance of a promising result. If the penultimate stage is promising, then the other company is willing to pay Proto £100 million for the intellectual property rights. If the penultimate stage is poor, then Proto estimate a final stage would only have a 0.5 chance of success. If the penultimate stage is promising, then the final stage has a 0.7 chance of success. The payoff after costs for a successful final stage is estimated at £140 million, and the payoff after costs for a failed final stage is estimated at £0. The other company would not purchase the intellectual rights from Proto if the penultimate stage were unsuccessful. Draw and roll back a decision tree to advise Proto Pharm whether to fund the penultimate stage or to sell the intellectual property to the other company.

Q9.4 A company classifies 30 % of its employees as above average, 40 % as average, and 30 % as below average. Each employee works in one of three functions: Operations, Marketing, or Finance. To recognise its employees, the company holds three celebration days at the end of each year. Day 1 is attended by above-average employees, day 2 by average employees, and day 3 by below-average employees. Of those attending the day 1 celebration, 30 % were from Operations, 40 % from Marketing, and 30 % from Finance. On day 2 the attendance was 40 %, 20 %, and 40 %, and on day 3 it was 50 %, 20 %, and 30 %.

What percentage of the employees in each function are classified as above average, average, or below average?

Q9.5 Brunch-Ease is a growing fast food company and has to decide whether to buy a market survey before expanding into a new geographic market. Luis Gomez, the finance officer, expects one of three outcomes if the company expands: poor sales, medium sales, or high sales. Of other fast food outlets opening in the area, 60 % have had poor sales, 15 % medium sales, and 25 % high sales. Experience indicates that the average loss resulting from poor sales is £90 000. The profit resulting from medium sales is expected to be £400 000. The profit from high sales is forecast as £900 000. If Luis decides not to expand, then Brunch-Ease can sell options it holds to rent prime locations to another company for £170 000. Luis can buy a survey report of the new market for £60 000. The survey report will rate the market conditions as either favourable or unfavourable but say nothing about whether the sales would be poor, medium, or high. Brunch-Ease is a member of a business network that issues information on the reliability of market surveys. The business network estimates that, if poor sales were going to occur, then a survey would indicate favourable market conditions only 5 % of the time. If sales were going to be medium, then a survey would indicate favourable conditions 30 % of the time. Finally, if sales were going to be high, a survey would suggest favourable conditions 65 % of the time.

What course of action should Luis take?

Activities

A9.1 Imagine that you have carried out the analysis resulting in Figures 9.6 and 9.10. Write a brief report summarising your results and making a recommendation.

A9.2 Prepare a 5–10 minute presentation discussing the suitability of decision tree analysis, or other decision-taking approaches, to choosing a form of mortgage. A starting paper might be:

Heian, BC. & Gale, JR. (1988) Mortgage selection using a decision-tree approach: an extension. *Interfaces* **18**(4), 72–83.

A9.3 Develop a decision tree for the *Monty Hall* problem. Discuss whether this is a useful approach. Discuss possible generalisations in terms of quantity and quality of payoffs.

A9.4 Identify commercial software packages to aid decision tree and Monte Carlo modelling. Investigate the software and then write a brief memorandum to a (fictitious) superior justifying the purchase of one of the products. Among others, some useful websites include:

www.treeplan.com
www.treeage.com
www.palisade.com
www.decisioneering.com

A9.5 One suggestion for combining qualitative and quantitative data in a decision tree is the *expected commercial value*. Justify whether this is useful.

Cooper, R., Edgett, S., & Kleinschmidt, E. (1997) Portfolio management in new product development: lessons from the leaders I. *Research-Technology Management* **40**(5), 16–28.

A9.6 In Chapter 9 it has been assumed that monies are already expressed as present values. It is often the case that such monetary values (profits, costs, cash flows, exercise prices, etc.) are initially in terms of their future values and must be discounted back to a present value before proceeding with the decision tree rollback. Arithmetically this is a simple step; if a cash flow were to occur immediately, such as the purchasing of the market research survey or the option to buy the land in Figure 9.10, then it would not be discounted at all. On the other hand, if a cash flow were to occur at year n, then it would be discounted for n years to be put in present value terms within the decision tree. The difficulty, however, is choosing the appropriate discount rate for all or parts of the tree; different branches of the tree have different risk profiles and hence should have different discount rates applied. One approach is to include the discount rate within the sensitivity analysis. Another suggested approach is to use real options analysis, although this has also been questioned. Research the issue of discount rates in decision trees. Starting papers might include:

Dixit, AK. & Pindyck, RS. (1995) The options approach to capital investment. *Harvard Business Review* **73**(3), 105–115.

Jagle, AJ. (1999) Shareholder value, real options, and innovation in technology intensive companies. *R&D Management* **29**(3), 271–287.

Steffens, PR. & Douglas, EJ. (2007) Valuing technology investments: use real options thinking but forget real options valuation. *International Journal of Technoentrepreneurship* **1**(1), 58–77.

Reyck, BD., Degraeve, Z., & Vandenborre, R. (2008) Project options valuation with net present value and decision tree analysis. *European Journal of Operational Research* **184**, 341–355.

And for motivation:

Wilkinson, M. (2006) Stern's report is based on flawed figures. *Financial Times* 3 November 2006. Available online: www.ft.com/cms/s/0/48bf3b58-6ae0-11db-83d9-0000779e2340.html [accessed 9 July 2008].

A9.7 Build a quincunx. Inspiration might be sought from:

Kunert, J., Montag, A., & Pöhlmann, S. (2001) The quincunx: history and mathematics. *Statistical Papers* **42**, 143–169.

Having constructed a quincunx, develop a computer simulation of it. What represents first-order uncertainty, and what represents second-order uncertainty?

A9.8 This activity aims to demonstrate the basics of Monte Carlo simulation within spreadsheet modelling. In practice there are many commercial suppliers of tools (see, for example, Activity **A9.4** above) with which to undertake simulations. However, the approach here is directed towards clarifying the essence of such simulations, rather than the exact approach of any particular product.

(a) In a new Excel Workbook, remind yourself of worksheet functions RAND, NORMINV, and BETAINV, the worksheet array formula FREQUENCY, and the plotting of column charts.

(b) A company is estimating its profit for the coming year using the following formula:

$$Profit = (Price - Variable\ Costs) \times Number\ of\ Sales - Fixed\ Costs$$

Given that $Price = £20$, $Variable\ Costs = £10$, $Number\ of\ Sales = 100\,000$, and $Fixed\ Costs = £800\,000$, the estimated profit is

$$Profit = (20 - 10) \times 100\,000 - 800\,000 = £200\,000$$

The company also wishes investors to know the probability of the company not reaching this profit, and the probability of the company making a loss. To this end, probability distributions have been associated with each of the four input parameters, each of which is considered to be essentially independent of the others. *Price* is fixed at £20, *Variable Costs* can be modelled as a beta distribution over the range 0–40 with shape parameters 20 and 60, *Number of Sales* can be modelled as a beta distribution over the range 0–110 000 with shape parameters 20 and 2, and *Fixed Costs* can be modelled as a normal distribution with a mean of 800 000 and a standard deviation of 100 000.

Open a new Excel Workbook, rename the worksheet 'Profit Simulation', and format the cells A1 to M1 as bold.

Each row will represent one simulation. Enter the following:

- into A1 type 'Random VC';
- into B1 type 'Variable Cost';
- into C1 type 'Random S';
- into D1 type 'Sales';

- into E1 type 'Random FC';
- into F1 type 'Fixed Costs';
- into G1 type 'Profit'.

Columns A, C, and E will be used to generate random numbers uniformly distributed on the interval (0, 1). Columns B, D, and E will use Excel's inverse cumulative distribution functions to generate the corresponding values of the input parameters. Enter the following:

- into A2 type '=RAND()';
- into C2 type '=RAND()';
- into E2 type '=RAND()';
- into B2 type '=BETAINV($A2,20,60,0,40)';
- into D2 type '=BETAINV($C2,20,2,0,110000)';
- into F2 type '=NORMINV($E2,800000,100000)'.

Column G will show the profit from each simulation:

- into G2 type '=(20-$B2)*$D2-$F2'.

More simulations can be carried out, but here 2000 will be performed.

Select cells A2 to G2, move the cursor to the bottom right of G2 until it becomes a black cross, and then click and drag down to cell G2001.

Each of the values in column G represents a simulated *Profit*. some will be similar to £200 000, as in the deterministic calculation above, others are markedly different and allow the company to estimate the required probabilities. Enter the following:

- into H1 type 'Average';
- into I1 type 'Bin';
- into K1 type 'Frequency';
- into L1 type 'Probability';
- into M1 type 'Cumulative';
- into H2 type '=AVERAGE($G2:$G2001)'.

In cell H2 it will be seen that the average of 2000 simulations is approximately £200 000.

- into cell I2 type '−1000000';
- into cell I3 type '−900000'.

Select cells I2 and I3, move the cursor to the bottom right of I3 until it becomes a black cross, and then click and drag down to cell I22. Each intermediate cell will increase by 100 000, so that I22 finishes with 1,000,000.

- into cell I23 type 'more';
- into cell K2 type '=FREQUENCY($G2:$G2001,$I2:$I22)'.

Select cells K2 to K23, press function key F2, then press CTRL+SHIFT+ENTER. Cells K2 to K23 will now contain frequency count data for each of the bins. To convert to estimated probabilities, these need to be divided by the total number of counts, which in this case is 2000.

- into cell L2 type '=K2/2000';
- into cell M2 type '=SUM($L$2:$L2)'.

Select cells L2 and M2, move the cursor to the bottom right of M2 until it becomes a black cross, and then click and drag down to cell M23.

Cell M12 contains an estimate of achieving a loss, and cell M14 shows an estimate of the profit being less than £200 000. The results can be summarised in a histogram.

Select cells I1 to I23 and L1 to L23, plot a clustered column chart, and change the gap width to zero (in Excel 2007, right click on one of the columns, select 'Format Data Series').

Excel updates the random numbers generated whenever there is a change in the spreadsheet, or by pressing the function key F9.

For each set of 2000 simulated results it can be seen that the expected value (cell H2) is ~£200 000, the probability of achieving a loss (cell M12) is ~0.19, and the probability of not reaching £200 000 profit (M14) is ~0.49. Nevertheless, the results obtained do vary by ±5 % from these. The Monte Carlo simulation technique then not only has reproduced the deterministic result but also has provided an indication of the potential variation in the profits for the forthcoming year.

CHAPTER 10

Sequential Games

Objectives

- *To understand the conceptual differences between simultaneous and sequential games.*
- *To represent sequential games in extensive form and find the solution using rollback.*
- *To incorporate asymmetry of information into the game and find an appropriate solution.*
- *To understand the concepts of signalling, signal jamming, and screening.*
- *To understand how sequential games can be used to analyse situations where outcomes are negotiated.*

Introduction

Unlike simultaneous games, in which players choose strategies at precisely the same point in time, sequential games require that the players choose strategies consecutively. As a consequence there is a player who will make the first choice, and all subsequent choices of other players are affected by the order in which the choices are made. Therefore, players must take into account the order in which strategies are chosen when selecting their strategy.

Sequential games are used for analysing situations where there is an opportunity for one player to choose a strategy before other players make a choice. As such, players who pick first may have an advantage, as their choice may force the other players to select strategies that are more beneficial to the first player. An example of such a situation is the case of first-mover advantage where a company may gain a significant advantage by being the first entrant in a market segment.

In situations where decisions are made sequentially, the approach taken by players to find their optimal choice is different to that used when decisions are taken simultaneously. Players should 'look ahead and reason back' (Dixit & Nalebuff, 1991, p. 34). So players should assess the optimal choices made by other players in the reverse of the order in which the decisions are made. Sequential games are therefore represented by game trees, rather like the decision trees already encountered. They are not presented in matrix form, as it can be difficult to ascertain in which order the choices are being made. This form of representation is known as extensive form.

Extensive Form

In order to see exactly how competitive situations where choices are made sequentially can be formulated in game theoretic terms, consider the following example. Company A produces product M and the management team are currently deciding whether to set production capacity 'high' or 'low'. Complicating this decision is the fact that Company A's direct rival, Company B, is also choosing its production capacity. Depending upon the choice each company makes, the payoffs they will receive are detailed in Figure 10.1.

		Company B	
		H	L
Company A	H	50, 50	200, 75
	L	75, 200	100, 100

Figure 10.1 Profit payoffs.

A swift analysis using best response (see Chapter 7) reveals that, if Company A and Company B make their choices simultaneously, there are two equilibria: (high, low) and (low, high). As far as Company A is concerned, the equilibrium of (high, low) is the preferable outcome. Can Company A influence the outcome in order to arrive at the most desirable outcome? The answer is 'yes', by choosing a strategy before Company B settles on its strategy. This changes the nature of the game from simultaneous to sequential and requires a modified representation of the game.

Figure 10.2 shows the extensive form of the game, which indicates the order in which the decisions are taken. Company A makes the first choice of strategy, and hence its choice is defined first, and then Company B will find itself at point B_1 or at point B_2 and the available choices are defined accordingly. Consequently, Company A can force the best outcome by choosing first and by choosing 'high'. Provided Company B chooses rationally, the company would choose 'low', thereby arriving at the equilibrium that provides the best outcome for Company A. In this case, Company A has gained an advantage by choosing its strategy before the other player.

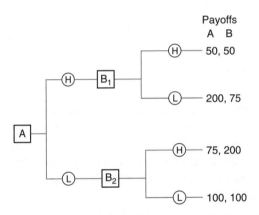

Figure 10.2   Extensive form.

Any such game can be represented in this form when the players in the game do not make decisions simultaneously. The format generally followed is that the decisions are represented in the order in which they are taken from left to right.

Rollback Revisited

In the previous example, the choice of strategy that would be made by Company A was clear: the company selected the strategy that would force the outcome that was most favourable. In other situations, however, the choices may be more complex. In these situations, rollback can be used to help determine the best choice the company can make.

Consider the example shown in Figure 10.3. Company A has two competitors, Company B and Company C.

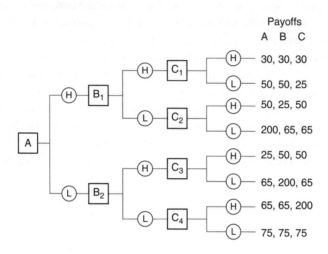

Figure 10.3 Rollback example – full game tree.

Although each company faces only two strategy choices, this will result in seven potential decision nodes with eight possible outcomes. Each decision node represents a *subgame* and in every subgame, all players are aware of the decision taken in the previous subgames. Assuming that the companies choose in the order A, B, and C, before Company A makes its choice, the rollback technique can be applied in order to determine its best choice.

The first step is to consider the possible choices made by Company C. At point C_1, Company C will choose 'high', and at C_2 it will choose 'low', as this results in the highest payoffs for each subgame. Similarly, it will choose 'low' at C_3 and 'high' at C_4. Hence, the other choices can now be discounted from the analysis (see Figure 10.4).

The same logic can now be applied to the choices of Company B, resulting in a choice of 'low' at B_1 and 'high' at B_2. Eliminating the non-optimal choices for B leads to Figure 10.5.

It is now clear that Company A should choose 'high', resulting in the following set of strategy choices:

- Company A – 'high';
- Company B – 'low';
- Company C – 'low'.

This set of strategies is known as a *subgame perfect Nash equilibrium*, which represents the Nash equilibrium of all the player's strategies in every subgame. Hence,

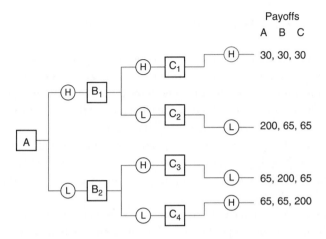

Figure 10.4   Rollback example – optimal choices for C.

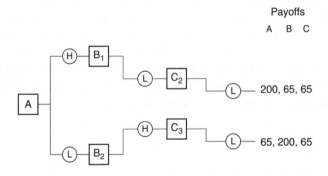

Figure 10.5   Rollback example – optimal choices for B and C.

all players are doing the best they can while accounting for the choices made by the other players and the order in which these are made.

In this example, the order of choice was fixed. It need not be so, and players may use this type of analysis in order to decide if they can gain an advantage by selecting a strategy at a particular point in the process. There are, for example, cases where making the second choice may be advantageous: allowing a competitor to try out a new product within a market before devoting costly resources on the development of a product that may not be popular may save an expensive mistake. This will depend upon the availability of suitable information in order to determine the payoffs, although it is not always necessary to estimate exact payoffs; knowing relative magnitudes may be sufficient (there is a related activity at the end of the chapter for the interested reader).

Asymmetry of Information

Real situations are rarely simple in the manner of the games presented here, and it does not always follow that players who make strategy choices later in the game have little or no influence over the outcome of the game. The underlying assumption here, and with the game theory discussed in Chapter 7, is that all players have access to the same information about the state of the game and the choices being made. This, however, is not true in many cases. Very often, players will hold an advantage over other players by being in possession of information that is not commonly known. This is known as *asymmetry of information* and can, with a little effort, be incorporated into the analysis.

Consider the situation of Company A, currently the market leader for a particular product, which is facing competition from a rival, Company B, wishing to enter the market. Company B may be a weak competitor, in which case Company A can pursue an aggressive marketing campaign, thereby preventing Company B from gaining any share of the market. This approach is expensive, however, and, if Company B happens to be a strong competitor, this will not prevent from gaining some share of the market. As a consequence, Company A would sacrifice a large proportion of its market share to Company B. Company A does have an alternative choice, that is, to continue with its current marketing campaign, which is much less expensive but will not prevent Company B from entering the market. Nevertheless, since Company A is the current market leader, if B is a weak competitor, then A will retain the majority of the market share.

To summarise the situation:

- Company B is in one of two states:

    o a <u>weak</u> state;
    o a <u>strong</u> state.

- Company A has two choices:

    o choose an <u>aggressive</u> marketing campaign;
    o continue with the <u>current</u> marketing campaign.

- Company B has two choices:

    o <u>enter</u> the market;
    o do <u>not enter</u> the market.

From the point of view of Company A, asymmetry of information arises as a consequence of the unknown state of Company B. The choice that Company A has to make must now not only take the possible choices of their rival into account but also the possible state of their rival. Company B knows whether it is weak or strong and therefore has an advantage over Company A.

The entire market is worth £100 million, and Company A currently has a 70 % market share. If Company B enters the market and is strong, Company A will be left with 53 % of the market share if it chooses an aggressive campaign, and 51 % if it continues with its current strategy. If Company B enters the market and is weak, Company A will continue to take 70 % of the market share if it chooses an aggressive campaign, and 62 % if it continues with its current campaign. The current marketing campaign costs Company A £2 million, and a new, aggressive marketing campaign will cost £5 million.

If Company B is strong and chooses to enter the market, it will take 25 % of the market share if Company A chooses to continue with its current marketing campaign, and 20 % if Company A chooses an aggressive marketing campaign. If Company B is weak, it will fail to take any of the market if Company A chooses an aggressive campaign, and will take 10 % if Company A continues with its current campaign. Entering the market will cost Company B £5 million. If, however, Company B chooses not to enter the market, it will get 0 % of the market share, regardless of whether it is weak or strong, and Company A will continue to take 70 % of the market, regardless of the chosen marketing strategy.

The first step is to calculate the payoffs. This process can be summarised in the two tables in Figure 10.6.

		Company B – Strong	
		Enter	**Not enter**
Company A	**Aggressive**	53 – 5, 20 – 5	70 – 5, 0
	Current	51 – 2, 25 – 5	70 – 2, 0

		Company B – Weak	
		Enter	**Not enter**
Company A	**Aggressive**	70 – 5, 0 – 5	70 – 5, 0
	Current	62 – 2, 10 – 5	70 – 2, 0

Figure 10.6 Payoff calculation in £ million.

For example, if Company B is strong and chooses to enter the market when Company A has chosen to invest in an aggressive marketing campaign, then Company A will take 53 % of the market (worth £53 million), but it will cost £5 million for the marketing campaign, leaving them with 53 – 5 = £48 million. Company B will take 20 % of the market (worth £20 million), and it will cost £5 million to enter the market, leaving them with $20 - 5 = £15$ million.

Since this is a sequential game (Company A chooses its marketing campaign first) and there is asymmetry of information (Company B's state is not known to Company A), the full structure of the game is best represented in terms of a game tree (see Figure 10.7).

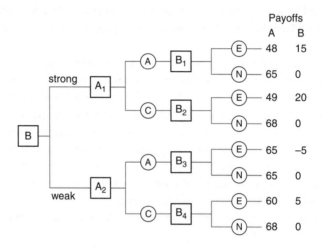

Figure 10.7   Initial game tree.

The first branch of the tree indicates the possible states of Company B (remember that this process will assist Company A in its decision-making process). This then allows the two possible payoff matrices shown in Figure 10.6 to be incorporated in the same way as in the previous examples of sequential games already presented.

Once the tree has been constructed, the next step requires the elimination of the outcomes that will never be reached, and hence the possible choices of Company B are determined. Since Company B is making its choice after Company A and knows with certainty whether it is 'weak' or 'strong', the standard best response process can be used to eliminate the choices that Company B will never make. Looking at the game tree, it is clear that, if Company B is strong, it will always choose to enter the market. If Company B is weak, it will only choose to enter the market if Company A chooses to continue with its current marketing campaign (see Figure 10.8).

Company A is in a different situation, since its choice is subject to uncertainty, which therefore needs to be incorporated into the game tree. This is achieved by assigning a probability to the state of Company B. It is assumed that the probability of Company B being strong is p, and hence the probability that Company B is weak is equal to $1 - p$ (see Figure 10.9).

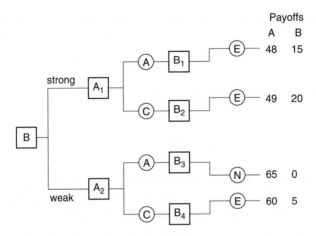

Figure 10.8 Subgame removal.

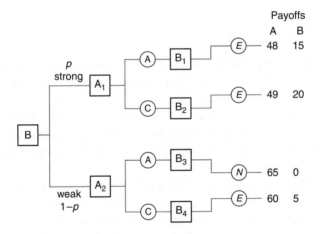

Figure 10.9 Incorporating uncertainty.

Company A's choice can be resolved in a similar fashion to the approach taken to determine mixed strategies. The first step requires that the expected payoffs of Company A are calculated for each possible strategy choice.

Company A's expected payoff from choosing an aggressive marketing campaign is given by

$$E(A) = 48p + 65\,(1 - p)$$

Similarly, Company A's expected payoff from continuing with its current marketing campaign is given by

$$E(C) = 49p + 60\,(1 - p)$$

Company A should choose an aggressive campaign if $E(A) > E(C)$, and therefore

$$48p + 65(1 - p) > 49p + 60(1 - p)$$

Rearranging this equation results in the following:

$$p < \frac{5}{6} \quad \text{and hence} \quad p < 0.83$$

This suggests that, if Company A believes that the probability that Company B is strong is less than 0.83, then Company A should choose an aggressive strategy. Hence, unless Company A is reasonably certain that Company B is strong (i.e. $p > 0.83$), it should not choose to continue with its current strategy.

Signals

With situations of asymmetric uncertainty, it is possible to gain more information about the game by observing signals. Signals are actions taken by players that give credible evidence of the state that they are in. These actions may not be chosen deliberately by the player and may be involuntary. For example, a manufacturing company choosing to downsize its production capacity might indicate that the company is in a weak position. The strategy of choosing these actions is known as *signalling*.

Recalling the previous example, Company B may be in one of two states, either 'weak' or 'strong'. Assume now that Company A observes a signal from Company B. There is a chance of observing this signal whether Company B is weak or strong. Hence, a probability is assigned to the chance of observing the signal in each of the states. So it is assumed that the probability of Company B being 'strong' and the signal being observed is q, and the probability that Company B is 'weak' and the signal being observed is r. Note that q and r do not need to sum to 1, since these probabilities represent independent events.

This situation is summarised in Figure 10.10. So, for example, the probability of Company B being strong and Company A observing the signal is pq. Bayes' theorem can now be used to calculate an updated probability for the state of Company B. In general terms, if there are two conditions, α and β, and an observation χ, then the probability of being in condition α given that an observation χ is made is

$$\text{Prob}(\alpha \mid \chi) = \frac{\text{Prob}(\alpha)\,\text{Prob}(\chi \mid \alpha)}{\text{Prob}(\alpha)\,\text{Prob}(\chi \mid \alpha) + \text{Prob}(\beta)\,\text{Prob}(\chi \mid \beta)}$$

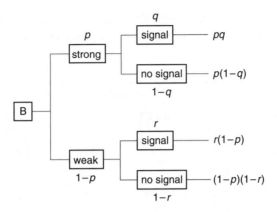

Figure 10.10 Signal probabilities.

Thus, in specific terms, the probability of Company B being 'strong' given that Company A observes a signal is

$$\text{Prob(strong}|\text{signal)} = \frac{\text{Prob(strong) Prob(signal}|\text{strong)}}{\text{Prob(strong) Prob(signal}|\text{strong)} + \text{Prob(weak) Prob(signal}|\text{weak)}}$$

The numerator is the probability of Company B being strong and the signal being observed, and the denominator is simply the probability of observing a signal regardless of whether the company is weak or strong.

Now

$$\text{Prob(strong)} = p$$

$$\text{Prob(weak)} = 1 - p$$

$$\text{Prob(signal } | \text{ strong)} = q$$

$$\text{Prob(signal } | \text{ weak)} = r$$

Hence

$$\text{Prob(strong}|\text{signal)} = \frac{pq}{pq + r(1 - p)}$$

This updated probability is used in place of p in the calculation of the choice of strategy. So, for this example, recalling that Company A should choose an aggressive strategy if $p < 0.83$, if a signal is observed, this can be updated to the following:

$$\frac{pq}{pq + r(1 - p)} < 0.83$$

By substituting some example probabilities into this formula, it is possible to note the effect the observation of the signal has on the probability (Figure 10.11).

p	Updated p					
	$q = 1$ $r = 0$	$q = 0$ $r = 1$	$q = 0.5$ $r = 0.5$	$q = 0.9$ $r = 0.3$	$q = 0.3$ $r = 0.9$	$q = 0.75$ $r = 0.25$
0.00	1.00	0.00	0.00	0.00	0.00	0.00
0.10	1.00	0.00	0.10	0.25	0.04	0.25
0.20	1.00	0.00	0.20	0.43	0.08	0.43
0.30	1.00	0.00	0.30	0.56	0.13	0.56
0.40	1.00	0.00	0.40	0.67	0.18	0.67
0.50	1.00	0.00	0.50	0.75	0.25	0.75
0.60	1.00	0.00	0.60	0.82	0.33	0.82
0.70	1.00	0.00	0.70	0.88	0.44	0.88
0.80	1.00	0.00	0.80	0.92	0.57	0.92
0.90	1.00	0.00	0.90	0.96	0.75	0.96
1.00	1.00	0.00	1.00	1.00	1.00	1.00

Figure 10.11 Updated probabilities.

Recalling that the sum of q and r does not have to be equal to 1 since these two probabilities represent independent events, it is possible that a signal is always observed regardless of whether Company B is 'strong' or 'weak' (i.e. $q = 1$ and $r = 1$). In this circumstance, the signal would add no information to the situation and would be irrelevant. In general, if the probability that the signal is observed and Company B is strong is equal to the probability that the signal is observed and Company B is weak, this does not add any other information to the situation, and the updated p is the same as the original p.

If the likelihood of observing the signal and Company B being strong is known to be certain (i.e. $q = 1$), and it is also known that a signal will never be observed if Company B is weak (i.e. $r = 0$), it is clear that it is known with certainty that Company B is strong.

If, however, the likelihood of observing the signal and Company B being 'strong' is close to certainty ($q = 0.9$) and it is unlikely that a signal would be observed if Company B is 'weak', the updated p will be closer to 1 when compared with the original p.

This is because the additional information means that, if a signal is observed, it is more likely that Company B will be 'strong' (i.e. the updated p will be closer to 1).

Observing signals can provide additional information when determining the choice of strategy. Given that many of the results shown here are intuitive, it is tempting to rely entirely on intuition. Nevertheless, humans are notoriously poor at judging uncertain situations, and so these mathematical techniques provide an approach that circumvents much of the intuition that could be applied in situations such as this. The calculation of both the initial probability and the probabilities associated with the observation of the signal should be based on data and existing expert knowledge to provide the best outcome.

Signal Jamming and Screening

The analysis presented here implicitly assumes the observed signals are 'truthful' and therefore are indicative of being in a certain state. This cannot always be assumed, since players may not wish to give away their information advantage. In this case, a player may choose to take actions that deceive other players, either by revealing false information or by concealing true information that is detrimental to the player. This strategy is often known as *signal jamming*. For example, employees might conceal their incompetence by blaming other employees.

It may therefore be necessary, as a player at an information disadvantage, to choose a strategy that induces other players to reveal true information. For example, an employer may wish to induce potential employees to reveal true information about their abilities by testing them prior to employing them. A strategy that helps to determine whether a signal is 'truthful' is known as screening.

In general, a signal is only credible if the cost of the signal is higher than the cost of signal jamming. Consider the case of a company that offers free extended warranties for their products. This acts as a credible signal of the quality of the products, since, if the company's products were of poor quality, the cost of honouring the warranties would be considerable and much higher than would be the case were this signal not a credible indication of high-quality products.

Bargaining

The formulation of sequential games lends itself to the analysis of situations involving players who are engaged in negotiating the outcome of their interaction, since in these circumstances decisions are very often taken sequentially. To engage in a bargaining process, it must be in the interests of all players to reach a mutually beneficial outcome, i.e. the payoffs derived from a negotiated outcome must be higher than those that could be achieved individually. This process therefore results in a surplus, and game theory can be used to aid in the division of this surplus between the players. Assuming rationality implies that there is a conflict of interest, since all players want a larger share of this surplus than their competitors would want them to have.

As with other branches of game theory, bargaining can be cooperative or non-cooperative. When bargaining cooperatively, all agents choose and implement their strategies jointly to reach the beneficial outcome. In these situations, an independent third party may be involved to help to determine and enforce the optimal outcome. These types of game are essentially simultaneous in nature, where all outcomes from all possible combinations of strategies are considered and the best outcome is chosen. A cooperative solution is possible if outcomes are enforceable. Since these games are simultaneous in nature, they are left as an investigation for the interested reader.

Of more interest within the business environment are non-cooperative bargaining games, where all players choose their strategy without involvement from others. A process of negotiation is then entered into where players make 'offers' and 'counteroffers' until an agreement is reached or the process breaks down. These types of game are clearly sequential in nature, as agents take turns to make offers.

An important aspect of non-cooperative bargaining is time. The surplus that is being divided degenerates during each round. Although the reasons for this are often complex, costs such as legal and arbitrator fees and loss of productivity during the negotiating process will cause costs to increase and therefore will cause the surplus to decrease over time.

Consider the following example where the employees of a company are negotiating a pay rise with their employers. The surplus being negotiated is the estimated contribution of the skilled employees over and above what might be contributed if the employees were less skilled. It is assumed that the surplus reduces in each round such that it disappears if an agreement is not reached in the final round. This may appear unrealistic, but, if the negotiation process breaks down, both employers and employees will be in a situation where strikes and redundancies are a reality, leading to lost productivity and profits.

Assuming that employers make the first offer, consider a single-round negotiation process where the company makes the only offer. Since there is only one round of negotiation, the surplus will disappear after this round, and hence the offer made will have to be accepted by the employees or the negotiation process will break down, leaving no surplus. This is a particularly extreme situation. The employees will have to accept any positive amount of surplus unless the company offers nothing, in which case the employees will be indifferent between accepting and rejecting the offer.

Now consider the situation where there are two rounds of negotiation, and hence, after the first round, only half of the surplus remains. The choices made by each of the agents in the negotiation process can be determined by using backward induction. Assume again that the company makes the first offer. Since the employees then make the offer in the last round, they are aware that only 50 % of the surplus remains, and so they demand the full 50 %, forcing the employers to accept or face a breakdown in negotiations.

Rolling back to the first round, the employers make an offer, aware of the fact that the workers are only expecting 50 % of the surplus. Consequently, the employers make an offer of 50 % in the first round, leaving 50 % for the employers themselves. Hence, with a two-round negotiation process, the surplus will be split in half between employers and employees.

Consider a three-round negotiation process, summarised in Figure 10.12.

Rounds remaining	Surplus remaining	Offer made by	Employees receive	Employers receive
1	33.3 %	Employers	0	33.3 %
2	66.7 %	Employees	33.3 %	33.3 %
3	100 %	Employers	33.3 %	66.7 %

Figure 10.12 Three-round negotiation process.

In this case the offer in the last round is made by the employers, assuming that the employers also make the first offer. Since this is a three-round process, the surplus is therefore reduced by one-third of the total value of the surplus during each round. So the employers know that there is 33.3 % remaining in the last round and make an offer demanding this amount. Consequently, in the penultimate round, the employees are aware that the employers will demand 33.3 %, so this is the offer made, leaving 33.3 % for the employees. In the first round, given that the employers know that the employees expect to get 33.3 % in round 2, the employers make this offer, which leaves 66.6 % for them. Hence, the analysis reveals that the surplus will be split in favour of the employers.

Similarly, a four-round negotiation process is determined as in Figure 10.13.

This process can be carried out for any number of rounds, but what becomes clear as the number of rounds increases is that the optimal split is approximately half each for the employers and employees. Hence, both the employers and employees can determine that they should offer and accept 50 % during the first round to ensure that the greatest amount of surplus is available.

Rounds remaining	Surplus remaining	Offer made by	Employees receive	Employers receive
1	25 %	Employees	25 %	0
2	50 %	Employers	25 %	25 %
3	75 %	Employees	50 %	25 %
4	100 %	Employers	50 %	50 %

Figure 10.13 Four-round negotiation process.

Of course, reality is never quite this straightforward. Although this analysis does include the time value of money in terms of the degeneration of the surplus, it does not account for the relative *bargaining power* of the players. Bargaining power is as a consequence of many factors but results mainly from the availability of alternative options should the negotiation process break down, the cost to each player of delayed outcomes, and the information available to the players and their beliefs about the other players. For example, if a player has attractive options in the event of the failure of the negotiation process, the player is then not as dependent upon a bargained solution. Consequently, this player is in a stronger bargaining position.

The relative bargaining power of each of the agents in the game determines how the division of the surplus will deviate from an even split between the agents in the game. Nevertheless, quantifying bargaining power is very difficult, and so the use of game theory here is as a descriptive rather than a prescriptive tool.

Summary

This chapter has introduced the concept of a sequential game in which the players make decisions in an alternating sequence. This type of game is particularly useful for analysing situations of negotiation, where the interested parties make offers and counteroffers. The games are represented in terms of a game tree that is known as the extensive form and is closely related to the decision trees met earlier in this text. The method of rollback was employed to find the optimal choices of the players.

Sequential games are also useful for examining and assessing optimal choices made in conditions of asymmetry of information between players. Uncertainty regarding characteristics of other players can be incorporated in a sequential format, and then optimal choices can be determined that take the uncertainty into account. Strategies employed by players to influence the game, such as signalling, signal jamming, and screening, all of which involve concealing, revealing, or determining the validity of information, were discussed and, where possible, incorporated into the analysis.

The chapter concluded with a discussion of how negotiation processes can be modelled using the ideas of sequential game theory. A negotiation process is a non-cooperative interaction between players where the players are trying to divide a surplus. The surplus arises because of the negotiation process, since without an incentive there would be no negotiation process. The concept of bargaining power was introduced, and it was demonstrated that, provided the bargaining power of the players was the same, the optimal negotiated outcome resulted in an even split of the surplus.

Further Reading

- The following texts present alternative formulations of the material contained in this chapter:

  Dixit, AK. & Skeath, S. (2004) *Games of Strategy*, 2nd edition. W.W. Norton & Company, New York/London.

  Carmichael, F. (2004) *A Guide to Game Theory*. FT/Prentice Hall: Harlow, UK.

- The following texts provide interesting, but less technical, discussions of game theory including sequential games and bargaining:

  Dixit, AK. & Nalebuff, BJ. (1991) *Thinking Strategically: The Competitive Edge in Business, Politics, and Everyday Life*. W.W. Norton & Company, New York/London.

  Axelrod, R. (1990) *The Evolution of Cooperation*. Penguin, London, UK.

- The following texts are classic game theory texts. They present the theory in its mathematical formulation and therefore are suitable for those who prefer this manner of presentation:

  Maynard Smith, J. (1982) *Evolution and the Theory of Games*. Cambridge University Press, Cambridge, UK.

  von Neumann, J. & Morgenstern, O. (2007) *Theory of Games and Economic Behavior (Princeton Classic Editions)*. Princeton University Press, Princeton, NJ.

- The following article discusses brinkmanship and how the strategy of making threats influences the relative bargaining power of the players:

  Schwarz, M. & Sonin, K. (2008) A theory of brinkmanship, conflicts, and commitments. *Journal of Law, Economics and Organization* **24**(1), 163–183.

- This article presents the entry deterrence example in a more technical framework and covers the use of game theory to analyse aspects of industrial organization such as collusion:

  Bagwell, K. & Wolinksy, A. (2002) Game theory and industrial organization, in *Handbook of Game Theory with Economic Applications*, ed. by Aumann, R. & Hart, S. Elsevier, Amsterdam, The Netherlands, pp. 1851–1895.

Questions

Q10.1 Company A and Company B are manufacturers of products that are rival goods. When choosing to set prices for these products, they can choose to set the price 'high' or 'low'. If both companies choose 'high' prices, both companies receive payoffs of £8 million. If both companies choose 'low' prices, payoffs of £4 million are received. If one company chooses 'high' and one chooses 'low', the company that chooses 'low' receives £10 million, while the other receives £2 million.

(a) Form this situation as a payoff matrix.
(b) Assuming that the choices are made simultaneously, find the Nash equilibrium.
(c) Assume that decisions are taken sequentially. Draw the game tree.
(d) Your company is making the first decision. Use the rollback method to determine your optimal choice.
(e) Is there any difference between the choices you would make if the decisions were taken simultaneously or sequentially? Why do you think that this is the case?

Q10.2 Company B chooses to change the market in which it operates and enters a new market as a direct rival to Company C. Each company can choose to set a 'high' or 'low' price. In this case, the payoffs are as detailed in the following table:

		Company C	
		High	Low
Company B	High	7, 9	2, 4
	Low	4, 3	5, 8

Assuming the companies choose prices simultaneously, determine the equilibria.

(a) Assuming that Company B makes the first choice, construct a decision tree to illustrate the situation and use rollback to determine the optimal choice for Company B.

(b) Is there a difference between the choices made under the assumption of simultaneous decisions and sequential decisions? Why is this so?

(c) If Company C were choosing first, what choice would be made in order to reach the best outcome for it?

Q10.3 Consider the situation in the text of the employers bargaining for a pay rise with their employers.

(a) Use backward induction to determine the choices made in a five-, six-, seven-, and eight-round negotiation process, assuming the employers make the first offer.

(b) What do you notice about the outcome when an even number of rounds is used?

(c) If the employees make the first offer, does the optimal division of the surplus change?

(d) What would be the consequences of the employers discovering that the employees would rather accept a 20 % share than let the negotiation process break down?

Q10.4 Danielle owns a car sales company and currently employs Emily as an administrator with a salary of £20 000 per annum. Emily has, however, expressed an interest in becoming a salesperson, earning £30 000 per annum. Danielle needs to decide whether to 'offer' Emily the position of salesperson or 'not offer' the position. If Emily is offered the position, she can 'accept' or 'reject' the offer, and if she rejects the offer she will continue to work as an administrator and Danielle will incur no costs. If Danielle chooses not to offer Emily the position, she is aware that Emily will leave, as she has a job offer from another company where she would earn £25 000 per annum. If Emily leaves, Danielle will then be forced to search for a new administrator, which will result in costs of £1000. The situation is further complicated by the fact that Emily may be a 'good' salesperson, in which case her employment as a salesperson will result in a £10 000 gain for the company, or she may be a 'bad' salesperson, in which case her employment will result in a loss of £10 000 to the company. Danielle, however, is uncertain as to whether Emily would be 'good' or 'bad'.

(a) Represent this game in extensive form, remembering that the initial decision is being made by Danielle.

(b) Use the extensive form to determine Emily's best strategies.

(c) Use this information to determine in what circumstances Danielle should offer Emily the job.

(d) Consider strategies that both parties could use to influence the outcome of this game.

Q10.5 Reconsider the situation outlined in **Q10.1**, assuming that the decision to set prices is a simultaneous choice. However, we now also assume that the price-setting decision is taken annually.

(a) Assume that the decision is taken for three successive years. Both Company A and Company B know that the decision is only being taken for three successive years. Considering the choices that each company will make in the final round, reason back to determine their choice in the first round.

(b) Is this scenario realistic, and why?

(c) Assume now that the game will be repeated for three successive years without either company knowing when the repetitions will end. Can you reason backwards?

(d) What is the effect of knowing when the repetitions will end?

(e) If simultaneous games are repeated with the agents being unaware of when the repetitions will end, how might you induce your competitor to cooperate with you?

Q10.6 Company X is a direct rival to Company Y, and both are in the process of deciding how much to invest in the development of a new technology. Each company can choose to set a 'high' or 'low' level of investment. The payoffs are detailed in the following table:

		Company y	
		High	**Low**
Company X	**High**	50, 20	40, 30
	Low	20, 40	30, 10

(a) Assuming that the decisions are made simultaneously, find the equilibrium.

(b) Assuming that the decisions are taken sequentially and that X makes the first move, what strategy would X choose?

(c)   Assuming that X chooses first, represent the game in extensive form and use rollback to find the equilibrium.

(d)   Would Company X be able to reach a more desirable outcome if it made its decision after Company Y? Reformulate the game in extensive form, with Company Y choosing first, and test your answer.

(e)   Suggest how Company X could ensure that Company Y makes the first choice.

Activities

A10.1 The games presented here have not included scope for cooperation between agents, since most cases encountered in business will involve direct competition, whether between rival firms or between employees and employers. There is scope for considering cooperative situations where simultaneous choice games are repeated (see **Q10.4**). Investigate the issue of trigger strategies for repeated games.

A10.2 Brinkmanship is an extreme form of bargaining strategy that involves the creation of an intolerable level of risk for the other player(s). This is only usually employed when the breakdown of negotiation without an agreement would result in a catastrophic outcome. The Cuban missile crisis, which occurred during October 1962, offers an example of the use of such a strategy. Investigate the negotiation process in which the presidents of Russia and the USA engaged, and identify the point at which the level of risk was created and the means by which it was created.

A10.3 Although game theory is certainly an interesting method of analysing decisions, there are those who believe that it is of very little use in the 'real world' (for example, see Rubinstein, 2000). Investigate the ways in which game theory is employed outside the academic community, and determine if you believe that this is a valid point of view.

Appendix: Mathematics Revision

Sets

A *set* is a well-defined collection of objects, whether perceived or conceived. The objects are called *elements*. A set may be specified by listing the elements in curly brackets, e.g.

$$\{\text{Peter Drucker}, 55\,000, \alpha\}$$

A set with an infinite number of elements can be listed if there is a pattern such that all elements can be reasonably inferred:

$$\{1, 3, 5, 7, \ldots\}$$

Nevertheless, both finite and infinite sets can be expressed by a well-defined rule, e.g.

$$\{z: z \text{ supports Birmingham City Football Club}\}$$

specifies the set of all people who support Birmingham City Football Club. Similarly

$$\{y: y < 100\}$$

specifies the set of all y such that y is less than 100.

The elements of a set occur only once. Although the numbers $\{3, 1, 2, 2\}$ can be written with a repeated '2', the set only contains one '2', $\{3, 1, 2\}$. Furthermore, repetition and ordering of elements are irrelevant, such that two sets are equal if and only if they contain the same elements:[1]

$$\{\text{Drucker, Porter, Goldratt, Porter}\} = \{\text{Porter, Drucker, Goldratt}\}$$

---

[1] This is known as the *axiom of extensionality*.

The *empty* or *null* set contains no elements and is written as {} or Ø. Since two sets are the same if they contain the same elements, it follows that the empty set is unique.

Sets are often named with a capital letter:

$$A = \{\text{Peter Drucker}, 55\,000, \alpha\}$$

$$B = \{\text{Peter Drucker}, 55\,000, \alpha, \text{banana}\}$$

$$C = \{\text{apple, banana, cabbage}\}$$

and $\in$ is used to indicate that an element is a member of a set:

$$55000 \in A$$

$$\text{Penrose} \notin A$$

For two sets, A and B, if each element of A is also an element of B, then A is a *subset* of B:

$$\emptyset \subset A \subset B \subseteq B, \quad \text{where } A \neq B$$

The empty set is a subset of A, A is a subset of B (where A is not equal to B), and B is a subset of itself.

The sum or *union* of two sets is the set that contains all elements of both sets:

$$A \cup B = \{\text{Peter Drucker}, 55\,000, \alpha, \text{banana}\}$$

$$B \cup C = \{\text{Peter Drucker}, 55\,000, \alpha, \text{apple, banana, cabbage}\}$$

The *intersection* of two sets is the set containing the elements that are common to the two sets:

$$B \cap C = \{\text{banana}\}$$

The *difference* between two sets, X and Y, is the set of elements of X not included in Y:

$$C \backslash B = \{\text{apple, cabbage}\}$$

Note that, when defining the difference between two sets, the ordering of the sets in the expression is important, and hence X\Y is distinct from Y\X. A difference can be defined in which order does not matter, and this is known as a *symmetric difference*, where X Δ Y is the set of elements that are in X or in Y but are not contained in both sets:

$$C \Delta B = \{\text{Peter Drucker}, 55\,000, \alpha, \text{apple, cabbage}\}$$

A *universal set* (sometimes referred to simply as a *universe*) is a set that contains all the elements defined in the problem of interest. For example, if the problem was that of allocating work shifts to employees of a manufacturing plant, the universal set would contain all staff members, with, for example, subsets defined by the department the employees worked in. A universal set can be thought of as a frame of reference for the issue in question. The universal set is defined as the set of all elements and is often denoted by V. Any universal set (including the universal set) will also contain itself.

The *complement* of a set X, denoted by X^c, consists of all elements not contained in that set, for example if a universe is the positive integers and X is the set of even numbers, then X^c is the set of odd numbers.

The ideas of a set are sketched in Figure A.1.

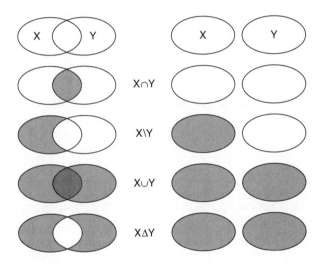

Figure A.1 Operations on sets.

Numbers

The set of natural numbers, $\mathbb{N}$, sometimes known as counting numbers, consists of elements of the set[2]

$$\{0, 1, 2, 3 \ldots\}$$

---

[2] Some definitions of the natural numbers include 0 and some do not. This largely depends upon the branch of mathematics in which the definition is encountered.

If $x, y, z \in \mathbb{N}$, then

- $x < y$ and $y < z \Rightarrow y < z$ (note that '$\Rightarrow$' is read 'implies', and hence A $\Rightarrow$ B means 'if A is true, then B is true')
- $x < y \Rightarrow x + z < y + z$
- $x < y$ and $z > 0 \Rightarrow x \times z < y \times z$

These are known as the *axioms of order* and make explicit the idea that natural numbers are ordered.

The set of natural numbers is *closed* under addition and multiplication. In other words, the addition or multiplication of any two elements of the natural numbers gives another natural number. The addition of '0' to a natural number leaves it unchanged; '0' is the identity under addition. Multiplication by '1' of a natural number leaves it unchanged; '1' is the identity under multiplication.

The set of *integer numbers*, $\mathbb{Z}$ (from zählen),

$$\{\ldots -3, -2, -1, 0, 1, 2, 3 \ldots\}$$

is *closed* under addition, subtraction, and multiplication. The integers can be thought of as the difference between two natural numbers. Introduction of the negative integers introduces an inverse under addition:

$$a + {}^-a = 0$$

The integers are *countable*, i.e. they can be placed in a one-to-one correspondence with the natural numbers.

The set of *rational numbers*, $\mathbb{Q}$ (from quotient), are numbers of the form

$$\frac{a}{b}, \quad \text{where } a, b \in \mathbb{Z} \text{ and } b \neq 0$$

The rational numbers are closed under addition, subtraction, multiplication, and division (other than by '0'). The rational numbers introduce an inverse under multiplication:

$$a \times \frac{1}{a} = 1$$

The rationals are countable, i.e. they can be placed in a one-to-one correspondence with the natural numbers.

The *irrational numbers* are numbers that cannot be expressed as the ratio of integers. Algebraic irrational numbers, such as $\sqrt{2}$, are roots to polynomial equations with rational coefficients. The algebraic numbers are countable. The transcendental numbers are not roots to any polynomial with rational coefficients. The transcendental numbers are not countable; they include 'π', 'e' and 'many' logarithms. An irrational number can be written as an infinite sum of rational numbers and hence does not repeat when expressed as a decimal.

The set of real numbers, $\mathbb{R}$, includes all the rational and irrational numbers.

The real numbers are closed under addition, subtraction, multiplication, and division (other than by '0').

The axioms of order encountered in the earlier part of this section also apply to real numbers and to all subsets of real numbers (the natural numbers are a subset of the real numbers).

Arithmetic

Addition and multiplication have some fundamental properties when performed on the real numbers. Let a and b be real numbers.

The *commutative* property is

$$a + b = b + a$$
$$a \times b = b \times a$$

The *associative* property is

$$(a + b) + c = a + (b + c)$$
$$(a \times b) \times c = a \times (b \times c)$$

The *distributive* property is

$$a \times (b + c) = (a \times b) + (a \times c)$$

When familiar with working with mathematical expressions it is easy to forget that the above properties are being applied. For instance, a well-known mnemonic for multiplying out brackets is *FOIL*:

$$F - \text{first terms}$$

$$O - \text{outer terms}$$

$$I - \text{inner terms}$$

$$L - \text{last terms}$$

so that

$$(a + b)(c + d) = ac + ad + bc + bd$$

This follows from the commutative and distributive properties:

$$(a + b)(c + d)$$
$$= (c + d)(a + b) \qquad \text{commutative}$$
$$= (c + d)a + (c + d)b \quad \text{distributive}$$
$$= a(c + d) + b(c + d) \quad \text{commutative}$$
$$= ac + ad + bc + bd \qquad \text{distributive}$$

By considering a real number line (Figure A.2) it is intuitively clear that the product of a positive and a negative number is a negative number, but it is less clear that the

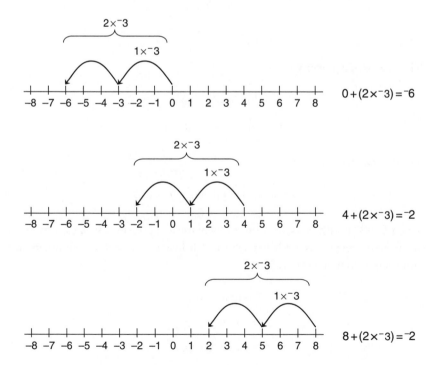

Figure A.2 Multiplication of a positive by a negative number.

product of two negative numbers is a positive number. The preceding result, though, is helpful in clarifying this, e.g.

$$(7 + {}^-3)(7 + {}^-3) = 16$$

$$(7 \times 7) + (7 \times {}^-3) + ({}^-3 \times 7) + ({}^-3 \times {}^-3) = 16$$

$$49 + {}^-21 + {}^-21 + ({}^-3 \times {}^-3) = 16$$

$$7 + ({}^-3 \times {}^-3) = 16$$

$$({}^-3 \times {}^-3) = 9$$

The associative property sometimes causes confusion when considering subtraction or division; these are not associative. Clarification comes by replacing subtraction with addition of the inverse, and division with multiplication of the inverse:

$$(10 - 8) - 2 = 0 \neq 4 = 10 - (8 - 2)$$

$$(10 + {}^-8) + {}^-2 = 0 = 0 = 10 + ({}^-8 + {}^-2)$$

$$(40 \div 5) \div 2 = 4 \neq 16 = 40 \div (5 \div 2)$$

$$(40 \times 1/5) \times 1/2 = 4 = 4 = 40 \times \left({}^1/_5 \times {}^1/_2 \right)$$

Several equivalent mnemonics exist to recall precedence in calculations:

B – brackets

I – indices (i.e. powers and roots)

D – division

M – multiplication

A – addition

S – subtraction

For example

$$5 \times 7 + 12 \div 4 = 35 + 3 = 38$$

Functions

A function is a rule that assigns to each and every element of a first set a unique element of a second set (Figure A.3); that is, a function can be one-to-one or many-to-one, but not one-to-many. The first set is called the *domain*, the set of arguments,

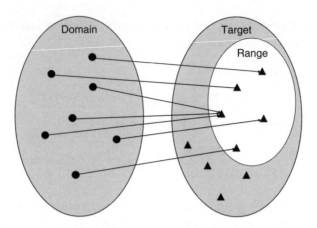

Figure A.3 Definition of a function.

or the set of independent variables. The second set is called the *target*. The *range* or image of the function is the set of values associated with the domain; it is a subset of the target set (for example, suppose the domain and target are the integers and the function is the second power or square). The elements of the domain and target may have different dimensions, e.g. the domain could comprise a pair of real numbers defining a patient's weight and height, and the target may be a real number defining the patient's body mass index.

Expressions, Equations, and Inequalities

An *expression* is a string that contains mathematical symbols, numbers, and variables; it can be thought of as mathematical phrase. The following are all expressions:

$$x$$

$$3 + 2x$$

$$\pi(x - 52)^2$$

An *equation* states that two expressions, either side of an '=' sign have the same value. Equations may be *identities* or *conditional*. Identities are equations which are true for all values assigned to variables, e.g.

$$(x + y)(x - y) = x^2 - y^2$$

In contrast, conditional equations are true for some values of variables, e.g.

$$x^2 - 2 = 0$$

is true for $x = \pm\sqrt{2}$, and

$$y - 5x - 15 = 0$$

is true for ordered pairs (x, y) that can be represented as a straight-line graph of gradient 5 passing through the points $(0, 15)$ and $(-3, 0)$.

Conditional equations are one common approach to describing functions, but not all conditional equations are functions. For an equation to represent a function, it must fulfil the criterion of associating a unique element of the second set with the first. Thus

$$y = \sqrt{x}, \quad x > 0$$

is not a function, but

$$y = \sqrt{x}, \quad x > 0, y > 0$$

is a function.

If a conditional equation is written in a form such that the expression to the left of the '=' sign is a single variable, it is said to be in *explicit* form, and that variable is termed the *dependent* variable. If all variables are grouped on one side of the '=' sign and a constant is on the other side, then the equation is said to be in *implicit* form:

$$\text{Implicit form:} \quad y - 5x - 15 = 0$$

$$\text{Explicit form:} \quad y = 5x + 15$$

Piecewise functions are those that are defined differently for different subsets of their domain. For example, a common piecewise function is the *absolute value function* or *modulus function*, which is defined as follows:

$$|x| = \begin{cases} x & \text{if } x \geq 0 \\ -x & \text{if } x < 0 \end{cases}$$

So, regardless of whether x is positive or negative, $|x|$ will always be positive.

An *inequality* compares two expressions either side of an inequality sign. There are four inequality signs:

$$x < y \quad x \text{ is strictly less than } y$$

$$x \leq y \quad x \text{ is less than or equal to } y$$

$$x > y \quad x \text{ is strictly greater than } y$$

$$x \geq y \quad x \text{ is greater than or equal to } y$$

For example

$$\{x: {}^{-}1 \le x \le 2\}$$

is the set of all x such that x is between $^{-}1$ and 2 inclusive of the endpoints -1 and 2 (this is also referred to as a *closed interval* and written as $[-1, 2]$),

$$\{x: {}^{-}1 < x < 2\}$$

is the set of all x such that x is strictly between $^{-}1$ and 2 excluding the endpoints -1 and 2 (this is also referred to as an *open interval* and written as $[-1, 2]$), and

$$|x| < 1$$

means that the absolute value, the modulus, of x is strictly less than 1 (equivalently, $-1 < x < 1$).

When dividing or multiplying both sides of an inequality by a negative number, the inequality sign switches direction:

$$-x < 1 \Rightarrow x > -1$$

Graphs

The relationship between sets of numbers can be shown with a graph. In the case of two sets, this is a plot with respect to two axes. For Cartesian coordinates the horizontal axis is often referred to as the x axis or *abscissa*, and the vertical axis as the y axis or *ordinate*. A conditional equation of two real variables results in a curve. If a continuous straight line drawn parallel to the y axis only crosses the curve at most at one point, then the curve represents a function $y = y(x)$, i.e. each value of x maps uniquely to one value of y. If this straight line were to cross the curve at more than one point, this curve would represent a one-to-many mapping rather than a function, i.e. the curve would define a relationship under which one value in the domain would be related to many values in the range.

The equation of a straight line is given by

$$y = mx + k$$

where m and k are constants. Here, m is the gradient of the line – for every unit that x increases, y increases by m; k is the intercept of the line – when $x = 0$, $y = k$, i.e. the line intercepts the y axis at k (Figure A.4).

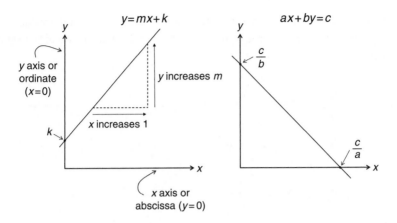

Figure A.4 Straight-line graphs.

Constraints (see Chapter 6) often occur with straight lines written in implicit form:

$$ax + by = c$$

where a, b, and c are all constants. Straight lines given in this form are simple to plot: setting $x = 0$ gives the intercept on the y axis at $\frac{c}{b}$; setting $y = 0$ gives the intercept on the x axis at $\frac{c}{a}$.

Summation and Product Notation

In situations where mathematical expressions require the addition or multiplication of many variables, summation (sigma) and product (pi) notation is used. For example, rather than writing the sum of five variables as, say,

$$v + w + x + y + z$$

subscripts rather than individual letters are used to represent the variables:

$$x_1 + x_2 + x_3 + x_4 + x_5$$

which can then be written as

$$\sum_{i=1}^{5} x_i = x_1 + x_2 + x_3 + x_4 + x_5$$

The notation is to be read as 'add together each of the terms from the value of the index specified at the base of the sigma until that specified at the top of the sigma'. For example,

$$\sum_{i=30}^{33} x_i = x_{30} + x_{31} + x_{32} + x_{33}$$

$$\sum_{i=0}^{5} x_{2i+1} = x_1 + x_3 + x_5 + x_7 + x_9 + x_{11}$$

$$\sum_{j=1}^{4} x_{\alpha j} = x_{\alpha 1} + x_{\alpha 2} + x_{\alpha 3} + x_{\alpha 4}$$

$$\sum_{j=1}^{6} x_{\alpha j} y_j = x_{\alpha 1} y_1 + x_{\alpha 2} y_2 + x_{\alpha 3} y_3 + x_{\alpha 4} y_4 + x_{\alpha 5} y_5 + x_{\alpha 6} y_6$$

(In passing it is worth recalling that the summation over j in the final example is a summation over a repeated index; in such situations some authors follow the Einstein convention and do not show the capital sigma, assuming that all repeated indices are to be summed over.)

Similarly, when wishing to specify the multiplication of several variables, then the pi notation is used. For example,

$$\prod_{i=m}^{n} x_i = x_m x_{m+1} x_{m+2} \cdots x_{n-1} x_n$$

Sequences, Limits, and Infinite Series

A *sequence* is a countable, ordered set, indexed by the natural numbers (often greater than zero), typically a succession of real numbers. The notation $<x_n>$ or (x_n) is used to indicate the sequence with nth term x_n, e.g.

$$\langle n^3 \rangle = 1, 8, 27, 64, \ldots \qquad \text{divergent}$$

$$\langle (^{-}1)^n \rangle = {}^{-}1, 1, {}^{-}1, 1, \ldots \qquad \text{divergent}$$

$$\left\langle 2 + \frac{1}{n} \right\rangle = 3, 2\tfrac{1}{2}, 2\tfrac{1}{3}, 2\tfrac{1}{4}, \ldots \qquad \text{convergent}$$

$$\left\langle \sqrt[+]{5} \right\rangle = \sqrt[+]{5}, \sqrt[+]{5}, \sqrt[+]{5}, \ldots \qquad \text{convergent}$$

The above examples illustrate concepts of divergent and convergent sequences. The sequence $<x_n>$ *converges* to a *limit* X if, for any small positive number ε, there exists an integer $N(\varepsilon)$ such that, for $n > N, X - \varepsilon < x_n < X + \varepsilon$. A divergent sequence is any sequence that does not converge.

A divergent sequence may, however, be *bounded*, i.e. there exists some real number, U, that is greater than or equal to every number in the sequence or less than or equal to every number in the sequence. In the former case, U would be an *upper bound*, and in the latter case it would be a *lower bound*. For example, the divergent sequence

$$\langle(^-1)^n\rangle = {}^-1, 1, {}^-1, 1, \ldots$$

has an upper bound of 1 and a lower bound of -1.

Addition of the terms in an infinite sequence defines an infinite *series*:

$$\sum_{i=1}^{\infty} x_i = x_1 + x_2 + x_3 + x_4 + \cdots$$

In some cases it is possible to define the sum of an infinite series. Define the nth *partial sum* as

$$S_n = \sum_{i=1}^{n} x_i = x_1 + x_2 + x_3 + \cdots + x_n$$

If the sequence $<s_n>$ has a limit S, then $\sum_{i=1}^{\infty} x_i$ is convergent with sum S, otherwise S is divergent. For example, consider the series $\sum_{i=1}^{\infty} a^i$ with $|a| < 1$. The partial sums are given by

$$S_n = \sum_{i=1}^{n} a^i = a + a^2 + \cdots + a^n$$

and hence

$$S_{n+1} - S_n = a^{n+1}$$

so

$$aS_n + a - S_n = a^{n+1}$$

giving

$$S_n = \frac{a(1 - a^n)}{1 - a}$$

With $|a| < 1$ as n tends to infinity,

$$S_n \to \frac{a}{1-a}$$

and hence

$$S = \frac{a}{1-a}$$

Factorial, Powers, Polynomials, Logarithm, and Exponential

The *factorial* function, $x!$, is the product of the first x natural numbers:

$$0! = 1$$

$$x! = x \times (x-1)!$$

So, for example,

$$0! = 1$$

$$1! = 1 \times 1 = 1$$

$$2! = 2 \times 1 = 2$$

$$3! = 3 \times 2 = 6$$

$$4! = 4 \times 6 = 24$$

In an expression b^p, b is called the *base* and p is called the *power* (or exponent or index). The power is the number of times the base is to be multiplied by itself:

$$x^3 = x \times x \times x$$

$$7^3 = 7 \times 7 \times 7$$

Multiplying powers of the same base is equivalent to adding the exponents:

$$x^4 \times x^3 = (x \times x \times x \times x) \times (x \times x \times x) = x^7$$

$$7^4 \times 7^3 = 7^7$$

$$4^5 \times 12^3 = 4^5 \times (4^3 \times 3^3) = (4^5 \times 4^3) \times 3^3 = 4^8 3^3$$

$$x^m \times x^n = x^{m+n}$$

Dividing powers of the same base is equivalent to subtracting powers:

$$x^4 \div x^3 = \frac{X \times X \times X \times X}{X \times X \times X} = x^1 = x$$

$$x^4 \div x^4 = \frac{X \times X \times X \times X}{X \times X \times X \times X} = 1 = x^0$$

$$x^4 \div x^5 = \frac{X \times X \times X \times X}{X \times X \times X \times X \times X} = \frac{1}{x} = x^{-1}$$

$$x^m \div x^n = x^{m-n}$$

Roots can be expressed as rational powers. Consider

$$y = x^3$$

Hence

$$y^1 = x^3$$

Hence

$$y^{(1/3+1/3+1/3)} = x^3$$

Hence

$$y^{1/3}y^{1/3}y^{1/3} = x^3$$

Hence

$$y^{1/3}y^{1/3}y^{1/3} = x \cdot x \cdot x$$

Hence

$$y^{1/3} = x$$

Generally,

$$x^{1/n} = \sqrt[n]{x}$$

A *polynomial* is an expression made up from variables raised to natural number powers and combined through addition, subtraction, and multiplication. The following are examples of polynomials:

$$x^3y + x^2 - y^2 + 144$$

$$y - 1$$

$$x^6 + 4x^4 + 4x^2 + 0$$

whereas

$$6x^2 + 3x^{1/2}$$

is not a polynomial. A polynomial equation is obtained when one polynomial expression is set equal to another polynomial expression. In the case of a single variable, a polynomial equation can be written in the form

$$\sum_{i=0}^{n} a_i x^i = a_0 + a_1 x + a_2 x^2 + \cdots + a_n x^n = 0$$

where n is the *degree* of the polynomial and a_i are the polynomial coefficients.

The *logarithm* function can be considered as the inverse to the power function. The logarithm of x is the power, p, to which a base, b, must be raised to give x:

$$x = b^p \iff \log_b (x) = p$$

The most commonly used bases are $b = 10$ and $b = e$, where e is the Euler number. So, for example,

$$\log_{10} (0.1) = -1 \quad \text{raise 10 to the power } ^-1 \text{ to give } 0.1$$
$$\log_{10} (1) = 0 \quad \text{raise 10 to the power 0 to give 1}$$
$$\log_{10} (10) = 1 \quad \text{raise 10 to the power 1 to give 10}$$
$$\log_{10} \left(\sqrt{10}\right) = \frac{1}{2} \quad \text{raise 10 to the power ½ to give } \sqrt{10}$$
$$\log_{10} (100) = 2 \quad \text{raise 10 to the power 2 to give 100}$$

Logarithms in base e are called natural (or Napierian) logarithms, and sometimes written as 'ln':

$$\log_e (x) \equiv \ln (x)$$

Adding logarithms in the same base is equivalent to multiplying their arguments:

$$\log_b (x) + \log_b (y) = \log_b (xy)$$

(Proof: if $x = b^p$, $y = b^q$, and $xy = b^{(p+q)}$, then $\log_b(x) = p$, $\log_b(y) = q$, and $\log_b (xy) = p + q$.)

Similarly, subtracting logarithms is equivalent to dividing their arguments:

$$\log_b (x) - \log_b (y) = \log_b \left(\frac{x}{y}\right)$$

The logarithm of a variable raised to a power equals the power multiplied by the logarithm of the variable:

$$\log_b (x^y) = y \log_b (x)$$

(Proof: if $x = b^p$ and $x^y = b^{yp}$, then $\log_b (x) = p$ and $\log_b (x^y) = yp$.)

Logarithms can be transformed between bases in the following way:

$$\log_c (x) = \frac{\log_b (x)}{\log_b (c)}$$

(Proof: $x = b^y = c^z$, so $\log_c (x) = z$ and $\log_b (x) = y = \log_b (c^z) = z \log_b (c) = \log_c (x) \log_b (c)$.)

The *exponential function* is the inverse of the natural logarithm, ln, where

$$\log_e (y) = \ln (y) = \int_1^y \frac{du}{u}, \quad y > 0$$

$$\log_e (e) = \ln (e) = 1 = \int_1^e \frac{du}{u} \quad \text{with } e \approx 2.7183$$

Alternatively, the exponential function can be defined as the sum of an infinite series that is convergent for all x:

$$\exp (x) = e^x = \sum_{i=0}^{\infty} \frac{x^i}{i!}$$

and if $x = 1$

$$e = \lim_{i \to \infty} \left(1 + \frac{1}{i}\right)^i = \sum_{i=0}^{\infty} \frac{1}{i!} = 1 + 1 + \frac{1}{2} + \frac{1}{6} + \frac{1}{24} + \cdots \approx 2.7183$$

Simultaneous Equations

Suppose there are two equations given in terms of the same two variables, say, x and y:

$$f (x, y) = 0$$

$$g (x, y) = 0$$

Independently, each of these equations can be seen as a conditional equation: for some x there are values of y such that the equation is true. In some cases it is possible

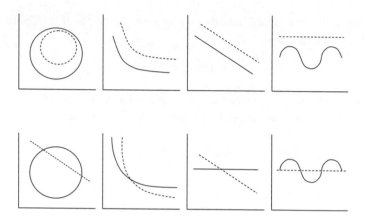

Figure A.5   Non-intersecting and intersecting curves.

to find x, y pairs that satisfy both conditional equations, in others this is not the case. Referring to Figure A.5, the upper four graphs illustrate the situation for which there are no x, y pairs that satisfy both equations; the lower graphs show the contrary situation. The lower left illustrates the case of a linear line cutting a circle at two points, or equivalently there are two x, y pairs that satisfy both the linear equation and the equation of the circle. The lower middle cases illustrate the situation of a single x, y pair satisfying two equations, while the lower right illustrates the case of an infinite number of solutions, assuming both curves continue as x tends to infinity. The last example is that of a *periodic function*. This is a function for which there exists some number, T, for which $f(x) = f(x + T)$ for all values of x. The number T is the period of the function. Common examples are the trigonometric functions, sine and cosine, which exhibit a period of 2π, which means that they result in the same value for inputs of x and $x + 2\pi$ for all values of x.

One approach to finding values of variables that simultaneously satisfy two equations is firstly to write one equation explicitly and then substitute this into the other equation and find the roots.

For example, suppose the two equations are a straight line and a circle:

$$y - 2x = 0$$

$$x^2 + y^2 - 5 = 0$$

Rewriting the first explicitly gives

$$y = 2x$$

Substituting into the second equation yields

$$5\left(x^2 - 1\right) = 0$$

to give the roots

$$x = \pm 1$$

Substituting back into either equation, two solution pairs are found:

$$x = +1, \quad y = +2$$
$$x = -1, \quad y = -2$$

Of particular interest is the case of two linear equations:

$$a_1 x + b_1 y + c_1 = 0$$
$$a_2 x + b_2 y + c_2 = 0$$

The earlier procedure could be applied, but it is often simpler (and readily generalised to systems of more equations) to proceed by an elimination technique. If $a_1 \neq a_2$, then multiply the first equation by a_2 and the second by a_1:

$$a_1 a_2 x + b_1 a_2 y + c_1 a_2 = 0$$
$$a_2 a_1 x + b_2 a_1 y + c_2 a_1 = 0$$

Subtracting one equation from the other eliminates the x variable:

$$(b_1 a_2 - b_2 a_1) y + (c_1 a_2 - c_2 a_1) = 0$$

This equation can then be solved for y:

$$y = \frac{c_2 a_1 - c_1 a_2}{b_1 a_2 - b_2 a_1}$$

Consider the two linear equations

$$2x + 3y - 8 = 0$$
$$9x + 4y - 17 = 0$$

Multiply the first equation by 9 and the second equation by 2 to give

$$18x + 27y - 72 = 0$$
$$18x + 8y - 34 = 0$$

Subtract one from the other:

$$19y - 38 = 0$$

resulting in

$$y = 2, \quad x = 1$$

Solving simultaneous linear equations is used in Chapters 6 and 7.

Differentiation

Differentiation refers to finding the *derivative* of a function. The derivative of a function is also known as the *differential coefficient*. For a function $y = f(x)$, the derivative, $f'(x)$, is defined by

$$f'(x) = \frac{dy}{dx} = \lim_{\Delta x \to 0} \frac{f(x + \Delta x) - f(x)}{\Delta x}$$

The derivative quantifies the rate of change in a function with respect to the independent variable (Figure A.6). For functions of a single variable, this is the gradient.

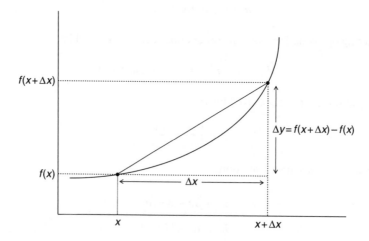

Figure A.6 Definition of differentiation.

In the case of a straight line (Figure A.7) it is immediately clear that this description gives the result consistent with the gradient above:

$$y = mx + k$$

$$\frac{dy}{dx} = \lim_{\Delta x \to 0} \frac{mx + m\Delta x + k - mx - k}{\Delta x} = \lim_{\Delta x \to 0} \frac{m\Delta x}{\Delta x} = m$$

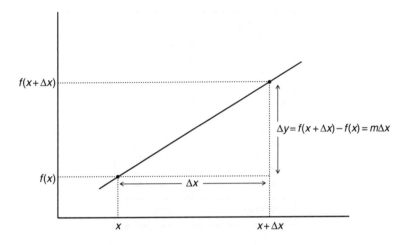

Figure A.7 Equivalence of gradient and derivative for a straight line.

It is broadly useful to be able to differentiate functions that can be expressed as equations. For example, suppose

$$f(x) = y = ax^2$$

Then

$$f'(x) = \frac{dy}{dx} = \lim_{\Delta x \to 0} \frac{a(x + \Delta x)^2 - ax^2}{\Delta x} = \lim_{\Delta x \to 0} (2a + a\Delta x) = 2a$$

The result is readily generalised for the case

$$f(x) = y = ax^n$$

Then

$$\frac{dy}{dx} = nax^{n-1}$$

The derivatives of some commonly met functions are shown in Figure A.8. The proof of such results often includes small 'tricks'. For example, it is useful firstly to express the exponential function as a polynomial before applying the definition of a derivative.

f(x)	f'(x)
ax^n	nax^{n-1}
e^{ax}	ae^{ax}
$\ln(ax) = \log_e(ax)$	$\dfrac{1}{x}$
$\sin(ax)$	$a\cos(ax)$
$\cos(ax)$	$-a\sin(ax)$
$\sinh(ax)$	$a\cosh(ax)$
$\cosh(ax)$	$a\sinh(ax)$

Figure A.8 Some standard derivatives.

In differentiating functions that are expressed in terms of two or more other functions, some useful general rules can be shown. For brevity, these are quoted here. Let a and b be constants, and let f and g be functions of x:

$$\frac{\mathrm{d}}{\mathrm{d}x}\big(af(x)\big) = af'(x)$$

$$\frac{\mathrm{d}}{\mathrm{d}x}\big(af(x) + bg(x)\big) = af'(x) + bg'(x)$$

$$\frac{\mathrm{d}}{\mathrm{d}x}\big(f(x)g(x)\big) = f(x)g'(x) + g(x)f'(x)$$

$$\frac{\mathrm{d}}{\mathrm{d}x}\left(\frac{f(x)}{g(x)}\right) = \frac{g(x)f'(x) - f(x)g'(x)}{(g(x))^2}$$

Stationary Points

Figure A.9 shows a graph of a function that possesses both a local and a global maximum, and both a local and a global minimum. At a local maximum a function achieves a higher value than any other within a neighbourhood of the independent variable. At a global maximum the function achieves its highest value for all values of the independent variable over which the function is defined. Equivalent definitions apply for local and global minima.

A *stationary point* is a point on a curve at which the differential is zero, i.e. at which the gradient is zero. Maxima and minima are stationary points. Consequently, the maxima and minima of a function can be found by differentiating the function, setting the result equal to zero, and solving for the independent variable. This result was

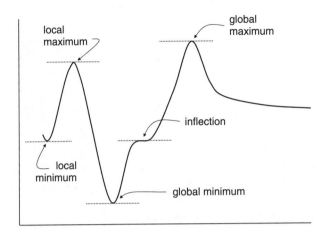

Figure A.9 Extrema of a function.

used extensively throughout Chapter 4, for example in the derivation of economic order quantity. As well as maxima and minima, a third type of stationary point is the inflection point.

Integration

Integration is the process of calculating integrals. An *indefinite integral* of a function $f(x)$ with respect to x is written as

$$\int f(x)\ dx$$

and is given, to within a constant, by a function $F(x)$ for which $f(x)$ is the derivative. In other words, integration can be considered as the converse of differentiation or antidifferentiation. For example,

$$\int x\ dx = \frac{x^2}{2} + \text{constant}$$

$$\frac{d}{dx}\left(\frac{x^2}{2} + \text{constant}\right) = \frac{d}{dx}\left(\frac{x^2}{2}\right) + \frac{d}{dx}(\text{constant}) = \frac{2x}{2} + 0 = x$$

The *fundamental theorem of calculus* states that

$$\int_a^b f(x)dx = \left[F(x)\right]_a^b = F(b) - F(a)$$

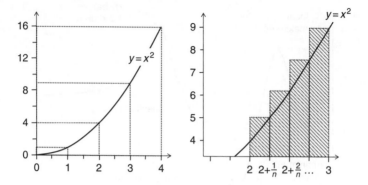

Figure A.10 Definite integration as the area under a curve.

This is practically important as it allows areas under a curve $f(x)$ to be found by identifying a function $F(x)$ for which $f(x)$ is the derivative. For example, if the area under the curve $y = x^2$ between $x = 2$ and $x = 3$ is required (Figure A.10), then this can be found by

$$\int_2^3 x^2 \, dx = \left[\frac{x^3}{3}\right]_2^3 = \frac{27}{3} - \frac{8}{3} = \frac{19}{3}$$

A more laborious route to this result would be to calculate the area under the curve as the sum of the area of n rectangles, which approximates the curve:

$$\sum_{i=1}^n \left(2 + \frac{i}{n}\right)^2 \frac{1}{n} = \sum_{i=1}^n \left(4 + \frac{4i}{n} + \frac{i^2}{n^2}\right) \frac{1}{n} = \frac{4}{n} \sum_{i=1}^n 1 + \frac{4}{n^2} \sum_{i=1}^n i + \frac{1}{n^3} \sum_{i=1}^n i^2$$

$$= 4 + \frac{2}{n^2} n(n+1) + \frac{1}{6n^3} n(n+1)(2n+1) = 4 + 2\left(1 + \frac{1}{n}\right)$$

$$+ \frac{1}{6}\left(1 + \frac{1}{n}\right)\left(2 + \frac{1}{n}\right)$$

as $n \to \infty$

$$= 4 + 2 + \frac{1}{3} = \frac{19}{3}$$

Some standard integrals are shown in Figure A.11.

Useful integration techniques include integration by *substitution, partial fractions,* and *integration by parts.*

$f(x)$	$F(x)$
ax^n	$\dfrac{ax^{n+1}}{n+1}$
e^{ax}	$\dfrac{e^{ax}}{a}$
$\dfrac{1}{x}$	$\ln(ax) = \log_e(ax)$

$\sin(ax)$	$\dfrac{-\cos(ax)}{a}$
$\cos(ax)$	$\dfrac{\sin(ax)}{a}$
$\sinh(ax)$	$\dfrac{\cosh(ax)}{a}$
$\cosh(ax)$	$\dfrac{\sinh(ax)}{a}$

Figure A.11　Some standard integrals.

Integration by Substitution

If the integrand is a function of the form $g(f(x))$, then let $f(x) = u$, and hence the integrand can be written as $g(u)$. Noting that

$$dx = \left(\frac{dx}{du}\right) du$$

it follows that

$$\int g\left(f(x)\right)dx = \int g(f(x)) \left(\frac{dx}{du}\right) du = \int g(u)du = G(u) = G\left(f(x)\right)$$

The final step requires that the $f(x)$ be substituted for u in the integrated function, and hence the name *integration by substitution*.

Integration by Partial Fractions

If the integrand is of the form $\dfrac{f(x)}{g(x)}$, where $f(x)$ and $g(x)$ are polynomials, then, provided the degree of $f(x)$ is less than or equal to the degree of $g(x)$, and $g(x)$ can be resolved into factors, there will exist a partial fraction expansion of the integrand, i.e.

$$\frac{f(x)}{g(x)} = \frac{a_1(x)}{b_1(x)} + \frac{a_2(x)}{b_2(x)} + \cdots + \frac{a_n(x)}{b_n(x)}$$

where n is the number of factors of $g(x)$. Hence

$$\int \frac{f(x)}{g(x)} dx = \int \frac{a_1(x)}{b_1(x)} dx + \int \frac{a_2(x)}{b_2(x)} dx + \cdots + \int \frac{a_n(x)}{b_n(x)} dx$$

Integration by Parts

If the integrand is of the form $F(x)g(x)$, where $g(x)$ is a derivative of some function $G(x)$, then

$$\int F(x)g(x)dx = F(x)G(x) - \int f(x)G(x)dx$$

where

$$f(x) = F'(x) \text{ and } g(x) = G'(x)$$

Differentiation under the Integral Sign

To differentiate under the integral sign, the *Leibniz integral rule* is used:

$$\frac{d}{du} \int_{a(u)}^{b(u)} f(x, u) \, dx = \int_{a(u)}^{b(u)} \frac{\partial}{\partial u} f(x, u) \, dx + f(b(u), u) \frac{db}{du} - f(a(u), u) \frac{da}{du}$$

where ∂ denotes partial differentiation (i.e. the derivative with respect to one argument of the function with all other arguments being kept constant).

Probability

Probability is measured on the interval [0, 1]. A probability of '0' indicates that an event is impossible, a probability of '1' indicates that an event is certain.

The mathematical or *combinatorial probability* of an event E_k occurring, $P(E_k)$, is given by

$$P(E_k) = \frac{\text{number of ways event } E_k \text{ can occur}}{\text{number of possible outcomes}}$$

assuming all outcomes are 'equally likely'. For example, if the *sample space* (i.e. the set of possible outcomes) is given by

$$O = \{1, 2, 3, 4, 5, 6\}$$

And the event E_k is given by

$$E_k = \{2\}$$

then

$$P(E_k) = 1/6$$

Empirical probability assumes that

$$P(E_k) \approx \frac{n_{E_k}}{n_T}$$

where n_{E_k} is the number of times an event E_k has occurred, and n_T is the number of experiments or trials carried out. If a die were thrown 30 times and the number '2' resulted 6 times, then

$$P(2) \approx \frac{1}{5}$$

Relative frequency probability is the empirical probability in the limit of an infinite number of trials:

$$P(E_k) = \lim_{n_T \to \infty} \frac{n_{E_k}}{n_T}$$

Two events, E_k and F, are *mutually exclusive* if the two events cannot occur simultaneously, i.e. the occurrence of one event precludes the occurrence of the other event, e.g. a student cannot pass and fail an exam simultaneously. For mutually exclusive events

$$P(F \cap E_k) = 0$$

Two events E_k and F are *independent* if the fact that E_k has occurred does not affect the probability of F occurring. For independent events

$$P(F \text{ and } E_k) = P(F \cap E_k) = P(F)P(E_k)$$

For example, if E_k is the outcome '2' for a first roll of a die, and F is the outcome '5' for a second roll of the die, then

$$P(F \cap E_k) = P(5)P(2) = 1/6 \times 1/6 = 1/36$$

The *conditional probability* is then defined as

$$P(F|E_k) = \frac{P(F \cap E_k)}{P(E_k)}$$

The *theorem of total probability* states that

$$P(F) = \sum_i P(F|E_i)P(E_i)$$

where the summation is taken over all i.

Bayes' theorem states that

$$P(E_k|F) = \frac{P(F|E_k)P(E_k)}{P(F)} = \frac{P(F|E_k)P(E_k)}{\sum_i P(F|E_i)P(E_i)}$$

For instance, given an achieved total of '>7' from two consecutive throws of a die, what is the probability that the first throw was '3'? A direct approach to this calculation is to observe that there are 15 ordered pairs that give rise to a total '>7', and that two of these have a first throw of '3', giving the probability as $\frac{2}{15}$ Alternatively, Bayes' theorem can be used. Let F be the event '>7', and let E_k be the event '3'. Then

$$P(3| > 7) = \frac{P(> 7|3)\,P(3)}{P(> 7)} = \frac{\frac{1}{3} \times \frac{1}{6}}{\frac{15}{36}} = \frac{2}{15}$$

Random Variables

For a discrete random variable, X, the probability of the variable taking a particular value is given by the *probability mass function* (pmf), $p_X(x)$, where

$$p_X(x) = P(X = X_i), \quad i = 1, \ldots, n$$

for n possible outcomes.

The probability that the random variable will be less than or equal to x is the *cumulative distribution function* (cdf):

$$F_X(x) = P(X \le x)$$

Figure A.12 shows the relationship between the pmf and cdf when the random variable is the total score from the roll of two dice.

x	2	3	4	5	6	7	8	9	10	11	12
$p_X(x)$	1/36	2/36	3/36	4/36	5/36	6/36	5/36	4/36	3/36	2/36	1/36
$F_X(x)$	1/36	3/36	6/36	10/36	15/36	21/36	26/36	30/36	33/36	35/36	36/36

Figure A.12 pmf and cdf for the roll of two dice.

The expected value or *mean* of X is

$$\mu = E(X) = \sum_{i=1}^{n} p_i X_i$$

and the *variance* of X is

$$\sigma^2 = \text{var}(X) = E\left((X_i - \mu)^2\right) = \sum_{i=1}^{n} p_i (X_i - \mu)^2 = E(X^2) - \mu^2$$

The distribution of relative frequency for a continuous random variable is described by a *probability density function* (pdf), which is the derivative of the cumulative distribution function:

$$F_X(x) = P(X \le x) \quad \text{and} \quad f_X(x) = F_X'(x)$$

The probability that the random variable falls within an interval $(a, b]$ is given by

$$P(a < x \le b) = \int_a^b f_X(x) dx$$

so that

$$P(x \le b) = \int_{-\infty}^b f_X(x) dx = F_X(x)$$

The expected value of X is given by

$$\mu = E(X) = \int_{-\infty}^{\infty} f_X(x) x \, dx$$

and the variance by

$$\sigma^2 = \int_{-\infty}^{\infty} f_X(x)(x - \mu)^2 \, dx$$

Bibliography

algebra, elementary (2008) *Encyclopædia Britannica. Deluxe Edition.* Encyclopædia Britannica, Chicago, IL.

analysis (2008) *Encyclopædia Britannica. Deluxe Edition.* Encyclopædia Britannica, Chicago, IL.

arithmetic (2008) *Encyclopædia Britannica. Deluxe Edition.* Encyclopædia Britannica, Chicago, IL.

Binmore, KG. (1982) *Mathematical Analysis: A Straightforward Approach.* Cambridge University Press, London, UK.

Borowski, EJ. & Borwein, JM. (2002) *Collins Dictionary of Mathematics.* HarperCollins Publishers, Glasgow, UK.

Bronshstein, IN. & Semendyayev, KA. (1997) *Handbook of Mathematics.* Springer-Verlag, Berlin, Germany.

Clapham, CRJ. (1973) *Introduction to Mathematical Analysis.* Routledge & Kegan Paul, London, UK.

Dennery, P. & Kryzwicki, A. (1996) *Mathematics for Physicists.* Dover Publications, New York, NY.

Eves, H. (1997) *Foundations and Fundamental Concepts of Mathematics.* Dover Publications, New York, NY.

Gowers, T. (2002). *Mathematics: A Very Short Introduction.* Oxford University Press, New York, NY.

probability theory (2008) *Encyclopædia Britannica. Deluxe Edition.* Encyclopædia Britannica, Chicago, IL.

set theory (2008) *Encyclopædia Britannica. Deluxe Edition.* Encyclopædia Britannica, Chicago, IL.

statistics (2008) *Encyclopædia Britannica. Deluxe Edition.* Encyclopædia Britannica, Chicago, IL.

Stewart, I. (1995) *Concepts of Modern Mathematics.* Dover Publications, New York, NY.

References

Arrow, K. & Hurwicz, L. (1972) Optimality criterion for decision making under ignorance, in *Uncertainty and Expectations in Economics. Essays in Honour of G.L.S. Shackle*, edited by Carter CF. & Ford JL. Blackwell, Oxford, UK.

Bazerman, MH. (2006) *Judgement in Managerial Decision Making*. John Wiley & Sons.

Bell, DE., Raiffa, H., & Tversky, A. (1988) *Decision Making: Descriptive, Normative and Prescriptive Interactions*. Cambridge University Press, Cambridge, UK.

Benton, WC. & Park, S. (1996) A classification of literature on determining the lot size under quantity discounts. *European Journal of Operational Research* **92**, 219–238.

Checkland, P. (1999) *Systems Thinking, Systems Practice: Includes a 30-year Retrospective*. John Wiley & Sons, Ltd, Chichester, UK.

Coates, JF. (2000) Scenario planning. *Technological Forecasting and Social Change* **65**, 115–123.

Dalkey, N. & Helmer, O. (1963) An experimental application of the Delphi method to the use of experts. *Management Science* **9**(3), 458–467.

Delbecq, AL. & Van de Ven, AH. (1971) A group process model for problem identification and program planning. *The Journal of Applied Behavioral Science* **7**(4), 466–492.

Dixit, AK. & Nalebuff, BJ. (1991) *Thinking Strategically: The Competitive Edge in Business, Politics, and Everyday Life*. W.W. Norton & Company, New York/London.

Dixit, AK. & Skeath, S. (1999) *Games of Strategy*. Norton, New York, NY.

Driouchi, T., Leseure, M., & Benett, D. (2009) A robustness framework for monitoring real options under uncertainty. *OMEGA* **37**(3), 698–710.

Eden, C. & Ackermann, F. (2001a) SODA – the principles, in *Rational Analysis for a Problematic World Revisited*, ed. by Rosenhead, J. & Mingers, J. John Wiley & Sons, Ltd, Chichester, UK.

Eden, C. & Ackermann, F. (2001b) SODA – journey making and mapping in practice, in *Rational Analysis for a Problematic World Revisited*, ed. by Rosenhead, J. & Mingers, J. John Wiley & Sons, Ltd, Chichester, UK.

Erlenkotter, D. (1989) An early classic misplaced: Ford W. Harris's economic order quantity model of 1915. *Management Science* **35**(7), 898–900.

Erlenkotter, D. (1990) Ford Whitman Harris and the economic order quantity model. *Operations Research* **38**(6), 937–946.

Field, RHG. & Andrews, JP. (1998) Testing the incremental validity of the Vroom–Jago versus Vroom–Yetton models of participation in decision making. *Journal of Behavioral Decision Making* **11**, 251–261.

Fransella, F., Bell, R., & Bannister, D. (2003). *A Manual for the Repertory Grid Technique,* 2nd edition. John Wiley & Sons, Ltd, Chichester, UK.

Gillies, D. (2000) *Philosophical Theories of Probability*. Routledge, London, UK.

Goodwin, P. & Wright, G. (2004) *Decision Analysis for Management Judgement,* 3rd edition. John Wiley & Sons, Ltd, Chichester, UK.

Gupta, SK. & Rosenhead, J. (1968) Robustness in sequential investment decisions. *Management Science* **15**(2), B18–B29.

Gustafson, DH., Shukla, RK., Delbecq, A., & Walster, GW. (1973) A comparative study of differences in subjective likelihood estimates made by individuals, interacting groups, Delphi groups, and nominal groups. *Organizational Behavior and Human Performance* **9**, 280–291.

Hacking, I. (2006) *The Emergence of Probability,* 2nd edition. Cambridge University Press, Cambridge, UK.

Harris, FW. (1913) How many parts to make at once. *Factory, The Magazine of Management* **10**(2), 135–136, 152; reprinted in *Operations Research* 1990, **38**(6), 947–950.

Hillier, FS. & Lieberman, GJ. (2006) *Introduction to Operations Research*. McGraw-Hill, New York, NY, Chapter 20.

Holt, CC. (2004). Forecasting seasonals and trends by exponentially weighted moving averages. *International Journal of Forecasting* **20**(5), 5–10.

Janis, IL. (1972) *Victims of Groupthink; a Psychological Study of Foreign-policy Decisions and Fiascoes*. Houghton Mifflin, Boston, MA.

Jones, PE. & Roelofsma, HMP. (2000) The potential for social contextual and group biases in team decision making: biases, conditions and psychological mechanisms. *Ergonomics* **43**(8), 1129–1152.

Kahneman, D., Slovic, P., & Tversky, A. (eds) (1982) *Judgement Under Uncertainty: Heuristics and Biases*. Cambridge University Press, Cambridge, UK.

Kahneman, D. & Tversky, A. (2002) *Choices, Values and Frames*. Cambridge University Press, Cambridge, UK.

Kelley, D. (1998) *The Art of Reasoning,* 3rd edition. W.W. Norton & Co., New York, NY.

Kelly, GA. (1955) *The Psychology of Personal Constructs*. Norton, New York, NY (both volumes reprinted in 1991 by Routledge, London, UK).

Khouja, M. (1999) The single-period (newsvendor) problem: literature review and suggestions for future research. *Omega, International Journal of Management Science* **27**(5), 537–553.

Klein, GA. (1989) Recognition-primed decisions, in *Advances in Man–Machine Systems Research, Vol. 5*, ed. by Rouse, WB. JAI Press, Greenwich, CT, pp. 47–92.

Klein, GA. (1998) *Sources of Power: How People Make Decisions*. MIT Press, Cambridge, MA.

Knight, FH. (1921) *Risk, Uncertainty and Profit*. Houghton Mifflin, New York, NY.

Linstone, HA. & Turoff, M. (eds) (1975) *The Delphi Method: Techniques and Applications*. Addison-Wesley Educational Publishers. Available at http://is.njit.edu/pubs/delphibook [accessed 19 February 2008].

MacNulty, CAR. (1977) Scenario development for corporate planning. *Futures* **9**(2), 128–136.

Makridakis, S., Wheelwright, SC., & Hyndman, RJ. (1998) *Forecasting Methods and Applications,* 3rd edition. John Wiley & Sons, Inc., New York, NY.

McKelvey, RD. & McLennan, A. (1996) Computation of equilibria in finite games, in *Handbook of Computational Economics, Vol. 1*, ed. by Amman, HM., Kendrick, DA., & Rust, J. Elsevier, Amsterdam, The Netherlands.

Mercer, D. (1995) Simpler scenarios. *Management Decision* **33**(4), 32–40.

Morgan, G. (2006) *Images of Organization*, updated edition. Sage Publications, Inc., Thousand Oaks, CA.

Moyer, K. (1996) Scenario planning at British Airways – a case study. *Long Range Planning* **29**(2), 172–181.

Nahmias, S. (2004) *Production and Operations Analysis*. McGraw-Hill, New York, NY.

O'Hagan, A., Buck, CE., Daneshkhah, A., *et al.* (2006) *Uncertain Judgements: Eliciting Experts' Probabilities*. John Wiley & Sons, Ltd, Chichester, UK.

Pecar, B. (1994) *Business Forecasting for Management*. McGraw-Hill, Maidenhead, UK.

Psillos, S. (2002) *Causation and Explanation*. Acumen Publishing, Chesham, UK.

Roach, B. (2005) Origin of the economic order quantity formula; transcription or transformation? *Management Decision* **43**(9), 1262–1268.

Rogers, P. & Blenko, M. (2006) Who has the D? How clear decision roles enhance organizational performance. *Harvard Business Review* **84**(1), 53–61.

Rosenhead, J. (1978) An education in robustness. *Journal of the Operational Research Society* **29**(2), 105–111.

Rosenhead, J. (2001a) Robustness analysis: keeping your options open, in *Rational Analysis for a Problematic World Revisited: Problem Structuring Methods for Complexity, Uncertainty, and Conflict*, ed. by Rosenhead, J. & Mingers, J. John Wiley & Sons, Ltd, Chichester, UK.

Rosenhead, J. (2001b) Robustness to the first degree, in *Rational Analysis for a Problematic World Revisited: Problem Structuring Methods for Complexity, Uncertainty, and Conflict*, ed. by Rosenhead, J. & Mingers, J. John Wiley & Sons, Ltd, Chichester, UK.

Rosenhead, J., Elton, M., & Gupta, SK. (1972) Robustness and optimality as criteria for strategic decisions. *Operational Research Quarterly* **23**(4), 413–431.

Rowe, G. & Wright, G. (1999) The Delphi technique as a forecasting tool: issues and analysis. *International Journal of Forecasting* **15**(4), 353–375.

Rowe, G., Wright, G., & McColl, A. (2005) Judgement change during Delphi-like procedures: the role of majority influence, expertise, and confidence. *Technological Forecasting and Social Change* **72**(4), 377–399.

Rubinstein, A. (2000) *Economics and Language: Five Essays*. Cambridge University Press, Cambridge, UK.

Savage, LJ. (1972) *The Foundation of Statistics*, new edition. Dover Publications, Inc., Mineola, NY.

Schenkerman, S. (1975) Constrained decision criteria. *Decision Sciences* **6**(1), 42–50.

Schwarber, PD. (2005) Leaders and the decision-making process. *Management Decision* **43**(7/8), 1086–1092.

Serrano, A. & Kraiselburd, S. (2007) *Economic Order Quantity and the Value of the Firm (31 July 2007)*. Available at SSRN: http://ssrn.com/abstract=1027547 (accessed 17 June 2008).

Shoemaker, PJH. (1995) Scenario planning: a tool for strategic thinking. *Sloan Management Review* **36**(2), 25–40.

Souren, R., Ahn, H., & Schmitz, C. (2005) Optimal product mix decisions based on the theory of constraints? Exposing rarely emphasized premises of throughput accounting. *International Journal of Production Research* **43**(2), 361–374.

Tannenbaum, R. & Schmidt, WH. (1958) How to choose a leadership pattern. *Harvard Business Review* **36**(2), 95–101.

Toulmin, S. (2003) *The Uses of Argument*. Cambridge, Cambridge University Press, UK.

Van de Ven, AH. & Delbecq, AL. (1971) Nominal versus interacting group processes for committee decision-making effectiveness. *Academy of Management Journal* **14** 203–212.

VanGundy, AB. (1988) *Techniques of Structured Problem Solving*, 2nd edition. Van Nostrand Reinhold, New York, NY.

Vroom, VH. (2003) Educating managers for decision making and leadership. *Management Decision* **41**(10), 968–978.

Vroom, VH. & Jago, AG. (1988) *The New Leadership: Managing Participation in Organizations*. Prentice Hall, Englewood Cliffs, NJ.

Vroom, VH. & Jago, AG. (2007) The role of situation in leadership. *American Psychologist* **62**(1), 17–24.

Vroom, VH. & Yetton, PW. (1973) *Leadership and Decision-Making*. University of Pittsburgh Press, Pittsburgh, PA.

Wald, A. (1945) Statistical decision functions which minimize the maximum risk. *The Annals of Mathematics* **46**(2), 265–280.

Wilson, RH. (1934) A scientific routine for stock control. *Harvard Business Review* **13**(1), 116–128.

Wong, HY. (2007) Using robustness analysis to structure online marketing and communication problems. *Journal of the Operational Research Society* **58**(5), 633–644.

Wong, HY. & Rosenhead, J. (2000) A rigorous definition of robustness analysis. *Journal of the Operational Research Society* **51**(2), 176–182.

Woodward, J. (2003) *Making Things Happen: A Theory of Causal Explanation*. Oxford University Press, Oxford, UK.

Index